AGÉNOR
DE MAULÉON

VOLUME TWO

ILLUSTRATED

1906
LONDON
J. M. DENT & CO.
29 & 30 BEDFORD STREET, W.C.

Copyright, 1897,
By Little, Brown, and Company.

The University Press, Cambridge, Mass., U. S. A.

In the interest of creating a more extensive selection of rare historical book reprints, we have chosen to reproduce this title even though it may possibly have occasional imperfections such as missing and blurred pages, missing text, poor pictures, markings, dark backgrounds and other reproduction issues beyond our control. Because this work is culturally important, we have made it available as a part of our commitment to protecting, preserving and promoting the world's literature. Thank you for your understanding.

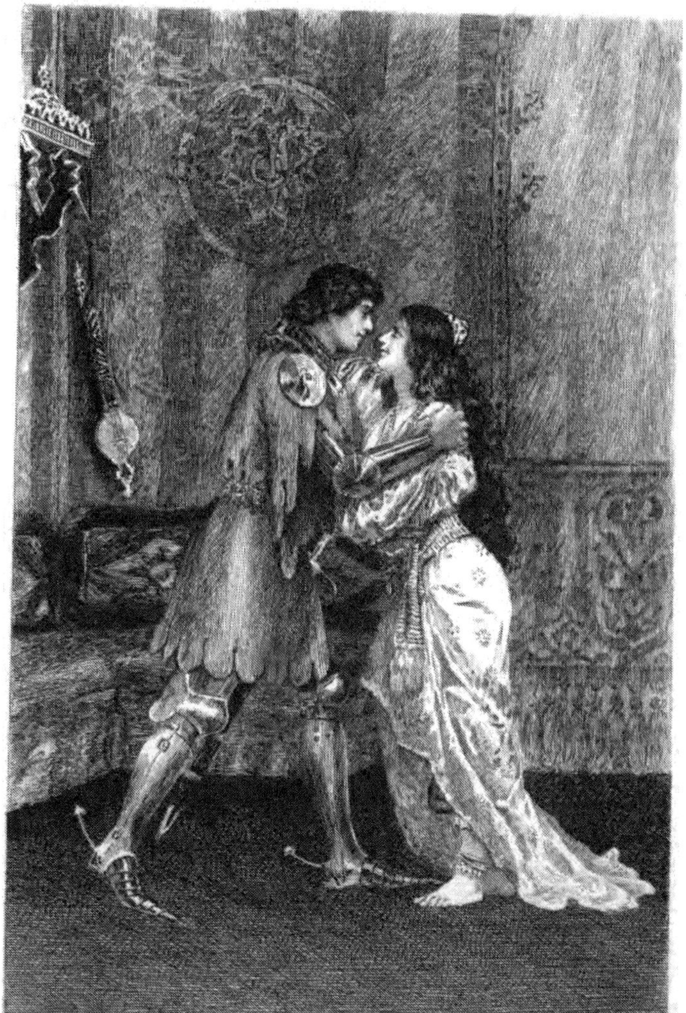

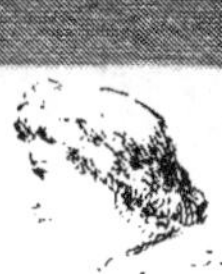

CONTENTS.

CHAPTER		PAGE
I.	How Don Pedro, after His Return, observed the Litter, and what followed	1
II.	How Mothril was appointed Leader of the Moorish Tribes, and Minister of the King Don Pedro	11
III.	How Agénor and Musaron conversed as they travelled through the Sierra Aracena	20
IV.	How Musaron found a Grotto, and what He found therein	28
V.	The Gypsies	36
VI.	The Queen of the Gypsies	45
VII.	How Agénor and the Unknown Traveller rode in Company, and the Things whereof they communed during the Journey	53
VIII.	The Varlet	60
IX.	The Bough of Orange	68
X.	The Audience	76
XI.	The Appointment	86
XII.	The Interview	99
XIII.	The Preparations for Battle	107
XIV.	The Battle	116
XV.	After the Battle	126
XVI.	A Treaty of Alliance	136
XVII.	The Truce	147

CONTENTS

CHAPTER		PAGE
XVIII.	THE JOURNEY	154
XIX.	MADAME TIPHAINE RAGUENEL	160
XX.	THE MESSENGER	165
XXI.	AÏSSA	170
XXII.	THE RETURN	176
XXIII.	RIANZARES	180
XXIV.	GILDAZ	187
XXV.	OF THE MISSION OF HAFIZ AND HOW HE HAD FULFILLED IT	192
XXVI.	HOW HAFIZ MISLED HIS TRAVELLING COMPANIONS	202
XXVII.	THE PATIO OF THE SUMMER PALACE	209
XXVIII.	AN EXPLANATION	217
XXIX.	THE RING OF DOÑA MARIA AND THE PONIARD OF AÏSSA	226
XXX.	THE PRISON OF THE GOOD CONSTABLE	238
XXXI.	THE RANSOM	247
XXXII.	HOW THE GOVERNOR, INSTEAD OF SURRENDERING A PRISONER, LIBERATED AN ENTIRE ARMY	252
XXXIII.	THE POLICY OF MUSARON	260
XXXIV.	HOW MOTHRIL'S CRIME HAD A HAPPY SUCCESS	263
XXXV.	HOW AGÉNOR LEARNED THAT HE ARRIVED TOO LATE	273
XXXVI.	THE PILGRIMS	280
XXXVII.	THE CAVERN OF MONTIEL	295
XXXVIII.	HOW CAVERLEY LOST HIS PURSE AND AGÉNOR HIS SWORD	305
XXXIX.	HAFIZ	315
XL.	THE PREPARATIONS	319
XLI.	STARVING TOLEDO	322
XLII.	THE BATTLE OF MONTIEL	330
XLIII.	A TRUCE	347
XLIV.	THE STRATAGEM OF THE VANQUISHED	354

CONTENTS.

CHAPTER		PAGE
XLV.	THE FLIGHT	363
XLVI.	A DIFFICULTY	368
XLVII.	THE DIPLOMACY OF LOVE	374
XLVIII.	WHAT WAS SEEN IN THE TENT OF LE BÈGUE DE VILAINE	380
XLIX.	THE MOOR'S RESOLUTION	386
L.	SWORD AND SHAFT	394
	EPILOGUE	401

ILLUSTRATIONS.

Vol. II.

"'Thou, thou!' she murmured" . . . . *Frontispiece*
    Drawn by J. Wagrez, etched by Teannin.

Charles V. of France . . . . *Page* 156
    From an engraving.

Bertrand du Guesclin 238
    From an old engraving.

AGÉNOR DE MAULÉON.

I.

HOW DON PEDRO, AFTER HIS RETURN, OBSERVED THE LITTER, AND WHAT FOLLOWED.

Don Pedro had reached Segovia, and his heart was full of deep bitterness and sorrow.

These first assaults, directed against his sovereignty of ten years' standing, had affected him more deeply than the reverses he was to suffer later, in battle, and through the desertion of his friends. And to be compelled to travel through Spain with the utmost precaution like some mere night prowler, — he, the king, accustomed to wander through Seville with no other guard than his sword, no other disguise than his mantle! His journey seemed to him a flight. And a king is lost who compromises thus with his own inviolability.

But at his side, like some spirit of old, breathing the breath of anger into the heart of Achilles, galloping when the other hastened his speed, pausing when it was slackened, — this was Mothril! Like some malign Genius, breathing hatred and fury, ever at the king's ear with some counsel poisoned with bitterness, offering him all the delicious after-fruits of vengeance, Mothril accompanied the king. His fruitful imagination, swift to discover evil, found an escape from every danger; his inexhaustible eloquence dived into the Orient and brought forth mysterious treasures, and he revealed to the fugitive a wealth, an abundance of resources and of power that had been unimagined by the king even in the brightest days of his fortune.

And through him the long and dusty road vanished as swiftly from their sight as the thread reeled by the spinner's hand. And Mothril, the child of the desert, knew where to find even at noon-day some grove of oaks and plantains, which concealed a cooling spring. And when they passed through a town, who but Mothril contrived to win for Don Pedro a greeting here and there, and demonstrations of fidelity, the last reflections of royalty's declining sun?

"They love me then," said the king, "or else they still fear me, which perhaps is better."

"Ah, when you are indeed king once more, you shall see how they will adore you, how they will tremble before you!" said Mothril, with inscrutable irony.

Meanwhile, during all these questionings and fears and hopes of Don Pedro, Mothril had joyfully remarked one fact: this was the complete silence of the king concerning Maria Padilla. That enchantress, whose mere presence exerted so great a power that many had attributed it to magic, in absence seemed to be exiled not merely from the king's heart but even from his memory. For Don Pedro, a man of ardent imagination, capricious, with the southern temperament, passionate in the strongest sense of that word, had yielded since the beginning of the journey with Mothril to the influence of another thought. That litter closed all the way from Bordeaux to Vittoria, that fugitive borne away by Mothril across the mountains, whose veil lifted twice or thrice by the wind had revealed an adorable Peri of the Orient, with velvety eyes and dusky black tresses and rich complexion which harmonized with eyes and hair, and the sound of the guzla vibrating through the darkness, its tender notes waking the silence, whilst Don Pedro himself, filled with anxiety, slept not, — all these things had by degrees driven all memory of Maria Padilla from Don Pedro's thoughts. It was not distance merely that had wrought such mischief for the absent mistress, it was the presence of the mysterious Unknown, whom Don Pedro's vivid and exalted imagination was quite ready to regard as some spirit under the spell of Mothril, still more potent enchanter than herself.

Thus they reached Segovia, their flight unhindered by any serious obstacle. In Segovia at least nothing was changed. The king found everything as he had left it: a throne within a palace, a fair city, archers, and respectful subjects ranged about them.

The king breathed again. The day following his arrival, they sighted a considerable number of troops. It was Caverley and his men; faithful to the oath given their sovereign, they came, bringing with them that national spirit which has ever been England's bulwark, and they came to ally themselves with the Black Prince, who was awaited by Don Pedro.

The evening before, on the way, a considerable corps of Moors, Andalusians, and soldiers from Granada had rallied; they had come to the aid of the king.

Soon arrived an emissary from the Prince of Wales, that indefatigable enemy of all things French, whom Charles V., throughout his reign, as well as King John, had to reckon with, the cause of every defeat which France suffered. The emissary brought great news for Don Pedro.

The Black Prince had assembled an army at Auch,

and for twelve days had been on the march, leading on this army. He was marching from the heart of Navarre, which he had been endeavoring to win over from Don Henry's side. He had sent on an emissary to Don Pedro to announce that his arrival might be expected.

Don Pedro's throne, which had been threatened for a moment by Henry of Trastamare's proclamation at Burgos, stood firm once more. And as his power was strengthened, from all parts of his dominion flocked those steadfast partisans of power, excellent men of their kind, who had almost started on their journey to Burgos to salute Don Henry, when they discovered that the times were not quite ripe for such a move, and that undue haste might cause them to leave behind a king not yet dethroned.

In addition to these, and their number was many, was a less compact but better chosen assemblage of faithful adherents, hearts as unyielding and pure and transparent as the diamond; for these a consecrated king remains a king until the day of his death, since having once sworn fidelity to their king, nothing but death can absolve them from slavish obedience. They may suffer and fear, they may even hate the *man*, but not the prince; and they wait patiently and loyally until God frees them from their promise by taking to Himself His Chosen One.

Such loyal spirits are easily recognized in all times and in every epoch. They are not outwardly as attractive as others; they speak with less emphasis, and having humbly and respectfully saluted the king upon his throne, they draw aside and, at the head of their vassals, await the hour when they shall go forth and be killed for the principal actor in the scene.

The only fact which tempered with a little coldness the reception these faithful servants gave Don Pedro, was the presence of the Moors, whose influence was now more powerful than ever with the king.

This warlike Saracen race surrounded Mothril as bees swarm about the hive which conceals their queen. They felt that they owed entirely to the subtle and audacious Moor the royal favor with which they were regarded. They were indeed a formidable body, and had everything to gain through civil war; and so they ran hither and thither with an enthusiasm and activity which the Christians admired, even while they envied them, and remained dumb and inactive witnesses.

Don Pedro found money again in the public treasury. He surrounded himself with all that illusive luxury which seduces some hearts merely to look upon, whilst it captivates ambition through self-interest. As the Prince of Wales was soon to enter Segovia, he had resolved upon such a magnificent feasting as should by its brilliancy efface the ephemeral grandeur of Henry's consecration, restore the people's confidence in himself, and compel them to confess that he was the only true king who possessed and dispensed most.

Meanwhile, Mothril was still bent upon that project long before conceived, that scheme which was to ensnare the senses of Don Pedro, whose intelligence already owned his sway completely.

Every night Aïssa's guzla was heard, and since — true daughter of the Orient! — she knew no songs but lays of love, these sounds borne upon the breeze caressed the prince's solitude, and imparted to his fevered blood those overpowering sensations which yield a passing somnolence even to these energetic southern natures. Mothril knew that this hidden fire was consuming Don Pedro, and waited day by day for one word which should reveal it, but he waited vainly.

One day, however, Don Pedro said, abruptly and unexpectedly as though he had been tongue-tied before, and only a violent effort could remove the fetters silence had laid upon him, —

"Well, Mothril, still no news from Seville?"

One word revealed all the anxiety felt by Don Pedro; no news from Seville meant no news from Maria Padilla.

Mothril trembled. That very morning at his command a Nubian slave had been seized on the road between Toledo and Segovia, and thrown into the Adaja. He had been the bearer of a letter from Maria Padilla, intended for the king.

"No, sire," said Mothril.

Don Pedro relapsed into a gloomy reverie. Then, as if answering aloud the small voice within, he murmured, "So soon, then, can a woman efface from mind all memory of that consuming passion which moved me to sacrifice for her sake brother, wife, honor, and my crown. Yes, even my crown," he repeated; "for who snatches it from my head? Not the bastard alone, but the constable!"

And the menacing gesture which accompanied these words promised anything but good to Du Guesclin, if ever he should have the evil fortune to fall into Don Pedro's hands.

Mothril paid no attention to that; his attention was turned in another direction. "Doña Maria," he said, "desired above all things to be queen, and as it is believed in Seville that Your Highness is king no longer — "

"You have told me that already, Mothril, and I did not believe it."

"I repeat it, sire, and you are beginning to believe it!

I told it to you before, when first you commended me to the unfortunate Don Frederic at Coimbra."

" Mothril ! "

"You remember how reluctantly, I may even say with what repugnance, I fulfilled that order."

" Silence, Mothril, silence ! "

"But your honor had been compromised, my king, and — "

"Oh, yes! but Maria Padilla should not be charged with these crimes, — rather, that infamous pair."

"Certainly; but had it not been for Maria Padilla you would not have known of their guilt; for I should have kept silence, though not in ignorance."

"She still loved me, then, for she was jealous ! "

"You are a king, and upon the death of the unfortunate Blanche it was possible that she might become queen; besides, jealousy does not prove there is love. You were jealous of Doña Bianca. Did you love her, sire ? "

At that moment, as if Mothril's words had been the very signal for them, sounds of the guzla were heard, and Aïssa's words, too far away to be understood, reached Don Pedro's ears, — a murmur full of harmony, and musical as the rustling of leaves.

"Aïssa ! " murmured the king; "is not that Aïssa singing ? "

"Yes, seigneur, I believe so," said Mothril.

"Your daughter or your favorite slave, is she not ? " asked the king, distractedly.

Mothril shook his head with a smile. "Oh, no," he said, "one does not kneel before a daughter, sire. A wise man would scarcely clasp his hands before a slave gold had bought him."

"Then who is she ? " exclaimed Don Pedro; for his thoughts, concentrated for a moment upon the mysterious young girl, overleaped every barrier. "Accursed Moor, are you playing with me? Would you burn me with a red-hot iron, simply to see me bound like a bull for your pleasure?"

Mothril recoiled almost in terror, for the sally was abrupt and violent.

"Answer!" cried Don Pedro, overcome by one of those frenzies which change a king into a madman, a man into a wild beast.

"Sire, I dare not answer."

"Then bring this woman hither," exclaimed Don Pedro, "that I may ask herself."

"O seigneur!" exclaimed Mothril, as if terrified by this order.

"I am master. It shall be so."

"Seigneur, mercy!"

"Let her be here upon the hour, or I myself will seize her in her apartment."

"Seigneur," said Mothril, turning towards Don Pedro with the calm and solemn gravity of an Oriental, "Aïssa is of most noble blood. None dare lay profane hands upon her. Injure not Aïssa, Don Pedro."

"And how should my love injure this Moorish girl?" asked the king. "My wives were princes' daughters; more than once my mistress has been as nobly born as my wives."

"My lord," said Mothril, "were Aïssa my daughter, as thou believest, I would tell thee, 'King Don Pedro, spare my child, dishonor not thy servant.' And perchance, grateful to him who had so often given thee wise counsel, thou wouldst spare my child. But in Aïssa's veins flows the blood of a more exalted race than that of thy wives or thy mistresses! Aïssa is nobler born than a princess, for she is the daughter of King Mohammed, and descendant of great Mohammed the Prophet. Thou seest, Aïssa is more than princess, more than queen. I command thee, King Don Pedro, respect Aïssa."

Don Pedro paused, completely conquered by the proud authority of Mothril.

"Child of Mohammed, the King of Granada!" he murmured.

"Yes, child of that Mohammed, King of Granada, assassinated at thy command. Thou knowest I was in that great prince's service, and whilst thy soldiers were pillaging his palace, I saved the child. A slave was bearing her away in his mantle to sell her. This was nine years ago. Aïssa was scarcely seven years old. Thou hadst heard that I was a faithful servant and called me to thy court. God willed I should serve thee. Thou art my master, for thou art great among the great. I obeyed thee. But whilst I dwelt with my new master, the child of my former master has followed me always; she believes me to be her father, poor child! Reared in a harem, she never beheld the majestic face of the sultan who is no more. Now thou hast my secret which thy violence has wrested from me. But remember, King Don Pedro, that though I wait upon thee the devoted slave of thy least caprice, I would spring upon thee as a serpent to defend against thee the one object dearer to me than thou!"

"But I love Aïssa," exclaimed Don Pedro, beside himself.

"Love her, King Don Pedro, for thou mayst well; her blood is at least as noble as thine own. Love her, but win her of herself; I shall not hinder thee," said the Moor. "Thou art young, beautiful, mighty; why should not that virgin heart be thine? Will she not yield through love what thou wouldst obtain by violence?"

After these words, darted at him like a Parthian arrow and penetrating the deepest recesses of Don Pedro's heart, Mothril raised the hanging of the chamber, and went out backwards.

"But she will hate me, she must hate me if she knows that it is I who have slain her father."

"I never speak evil of the master whom I serve," said Mothril, his hand resting for a moment upon the lifted tapestry; "and Aïssa knows nothing about you, except that you are a good king and a great sultan."

He let the hangings fall, and for some time Don Pedro continued to hear Mothril's footsteps upon the flaggings, as he turned slowly and solemnly towards Aïssa's chamber.

II.

HOW MOTHRIL WAS APPOINTED LEADER OF THE MOORISH TRIBES, AND MINISTER OF THE KING DON PEDRO.

WE have stated that Mothril, upon leaving the king, directed his footsteps towards Aïssa's apartment.

The young girl, confined in her chamber, guarded by gratings, watched by her father, and deprived of her liberty, longed for a breath of air.

Aïssa had not the resources of the women of our own times; she could not obtain such news of the outer world as might take the place of intercourse with it. For her, to be deprived of the sight of Agénor meant death; deprived of the sound of his voice, her ears were closed to every sound that might have reached her from without her prison.

But a profound conviction animated her still. She believed that she had inspired in Agénor a love equal to her own, and she knew that he who had already found a means of reaching her for the third time would, unless death overtook him, find her again; and with that confidence in the future which belongs to youth, it seemed impossible to her that Agénor could die.

Nothing then remained for Aïssa except to wait and to hope.

The life of an Oriental woman is made up of perpetual dreaming, blended with moments of energized activity which now and then awake her, breaking in upon that slumber of the senses in which she dwells. If the poor captive had known what steps to take to discover Mauléon again, she certainly would have taken them; but, ignorant of everything as some Oriental flower, whose perfume and innocence she possessed, she knew no other instinct than that which bade her heart turn towards love, as her life's sun.

But to escape, obtain money, to question and to flee,— it never entered her mind to do any one of these things, for they seemed impossibilities to her.

And besides, where was Agénor? Where was she herself? She did not know. In Segovia, doubtless, but Segovia meant to her merely the name of a city, that was all. Where was that city? She knew not. In what province of Spain? She knew not; she did not even know the names of the different Spanish provinces. Had she not travelled five hundred leagues without knowing a single country through which she had crossed, and remembering only three points in the journey, the places where she had seen Agénor?

But how they had fixed themselves in her memory! Always she saw before her the banks of the Zezera, sister stream of the Tagus, with its bosky thickets of wild olive-trees where her litter had rested, its steep banks and gloomy stream which had listened to soft murmurs, which had heard the last sigh of the unfortunate page, and the convulsive heaving of her breast at Agénor's first words of love. Her heart leaped still to remember them.

And again she saw her chamber in the Alcazar, its lattice entwined with honeysuckle, its window looking upon a verdurous garden in whose midst bubbling waters were gleaming in marble basins. And again she saw the gardens of Bordeaux, with its tall trees and sombre leafage interposed between her and that lake of silvery light which the moon poured from high heaven.

Of all these various scenes, every note, every phase, each detail, each leaf almost, she seemed to see still.

But to tell whether these isolated points of light which seemed to illuminate the obscurity of her life, lay to her left or to her right, would have been impossible for this ignorant young girl, who had learned only what is learned within a harem,—the luxurious delights of the bath and the voluptuous dreams of idleness.

Mothril comprehended all this perfectly, otherwise he might have been seriously concerned regarding her.

He entered the young girl's chamber.

"Aïssa," he said, after he had prostrated himself according to his custom, "may I hope that you will hear, with some favor, what I am about to say?"

"I owe you all things; my life is bound to yours," answered the young girl, gazing at Mothril, as though she desired that he should read within her eyes that she spoke the truth.

"Does the life you are leading please you?" asked Mothril.

"How should it?" asked Aïssa, who evidently desired to know the object of this question.

"I wish to know whether it pleases you to live in confinement."

"Oh, no!" said Aïssa, quickly.

"Then you would like to change your condition."

"Certainly."

"And what would please you?"

Aïssa was silent. The one object of her desires she dared not name.

"You do not answer," said Mothril.

"I know not what to answer," she replied.

"How would you like," continued Mothril, "mounted upon a noble Spanish steed, to speed across Spain, followed by women and knights and hounds and music?"

"This is not what I desire most of all," answered the young girl; " but, after what I wish most, it would please me — that is, if — "

She paused.

" If what?" asked Mothril, curiously.

" Oh, nothing, nothing!" said the young girl, proudly.

But in spite of her reticence the Moor understood perfectly what the " if " signified.

" As long as you remain with me," continued Mothril, " and as long as I am supposed to be your father, although I have not that great honor, I shall be responsible for your happiness and your peace of mind; as long as that is so, the one thing you desire most you cannot have."

" And when will that be changed?" asked the young girl, with her naïve impatience.

" When a husband claims you."

She shook her head.

" That will never be," she said.

" You interrupt, señora," said Mothril, gravely, " although I was about to speak of matters which pertain to your happiness."

Aïssa fixed her gaze upon the Moor.

" I was about to say," he continued, " that a husband could give you liberty."

" Liberty!" repeated Aïssa.

" Perhaps you do not understand what that means," continued Mothril. " I will tell you. Liberty is the right to pass through the streets with your face uncovered, and without being imprisoned in a litter; it is the right to receive visits as do the women of France, to assist at the chase, at festivals, and to take part in great banquets in the company of fair knights."

As Mothril proceeded, a slight blush tinged the pallid hue of Aïssa's face.

"But, on the contrary," responded the young girl, "I have heard that the husband deprives the wife of these rights, instead of giving them."

"Yes, after he is her husband, that is true sometimes; but before that day, especially if he is of exalted rank, he permits his betrothed all those liberties I have mentioned. In Spain and in France, for instance, even the daughter of a Christian king listens to gallantry, and it is considered no dishonor to do so. The man who is to espouse her permits her to see for herself in advance the liberal and sumptuous life which he reserves, in store for her. Take, for example, Maria Padilla; do you remember her?"

Aïssa was listening now.

"Well?" asked the young girl.

"Very well! was not Maria Padilla the queen of feasts, the mighty mistress in the Alcazar, in Seville, mistress of each province, and of Spain? Do you not remember how often we saw her, through our lattice, whilst she exercised her beautiful Arabian courser, gathering about her for days at a time the knights whom she preferred, whilst you, as I was saying, you were hidden away, a recluse, who dared not cross the threshold of your chamber, seeing only your women, and daring to speak to no one of all that was upon your mind, or hidden in your heart?"

"Yes," said Aïssa; "but Doña Padilla loved Don Pedro, and when one loves in this land one is free, so it appears, to speak openly of her love to him whom she cares for. He chooses her, he does not buy her as in Africa. Doña Maria loved Don Pedro, I say, but I should not love him who would wish to espouse me."

"How do you know that, señora?"

"Who is he?" asked the young girl, quickly.

"Ah, you question most eagerly," said Mothril.

"And you are slow to answer," responded Aïssa.

"Well, as I was saying, Doña Maria was free."

"No, not free, for she loved."

"And through loving one becomes free, señora."

"How so?"

"At last one ceases to love, that is all."

Aïssa shrugged her shoulders as though Mothril's words were incredible.

"Doña Maria is free again, I tell you, for Don Pedro loves her no longer, and is no longer loved by her."

Aïssa raised her head in surprise; the Moor continued, —

"For you see, Aïssa, that their marriage has not been celebrated; and yet both of them were of noble station, and enjoyed all the distinction which rank and illustrious connections can confer."

"What are you driving at?" asked Aïssa.

"I would tell you what you have already comprehended perfectly," said Mothril.

"Speak, then."

"A great seigneur — "

"The king?"

"The very same, señora," answered Mothril, bowing.

"Would give me the place left vacant by Maria Padilla?"

"And his crown."

"As he gave it to Maria Padilla?"

"Doña Maria knew only how to win the promise of his crown; another, younger, fairer, wiser, will know how to win the crown itself."

"Ah, but what of her, if he loves her no longer, —

what will become of her?" asked the young girl, most pensively, her tapering fingers suddenly ceasing to twirl the beads of a chaplet of aloes-wood, incased in gold.

"Oh!" said Mothril, affecting a certain carelessness, "she has found happiness elsewhere. Some say that she is afraid of this war which has deprived her of the king's presence; others say, and this is more likely, that she loves some one else, and is about to wed him."

"Whom?"

"A knight of the Occident," answered Mothril.

Aïssa was plunged in a profound reverie, incited by the Moor's insidious words, which with magic potency revealed to her step by step all that delightful future which she had dreamed of, though through ignorance or timidity she had merely dared to raise for a moment the veil which separated her from it.

"Ah, they say that?" asked Aïssa in delight.

"Yes," said Mothril; "and they add that she exclaimed, upon regaining her freedom, 'Oh, what happiness the king's favor has brought me, for it lifted me out of the obscurity and silence in which I lived, to place me in this blaze of splendor where I have discovered my love!'"

"Yes, yes!" said the young girl, completely absorbed.

"And certainly," replied Mothril, "it was not in a harem or a convent that she found this happiness that has just come to her!"

"True," said Aïssa.

"Therefore, Aïssa, for the sake of your own happiness you will listen to the king."

"But the king will leave me time to reflect, will he not?"

"All the time you desire, and all the time a noble child like yourself ought to have. But remember, 't is a melancholy seigneur, whom his misfortunes have somewhat imbittered. Your speech is gentle, when you choose; choose your words well, Aïssa. Don Pedro is a powerful king, whose sensibilities must be treated tenderly, while his desires must be augmented."

"I will listen to the king, seigneur," answered the young girl.

"Good!" thought Mothril; "I was sure that ambition would speak if love did not. She loves her French knight sufficiently to seize this opportunity of seeing him again. True, at this moment she would sacrifice the monarch to the lover, but later I may perhaps be compelled to watch that she does not sacrifice the lover for the monarch."

"Then you do not refuse to see the king, Doña Aïssa?" he asked.

"His Highness shall find me his respectful servant," said the young girl.

"No, no, for you are the king's equal, remember that; only, remember as well, show no more of pride than of humility. Farewell! I go to tell the king that you will be present at the serenade which will be given him as usual this evening. All the court will be there, and a number of foreign nobles. Farewell, Doña Aïssa!"

"Who knows," murmured the young girl, "who knows whether I may not find Agénor among those nobles?"

Don Pedro, whose passions were sudden and violent, colored with delight like a young novice when that evening he saw the beautiful Moorish girl approaching the balcony, resplendent beneath her gold-embroidered veil, her wondrous pallor and black eyes effacing the charms of all the beauties of Segovia.

Aïssa seemed as accustomed to the homage of kings as though she were a queen. Her eyes met Don Pedro's quite frequently; her glance never wavered, and seemed to take in the entire assemblage. More than once that evening Don Pedro left the wisest counsellors and the fairest women to converse with the young girl, speaking in an undertone, to which she replied, unembarrassed and undisturbed, although perhaps she seemed somewhat absent-minded, for her thoughts were elsewhere.

Don Pedro gave her his hand to re-conduct her to her litter, and, after she had entered it, continued to converse with her through the silken curtains.

All night long the courtiers discussed the new mistress whom the king seemed about to give them, and before retiring Don Pedro announced publicly that henceforth he would confide all negotiations and the payment of his forces to his prime minister, Mothril, leader of the Moorish tribes employed in his service.

III.

HOW AGÉNOR AND MUSARON CONVERSED AS THEY TRAVELLED THROUGH THE SIERRA ARACENA.

WE have seen how Mauléon and his squire set out upon their journey by moonlight, hastening to obey the wish of the new King of Castile.

Nothing caused Musaron's heart to dilate with greater joy than the indiscreet sound of coins rattling about in his capacious leathern pouch, and this time the jingling was occasioned by no casual collision, but by the unctuous sound of a hundred big pieces, all dancing merrily together, and crowded into a bag whose very depths they filled; consequently Musaron's joy was great and sonorous in proportion to the amount of his money and the music it was making.

The road from Burgos to Segovia was a beautiful one, and had become much frequented even at this epoch; on account of these facts Mauléon considered it would not be prudent to follow the road too exactly. And so, in true Béarnese fashion, he plunged into the sierra, following the picturesque undulations of its western declivity, which extended from Coimbra to Tudela; dotted with flowers here and there, moss-grown and rocky, it seemed like an immense natural wrinkle upon the face of the mountains.

From the beginning of the journey, Musaron, who had counted upon the assistance of his crowns in making their way, as he understood the term, — Musaron was deeply disappointed. If the people of the cities and the plains had disgorged their wealth under the double pressure brought to bear by Henry and Don Pedro, what could remain for these mountaineers who had no wealth to give? And so our travellers, reduced to sheep's milk, the wretched wines grown on those poor mountain farms, and bread made of barley and millet, were not slow to regret the dangers of the plain, dangers which were mingled with delights, — roast kid, olla-podrida, and skins filled with good wine.

And Musaron began to lament bitterly that there were no enemies to attack. Agénor, who was thinking of other things, endured his grumbling without reply, but at last interrupted in his musing, deep as it was, by the ferocious rhodomontades of his squire, he had the misfortune to smile. That smile, in which there was a shade of incredulity, displeased Musaron mightily.

"I do not believe, seigneur," he said, pressing his lips together to impart to his features an expression of discontent so unusual, that it greatly belied the habitual good humor of his honest countenance, " I do not believe that monseigneur has ever doubted my bravery, and more than one exploit has given him proof of it."

Agénor made a sign of assent.

"Yes, more than one exploit," said Musaron. "Need I mention the Moor so skilfully perforated in the moat at Medina Sidonia, eh! or that other whom I butchered in the very chamber of poor Queen Blanche? Come, now! I say it with all modesty," he continued; "address and courage shall be my device if ever I am elevated to the rank of knighthood."

"That is all very true, my dear Musaron," said Agénor; "but what are you driving at with this long discourse, and these terrible frownings?"

"Seigneur," said Musaron, somewhat reassured by the note of sympathy in his master's voice, "you are not wearied already, are you, seigneur?"

"Of your society, my good Musaron? Very seldom. Of my own thoughts, never."

"Thank you, seigneur; but when I consider that there is not in sight a single suspicious-looking traveller whom we might, at the point of the lance, relieve of a good quarter of cold venison or a big skin filled with those delicious wines grown on the coast yonder, thinking of that, I grow very weary."

"Ah, I understand, Musaron, you are hungry, and your entrails have sounded this warning."

"Exactly so, señor, as they say here; look, now, below us, that fine road! To think that instead of wandering like vagabonds through these eternal gorges and under these inhospitable birch-trees, we might follow this path that descends for about a league, and find ourselves again on that plateau where yonder church rises! And look, monsieur, at that rich cloud of smoke rising to one side of it! Is there not within you a pious knight and a good Christian to whom that church appeals? Oh that delicious smoke! it smells savory even at this distance."

"Musaron," said Agénor, "I am no more in love with our surroundings or our society here than you are, but I will not expose my life to needless dangers. Serious perils there must be in the accomplishment of my mission. These mountains are arid enough, but they are safe."

"Eh, seigneur!" continued Musaron, who seemed determined not to yield without an argument. "In Heaven's name, descend with me but a third of the way; there you may await me, and I will push on to where yonder smoke rises, and obtain some provisions, and they will help us to have patience. Two hours only, and I will return. As for the tracks I shall leave, night will soon be upon us, and to-morrow we shall be far away."

"My dear Musaron," replied Agénor, "listen well. I will permit no turning aside, no roundabout road, until we have reached Segovia. At Segovia, sir sybarite, you shall have all you desire: expensive dainties, agreeable society. At Segovia you shall receive all the consideration due an ambassador's squire, which you are. But until we get there, straight ahead, if you please! And besides, is not the city which I see through the smoke, that beautiful tower and shining dome rising in the midst of it, Segovia itself? To-morrow evening we shall be there. It is not worth while for so little, to turn aside from our path."

"I will obey Your Lordship," said Musaron, dolefully, "for it is my duty and I love my duty; but if I might be permitted an observation wholly in the interests of Your Lordship—"

Agénor glanced at Musaron, and Musaron responded by a motion of the head which seemed to say, "What I have said, I will maintain!"

"Come, speak," said the young man.

Musaron hastened to respond.

"We have a proverb in my country and in yours, which warns the bell-ringer to try the little bells before he rings the big ones."

"Yes, and what does that proverb signify?"

"That before we enter Segovia, the great city, monseigneur, it would be prudent to try the village, as in all probability we may hear there some good piece of news, bearing upon the condition of our affairs. Oh, if

Your Lordship only knew what good things I presage merely from smelling the smoke of that village!"

Agénor was a man of good sense. The first reasons Musaron had given did not impress him greatly, but the last did; he reflected that Musaron's mind was bent upon going to the neighboring town, and that to disturb an idea once lodged in Musaron's brain would certainly disturb the well-regulated clock-work of his nature, and that this derangement of Musaron's ideas would compel the knight himself to endure that worst of evils under the sun, that thundercloud blacker and more inevitable than any tempest, — the ill-humor of a valet.

"Well," he said, "I will consent to what you ask, Musaron; depart, learn what is going on where we see the smoke rising, and return and tell me."

As Musaron had felt almost sure of gaining his point from the very beginning, he received this permission without any immoderate display of joy, and put his horse to a trot, following the windings of the little footpath which his eyes had devoured for a long time.

Agénor, the better to await his squire's return at ease, selected a charming amphitheatre of rocks, with birches here and there; in its centre was a carpet of fine mountain moss gleaming with those exquisite flowers which grow only upon the edge of a precipice, each one outvying its neighbor in loveliness; a stream transparent as glass slept for a moment in a natural basin, and then ran gurgling between the stones. Agénor quenched his thirst, and, removing his helmet, he lay down beneath the rustling leafage of a green oak at the foot of a mossy stump.

As some knight of old, whose adventures are recorded in fable and romantic legends, the young man was soon lost in thoughts of love, which by degrees absorbed him so profoundly, that imperceptibly almost he passed from reverie to rapture and from rapture to slumber.

At Agénor's age one rarely sleeps without dreaming; and hardly had the young man fallen asleep when he dreamed that he had arrived in Segovia, and that the King Don Pedro had caused him to be put in irons and thrown into a narrow cell. Through its bars he could see Aïssa, but scarcely had that beautiful vision brightened the gloom of his dungeon when Mothril appeared to banish this consoling image, and a combat ensued between himself and the Moor. In the midst of it, just as he was about to succumb, galloping was heard, announcing the arrival of unexpected aid.

"Seigneur, seigneur!" cried the voice. Agénor opened his eyes. Musaron was before him. And a curious appearance the worthy squire presented: he was planted upon his horse, whose movements he was no longer able to direct save with his knees, for his hands were spread before him as though he were playing blindman's-buff; in one elbow he held a skin, tied at the four ends, in the other a cloth knotted at the four corners, and holding a bundle of raisins and smoked tongues; and, as though he were presenting a pair of pistols, he held in one hand a fat goose, and in the other a loaf of bread that would have sufficed six men.

"Seigneur, seigneur," cried Musaron, " great news!"

"What now?" exclaimed the knight, donning his helmet again, and laying his hand upon his sword, as though a hostile army was close upon Musaron's heels.

"Oh, I was surely inspired! and when I think that if I had not insisted, we might have gone on without — "

"Come, what is it, cursed babbler?" cried Agénor, impatiently.

"What is it? Surely the Lord himself led me to that village!"

"But what did you learn there? 'S death! speak."

"I learned that the King Don Pedro, or, I should say, the ex-King Don Pedro—"

"Well, what of him?"

"Is no longer at Segovia!"

"Indeed! is that so?" asked Mauléon, disdainfully.

"Yes, seigneur; the alcalde returned yesterday from a visit paid to Don Pedro with all the notables of the town. Don Pedro passed them on the plain below, coming from Segovia."

"But going whither?"

"To Soria."

"With his court?"

"With his court."

"And," continued the young man, hesitatingly, "with Mothril?"

"Very likely."

"And doubtless," stammered the young man, "with Mothril was—"

"His litter? I suppose so, for he does not permit it to leave his sight except when he sleeps. Oh, it is very well guarded at present!"

"What do you mean?"

"The king himself keeps guard."

"Over the litter?"

"Certainly. He escorts it on horseback. He was beside it when he received the deputation from the town."

"Well, my dear Musaron, let us go to Soria," said Agénor, with a smile that scarcely concealed the uneasiness he was beginning to feel.

"Yes, monseigneur, but we can no longer follow the

same road; we must turn our backs upon Soria for the present, for I learned in the village that we must cut the mountain on our left, and enter a defile parallel to the plain. This will save us the fording of two rivers and eleven leagues of road."

"As you will. I consent to accept you for guide; but consider well, my good Musaron, the responsibility you are taking."

"And having pondered it well, seigneur, I must tell you that we ought to spend the night in the village; for it begins to grow chill, night is falling fast, and in an hour more darkness will be upon us."

"Let us make the most then of the hour that remains to us, Musaron, and since you are so well instructed, lead on!"

"But you have not dined, seigneur," said Musaron, making a last effort.

"We will do so when we have found a suitable spot. Come, march, Musaron, march!"

Musaron did not reply. There was a certain intonation in Agénor's voice which he knew perfectly well, and when it accompanied any command there was nothing further to be said.

The squire, by a series of moves, each one cleverer than the one that preceded it, contrived to hold his master's stirrup, without parting with a single one of the bundles with which he was burdened; and, holding them all, he mounted his own horse, maintaining his equilibrium through some miracle. He then led the way and plunged bravely into the mountain gorge that was to save them eleven leagues' journey and the fording of two rivers.

IV.

HOW MUSARON FOUND A GROTTO, AND WHAT HE FOUND THEREIN.

THE travellers had still nearly an hour of daylight, as Musaron had stated, and, for a time, the sun remained long enough above the horizon to enable them to keep their course; but, as soon as the reflection of its rays, growing ever dimmer, forsook the topmost peak of the sierra, night came upon them with a swiftness the more appalling, because Musaron and his master had become fully aware, during this last hour of the expiring day, how steep, and, therefore, how dangerous, was the road they were following.

So, when they had jogged along in the dusk for a quarter of an hour, Musaron suddenly reined in his horse and said, —

"Oh, oh, Seigneur Agénor, the road grows worse and worse, or rather there is no road at all! We shall certainly be killed if you insist on going farther."

"The devil!" exclaimed Agénor. "I am not hard to please, as you know; but the entertainment promised by these quarters is likely to be just a little too rural. Cannot we push on?"

"Impossible! We are on a sort of table-land with precipices on every side of it. Let us bide here, or rather make a simple halt; and you may trust to my mountain training, monseigneur, to find you a place where you may spend the night."

"Have you seen again some good fat smoke?" asked Agénor, smiling.

"No, but I am on the track of a pretty grotto with curtains of ivy and moss-clad walls."

"Whence we shall have to chase a multitude of owls and lizards and serpents."

"By my faith, that need not trouble you, monseigneur! When I consider the time it is, and the place where we are, it is not what flies or scratches or creeps that frightens me; it is what walks. Besides, you are not so superstitious as to be afraid of owls, and I believe the lizards and serpents would have but a sorry time of it, biting at your mailed legs."

"Well, then," said Agénor, "let us call a halt."

Musaron alighted and fastened the bridle of his steed to a stone, while his master, standing up in the stirrups, and looking not unlike an equestrian statue, awaited the issue with cool, determined courage.

The squire set about exploring the neighborhood with that instinctive good-will which gives a tenfold energy to persistent effort.

A quarter of an hour had scarcely elapsed when he returned, with the air of a conqueror, a naked sword in his hand.

"This way, monseigneur, this way," said he; "come and let me show you our alcazar."

"What the devil is the matter with you?" asked the knight. "You look as if you were wet to the skin."

"I have, monseigneur, been fighting my way through a very forest of creepers and woodbine, and I had much ado that they did not make me their prisoner. But, what with cutting and thrusting right vigorously, I forced a passage. Still, I could not help the damp leaves shaking their dewy burden on my head in showers. I have succeeded, however. After a dozen bats had escaped, whirring by my ears, the fortress was taken. Come with me, and you can feast your eyes upon a really wonderful gallery, the floor of which is carpeted with the finest sand."

"Ah, indeed!" said the knight, following his squire obediently, but not at all certain that he could rely on his delectable promises.

Agénor did wrong to doubt. He had hardly walked a hundred paces down a rather steep declivity, when, at a spot where the path seemed to be barred by a wall, he began to feel a pile of fresh leaves under his feet, as well as heaps of little branches, — proof positive of the slaughter Musaron had made among the trees; while, at intervals, the gusts of air that fanned his face told him of the presence of large-sized bats, silently beating their wings, and waiting impatiently for the hour that would again give them possession of their abode.

"Why," said Agénor, "it is the cavern of the enchanter Maugis!"

"Discovered by me, monseigneur, by me, the first discoverer. Devil take me if ever man has thought of setting foot here before! These creepers date from the beginning of the world."

"Very well," returned Agénor, laughing; "but, though this grotto be unknown to men — "

"Oh, that I answer for!"

"Can you say the same of wolves?"

"Humph!" returned Musaron.

"Or of those little red bears — the mountain breed, you know — that are found in the Pyrenees?"

"The devil!"

"Or of those catamounts that open the throats of sleeping travellers and suck their blood?"

"I'll tell you what we must do, sir knight. One of us must keep watch while the other sleeps."

"It would be prudent to do so."

"And now, have you aught else against the cavern of Maugis?"

"Absolutely nothing; I deem it a rather pleasant place, on the contrary."

"Then, let us enter," said Musaron.

"Let us enter, by all means," said the knight.

Both alighted and entered, feeling their way with many precautions, the knight using for this purpose the end of his lance, the squire the end of his sword. After advancing about twenty yards, they came upon a solid, impenetrable wall, which looked as if it had been hewn out of the rock itself, without any apparent opening through which noxious animals could make their escape.

This cavern was divided into two parts: the entrance to the first was through a sort of porch. A gap, not unlike a door, led into the second chamber, the roof of which rose to the same height as that of the first excavation, once the gap was cleared.

Evidently, it had been, in the early days of Christianity, one of those grottos in which pious hermits, intent on working out their salvation in solitude, sought shelter.

"God be praised!" cried Musaron, "our bed-chamber is quite secure."

"In that case, see to the stabling of the horses, and lay the cloth, for I am hungry," said Agénor.

Musaron at once obeyed, and led in the two horses, which he "stabled," to use the expression of his master, in the porch of the grotto.

Then, this business done with, he turned his hands to the more important matter of getting supper ready.

"What are you saying?" asked Agénor, who could hear a good deal of muttering and grumbling coming from the direction in which Musaron was executing the orders of his master.

"I am saying, sir knight, what a fool I was not to think of providing myself with some wax, so that we might have a taper to let us see what we are doing. Luckily, there is nothing to hinder us from making a fire."

"Can you think of such a thing, Musaron,—making a fire?"

"A fire keeps wild beasts away. That is a truth, the justice of which I have had plenty of opportunities of testing."

"Yes, but it attracts men; and I confess that, at present, I am more in dread of an onslaught from a band of English or Morisco savages than I am of a pack of wolves."

"*Mordieu!*" exclaimed Musaron. "Still, it is very sad, monseigneur, to have to eat such fine things without seeing them."

"Pshaw!" retorted Agénor; "your hungry stomach may have no ears, but, rest assured, it has eyes."

Musaron, most docile of squires when one went the right way to work with him, or when he was told to do just the thing he wanted to do, freely acknowledged this time the solidity of his master's reasoning, and began arranging their repast in the entrance to the second cavern, in order that, if a last stray glimmer of light happened to be about outside, it might, perhaps, make its way to them.

As soon as the horses received permission, then, to bury their noses in the sack of oats which Musaron carried on the crupper, knight and squire fell to with a will. Indeed, Agénor, being young and vigorous, showed such prowess as a trencherman that a lover of the present day would, perhaps, have blushed only to look at him; and such was the zeal of Musaron in following his leader, that he actually crunched the bones with the meat, alleging, by way of apology, that it was impossible to see what one was about in such darkness.

Suddenly, although Agénor kept up the music with spirit, the accompaniment on Musaron's side came to a stand.

"Well, then, Musaron! What ails you?" queried the knight.

"Seigneur," returned the squire, "methought I heard something, but no doubt I was mistaken. 'T is nothing."

And he set to work to make up for lost time.

However, it was not long till he stopped again, and, as he turned his back to the opening, Agénor was able to notice the fixedness of his attitude.

"What means this?" exclaimed the knight. "Are you growing mad?"

"No, seigneur, nor deaf either. I can hear, I tell you, and I do hear."

"Bah!" retorted the young man, "you are dreaming. 'T is some belated bat flapping its wings against the walls."

"Well, then!" answered Musaron, lowering his voice so that his master could hardly hear him, "not only do I hear, but I see."

"You see?"

"Yes, and if you will but just turn around you will see yourself."

The suggestion was uttered with such assurance that Agénor turned around immediately.

And, in fact, at the back of the cavern, which had seemed bathed in darkness, twinkled a gleam of light, — a light coming from a flame evidently, and making its way through a crevice in the rock.

The phenomenon was alarming enough to excite the apprehensions even of a person who had not made the reflection that at once occurred to Musaron.

"Though we have no light, there are others who have."

"And who are they?"

"Faith, our neighbors!"

"And you think this solitary grotto has tenants?"

"I would not make bold to say so, but the next one surely has."

"Come, explain your meaning."

"Surely you know right well, monseigneur, we are either on the crest of a mountain, or we are very close to one; now, every mountain has two slopes."

"Very well!"

"Follow my reasoning, then. This grotto has two entrances. Mere chance has brought about the imperfect separation between them which you see. We have made our way into the grotto by the eastern entrance; they have got in through the opening on the west."

"But, then, who are they?"

"I know not. We shall see, monseigneur. You did right in preventing me from making a fire. In fact, monseigneur, you are as wise as you are brave, and that is saying a good deal. But we had better look about us."

"Yes, by all means," said Agénor.

And both, not without feeling their hearts beating, pushed forward into the recesses of the cavern.

Musaron preceded his master, and was the first to

apply his eye to the cranny in the wall that divided the two grottos.

"Look!" he whispered; "it is well worth your while."

Agénor did so, and at once gave a start.

"What do you think now?" said Musaron.

"Hush!" answered Agénor.

V.

THE GYPSIES.

The sight our travellers saw was sufficient excuse for their astonishment, and certainly deserved the attention they paid it.

This was the spectacle that met their gaze through the fissure in the rock.

In the first place, they beheld a cavern, not unlike the one in which they were standing.

Two persons were sitting, or rather squatting, in the centre of this cavern in front of a casket, which rested upon a stone much wider than the casket, and one of these persons was endeavoring to fix a lighted taper on a corner of the stone. It was the light from this taper, which illuminated the whole interior, that had attracted the attention of Musaron and his master.

These two figures were wretchedly apparelled, and their heads were muffled up in the thick veils, of no definable color, which formed the distinctive badge of the gypsy women of the period. Agénor, then, came at once to the conclusion that they belonged to that wandering race; they were old, to judge from their deportment and gestures.

Two steps away from them, stood a third figure in an attitude of deep thoughtfulness, but, owing to the flickering light reflected on the face from the taper, it was impossible to tell the sex of this third individual.

Meanwhile, the two women laid some bundles of clothes upon the floor to serve as seats.

Everything had a sordid and ragged appearance; the casket alone offered a singular contrast to all this wretchedness; it was of ivory, and entirely inlaid with gold.

Next advanced a fourth figure, emerging from the obscurity at the back of the grotto, then looming up through the nebulous shadow farther on, and finally standing in the full light.

It approached one of the two women, made an inclination, and uttered some words which neither Agénor nor Musaron could hear.

The gypsy listened attentively, without stirring from her seat, and dismissed the new-comer with a gesture.

There was something in this gesture that excited the keenest interest in Agénor; it was at once noble and commanding.

The person who had remained standing bowed also, then followed the person who had spoken, and both disappeared into the depths of the grotto.

No sooner had they departed, than the woman of the imperious gesture rose in turn, and placed her foot on the stone.

Every act of these people could be seen clearly enough, but, as we have said, it was impossible to hear their words, which came to the ear only in confused murmurs.

The two gypsies were now alone.

"I would venture a wager, monseigneur," whispered Musaron, "that these two old witches can reckon three hundred years between them. Gypsies are as long-lived as crows."

"In fact," returned Agénor, "they do not seem young."

During this time, the second woman, instead of rising like the first, fell on her knees and began unlacing the deer-skin buskin which covered the foot of her companion, running up somewhat above the ankle.

"By my faith, look, if you wish!" said Agénor; "I give it up; nothing is so ugly as an old woman's foot."

The knight took a step backward, but Musaron, more inquisitive than his master, remained where he was.

After a moment's inspection, he broke silence.

"By my faith, sir knight! that which I see is not at all as dreadful as you might think. Oh, no! quite the contrary, it is charming. Just look and you'll see!"

Agénor plucked up his courage and looked.

"Why," said he, "this is simply wonderful! Never have I beheld ankle so perfectly exquisite. The gypsies are really a magnificent race."

The old woman next proceeded to steep a piece of linen of the most delicate texture in a stream of water rolling in diamond drops down a rock, and returned to wash the foot which she had exposed to view.

Then she opened the box, inlaid with gold, and took from it certain perfumes wherewith she gently rubbed that foot, which aroused the astonishment as well as the admiration of the two travellers

"Perfumes! balms! Mark you that, monseigneur?" cried Musaron.

"What can this mean?" murmured Agénor, as he saw the old gypsy bringing to view a second foot not less white and dainty than the first.

"Sir knight," said Musaron, "you are gazing on the toilet of the queen of the gypsies. But stay! In a moment she will be disrobed."

And, in fact, the old woman, after washing, drying, and perfuming the second foot, as she had done the first, gave her attention to the veil, which she removed with every possible precaution, and with an air of boundless respect.

The absence of the veil, instead of disclosing the wrinkled visage of a centenarian, as Musaron had predicted, unmasked a winsome face, brown eyes, rosy cheeks, and an aquiline nose of the purest Iberian type; and the two travellers had before them a woman of from twenty-six to twenty-eight years, in all the splendor of her marvellous beauty.

While they stood rapt in ecstasy in the presence of this entrancing vision, the old gypsy spread a carpet of camel's hair on the floor of the cavern. Although in length it was about ten feet, it would have passed through the finger-ring of a young girl; it was woven of that tissue of which the Arabs alone possessed the secret at the time, and was made out of the hair of a still-born camel. After placing both the feet of her companion on this magnificent carpet, the old gypsy, having, as we have already stated, removed the veil from her face, set about taking away the one that covered her bosom.

As long as this latter fabric remained in its proper place, Musaron held his breath, but, when it fell, he could not repress a cry of admiration.

No sooner was this cry uttered — it was undoubtedly heard by the two women — than the light was extinguished and the cavern buried in the profoundest darkness, — a darkness that ingulfed this mysterious scene as thoroughly as if it had been swallowed up in the waters of oblivion.

Musaron had the impression that a violent kick was aimed at him out of the shadow, which, owing to a dexterous movement on his side, missed him and reached the wall, and that the kick was accompanied by this energetic apostrophe uttered in his master's angriest tone, —

"Blockhead!"

He believed, or affected to believe, that this was an order to retire to his couch, as well as a punishment for his indiscretion.

Accordingly, he retreated quietly, wrapped his cloak about him, and lay down upon the bed of leaves which he had carefully provided for himself some time before. At the end of five minutes, when he had given up all hopes of seeing the taper lit again, Agénor came and stretched himself alongside his squire.

Musaron thought the moment propitious for getting his fault pardoned by giving an exhibition of his superior perspicacity.

"This is how the matter stands," he said, doubtless expressing aloud what Agénor was saying to himself in a whisper: "they followed — and in this I challenge contradiction — they followed, I repeat, a path on the other side of the mountain exactly parallel to ours, and they discovered on the other slope an opening parallel to the opening of the cavern in which we at present dwell; this cavern of ours is, as you see, bisected in the middle by a rock, which the caprice of nature or the fantasy of man has wedged in where it is, to serve as a gigantic partition."

"Blockhead!" Agénor contented himself with repeating a second time.

However, as this second apostrophe was pronounced in a milder tone, the squire considered it a marked improvement on the first.

"Now," he continued, after rendering a silent homage to his own infallible tact, "now, what kind of women were they? Gypsies, indubitably. Oh, yes!

I grant they were gypsies; but how do you account for the perfumes and the balms, and the delicate white feet, and the exquisitely beautiful face, and the magnificent throat and breast which we barely caught a glimpse of, and which we might have contemplated at our leisure, when — idiot that I am! — "

Musaron thereupon dealt himself a stinging blow on the cheek.

Agénor could not keep from laughing. Musaron heard him.

"The queen of the gypsies!" he went on, more and more satisfied with himself; " it is scarcely probable, and yet I can hardly find any other explanation of that truly fairy-like vision which vanished into air because of my own stupidity. Oh, what a blockhead I am, indeed!"

And he gave himself a sound thump on the other cheek.

Agénor saw clearly that Musaron, in his way, quite as inquisitive as himself, was genuinely repentant, and he remembered that the Gospel wisheth the conversion and not the death of the sinner.

Moreover, from the moment Musaron applied to himself, after calm reflection, the unseemly epithet which his master had used, after a sudden gust of anger, the reparation appeared in every way adequate.

"But what is your opinion of these two women?" Musaron ventured, after a pause.

"My opinion is that the sordid garments of the younger of the two did not harmonize very well with the ravishing loveliness of which, unfortunately, we barely caught a glimpse."

Musaron heaved a profound sigh.

"And," continued Agénor, "that the balms and perfumes taken out of the casket harmonized still worse with that same filthy raiment; and all this leads me to think — "

Agénor paused.

"To think what, monseigneur?" queried Musaron. "'T would please me much, I confess, to have the opinion, in the present circumstance, of a knight so thoughtful and sagacious."

"And all this leads me to think," went on Agénor, yielding unconsciously, like Maître Corbeau, to the magic allurement of flattery, "that they are two travellers, one of whom is rich and of high estate, on their way to some distant city, and that the lady who is rich and of high estate has invented this disguise in order not to tempt the avarice of thieves or the lust of soldiers."

"Hold, hold, monseigneur!" said Musaron, not at all inclined to abandon the pre-eminent position which he rightly held in every discussion; "might not one of these women be of the kind that the gypsies make sale of, and of whose beauty they are as mindful as are the horse-dealers whose steeds of price are carefully groomed and caparisoned while faring from town to town?"

Clearly, to-night it was useless contending with Musaron, who deserved the laurel crown, not only for his flawless reasoning, but for the originality of his suggestions. So Agénor surrendered, giving it to be understood by his silence that he acknowledged himself beaten.

The fact is that Agénor, although deep down in his heart abided a love true and genuine, had allowed himself to be smitten, as might any man of twenty-five, by the sight of a pretty foot and a charming face. He was thoroughly discontented with his conduct, and remained buried in gloomy silence. As likely as not, the ingenious Musaron's opinion was correct, and the mysterious fair one was simply an adventuress, rambling about the country in the train of a band of gypsies, and dancing to perfection, with those adorable little dainty feet of hers, the egg-dance, or, perhaps, that of the tight-rope.

There was one circumstance, however, that scarcely harmonized with this conjecture; it was the respect paid the unknown by her companions. But Musaron, whose argumentative powers and irresistible logic drove the poor knight crazy, called his attention to the fact that they had both seen mountebanks who showed the greatest respect towards the monkey of the company, or towards the principal actor; and naturally, for it was the animal or the actor that brought in the money that fed the others.

And so the knight floundered about in this distressing uncertainty until, at length, gentle sleep, that kindly soother of the weary, came and wooed him from that power of thinking which he had been using so immoderately for the last two hours.

About four in the morning, the first beams of the dawning day spread a violet mantle over the sides of the grotto. This gleam of sunlight awoke Musaron, who awoke his master, who rubbed his eyes, got his wits together, and ran to the cleft in the rock.

But Musaron shook his head. This pantomime meant that he had been there before him.

"There's not a soul in it," he murmured, "not a soul!"

And the sun, in fact, was now high enough to illuminate the neighboring grotto, and prove the correctness of Musaron's observation; the cavern was empty, there could be no doubt of it.

The gypsies had risen earlier than the knight, and

had taken to their heels, and casket, perfumes, balms, everything, in fact, had vanished with them.

Musaron, in whose mind the realities of life overbore every other consideration, suggested breakfast; but, before he could develop the advantages of this proposal, they had reached the crest of the mountain, and, perched like some bird of prey on that elevation, he could discover its curves and windings, and the bluish expanse of the valley as well.

On a table-land, about three-quarters of a league from the height where Agénor stood, the eyes of the bird of prey, whose place our travellers may be said to have usurped, might have descried an ass, and a person riding on that ass, while three others went along on foot.

These four individuals who, in spite of the distance, were outlined with some degree of distinctness before the eyes of Agénor, could, in all probability, be none other than the four gypsies, who, having come up with the road along which the two travellers had journeyed the evening before, appeared now to be following the path Musaron had been told led to Soria.

"Quick, Musaron, quick!" cried Agénor. "To horse, and spare not spur! These are our night-birds; 't is meet we see how their plumage looks by day."

Musaron, who was conscious that he had to make amends for many faults, led forward the knight's steed ready saddled and bridled, mounted his own, and silently followed Agénor, who was soon galloping at a rattling pace.

In half an hour, both were within three hundred yards of the gypsies, who, for a moment, were hidden from them by a clump of trees.

VI.

THE QUEEN OF THE GYPSIES.

THE gypsies had turned around two or three times, a movement which showed that, if they had been seen, they had also seen; and this led Musaron to adventure the opinion, though with a timidity which was anything but usual with him, that, once they had moved past the clump of trees, they would no longer see the little band of vagrants, who would, for certain, disappear in some by-path known to them alone.

Musaron was not lucky in his predictions, for, the clump of trees once turned, the gypsies were in full view again, apparently, at least, going their way tranquilly.

However, Agénor noticed one change that had taken place: the woman he had seen from a distance on the ass, who, he felt sure, was the woman with the white feet and the beautiful face, was now walking with her companions, and in no way differed from them in gait or bearing.

"Ho, there!" cried Agénor; "ho, there, good folk!"

The men turned around, and the knight remarked that their hands sought their belts, from which hung two long cutlasses.

"Monseigneur," said Musaron, with his usual forethought, "did you see?"

"Perfectly," answered Agénor.

Then, addressing these two gypsies, —

"You need have no fear," he said. "I have come hither with no unfriendly intent, and, now that we have met, I am glad to tell you so, my brave fellows; if 't were otherwise, little would your cutlasses avail against my cuirass and shield, and but poorly could you defend yourselves against my lance and sword. Now that this is settled, where go you, my masters?"

One of the two men frowned, and was about to make some rude answer, when the other checked him and replied politely,—

"Do you follow us, seigneur, because you would have us point out the road you wish to take?"

"Certainly," said Agénor; "and also because we greatly desire to be honored with your company."

At this, Musaron indulged in one of his most significant grimaces.

"Well, then, seigneur," answered the polite gypsy, "we are going to Soria."

"Thanks! that suits us marvellously; for we, too, are going to Soria."

"Unfortunately," returned the gypsy, "your lordships travel much faster than we poor wayfarers."

"I have heard it said," answered Agénor, "that those of your nation can run afoot and overtake a rider, be he ever so well horsed."

"It is possible," said the gypsy; "but not when they have two old women with them."

Agénor and Musaron exchanged a glance, the glance of Musaron being accompanied by a grimace.

"What you say sounds true," answered Agénor, "and yet, you are but poorly accoutred for travelling. How can the women who are with you support such fatigue?"

"They are accustomed thereto, seigneur, and for a long time, since they are our mothers. We gypsies are born in sorrow, and sufferance is our portion from our birth."

"Ah! these are your mothers," said Agénor; "poor women!"

For a moment the knight feared that the beautiful gypsy had taken another route; but, almost immediately, his mind recurred to the woman he had seen riding on the ass, who had alighted as soon as she perceived him. It was but a sorry mount for the lady; but at least it had sufficed to spare the delicate little perfumed feet he had observed the night before.

He drew near the women; they quickened their pace.

"Let one of your mothers mount the ass," he said, "and the other shall ride behind me."

"The ass is laden with our wearing apparel," replied the gypsy, "and that is about as much as he can bear. As for your horse, señor, your excellency, doubtless, makes sport of us; it is too noble and goodly a beast to serve for a poor old gypsy."

Meanwhile, Agénor was observing the two women, and on the feet of one of them he recognized the deer-skin buskins he had noticed on the previous evening.

"It is she," he murmured; "certainly, this time I do not err."

"Come, good mother with the blue veil, accept the offer I make you: ride behind me you must, and if your ass is too heavily laden, then your companion can ride behind my squire."

"Thanks, señor," answered the gypsy, in a voice of such melody that if any doubt remained in the mind of the knight it must needs have vanished.

"In truth," exclaimed Agénor, in a tone of irony, that made the two women start and the two men lay their hands on their knives, "never heard I voice so sweet from the lips of an old woman before."

"Seigneur!" said the male gypsy who had not yet spoken, in a voice that trembled with anger.

"Oh! it boots not to be wrathful," Agénor went on calmly. "If I guess by her voice that your companion is young, I guess by the thickness of her veil that she is beautiful; that is no reason why you should play with your knives."

The two men took a step forward, as if to protect the young woman.

"Stop!" she said imperiously.

The two men halted.

"You are right, sir knight," she continued. "I am young, and, perhaps, I am beautiful also. But I would ask you what business it is of yours? and may I ask further by what right do you interfere with my journey, even though my years are some twenty or twenty-five less than they appear?"

But Agénor was for the moment struck dumb with surprise. Every inflection in the accents of this voice bespoke the superior woman, the woman born and accustomed to command.

At length the young man stammered,—

"Señora, you are not mistaken; I am a knight."

"I doubt not you are; but I am not a señora, though I be a little less ugly, perhaps, than the women of my race."

Agénor made a gesture of incredulity.

"Do the wives and daughters of persons of rank travel on foot?" asked the unknown.

"Oh! that is but a flimsy reason," answered Agénor; "just now you were riding."

"Granted," returned the young woman; "but, at least, you will admit that my raiment is not that of a woman of quality."

"Women of quality sometimes disguise themselves, madame, especially when it is the interest of women of quality to be taken for women of the people."

"Believe you that a woman of quality whose wonted attire is silk and velvet would consent to incase her feet in such boots as these ? "

And she put forward one of her deer-skin buskins.

" A boot may be unlaced at night-time, and the delicate foot that has been fatigued with walking during the day can be rubbed with perfumes and so relieved."

Had the fair traveller raised her veil, Agénor would have seen her cheeks flush an angry red, and her eyes flame in the purple circle that surrounded them.

" Perfumes ! " she murmured, with an anxious glance at her companion, while Musaron, who had not lost a single word of the dialogue, smiled slyly.

Agénor did not care to embarrass her further.

"Madame," said he, "a delightful perfume exhales from your person; that is what I meant, and naught else."

"Thanks for your courtesy, sir knight. But, since that is what you meant and naught else, the saying so ought to be enough to content you."

" Which signifies that you order me to withdraw, does it not, madame ? "

"It signifies that I recognize you for a Frenchman by your accent, and, still more, from your discourse. Now, it is perilous travelling with Frenchmen, when one is a poor maiden at all responsive to fair words and courteous dealing."

" And so you insist that I part from you ? "

" Yes, sir knight, very regretfully, but — I insist."

One of the two servants showed by his attitude, on hearing the lady's answer, that he was quite ready to support her in her insistence.

"I shall obey, señora," said Agénor; "not, believe me, because of the threatening airs of your two companions, whom it would please me well to encounter in less good company than yours, so that I might teach them to be less fond of touching their knives, but because of the mystery wherewith you elect to surround yourself, and which may be necessary for the execution of some project I would fain not thwart."

"You thwart no project, and risk unriddling no mystery, this I swear," answered the lady.

"Enough, madame," said Agénor. "Besides," he added, somewhat abashed at seeing the little effect produced by his knightly bearing, "besides, the tardy pace at which you journey would hinder me from reaching the court of the King Don Pedro with that speed which my duty urges."

"Ah! you ride to the court of Don Pedro?" cried the young woman, quickly.

"And that at once, señora. Permit me, on taking my leave, to wish you all the prosperity so amiable a person deserves."

The young woman appeared to adopt a sudden resolution, and raised her veil.

No sooner was this rude covering discarded than the beauty of her face and the distinction of her features shone forth with even more splendor than when Agénor first saw her, for her eyes had a caressing expression, and her mouth was smiling.

The knight reined in his steed, which had already taken a step forward.

"Stay, sir knight," she said, "it is easily perceived that you are a delicate and discreet cavalier; for you have, perhaps, guessed who I am, and yet you did not persecute me, as another would have done in your place."

"I have not guessed who you are, madame, but I have guessed who you are not."

"Well, sir knight, since you are so courteous, I am going to tell you the whole truth."

At these words the two servants exchanged a look of bewilderment; but the false gypsy went on, still smiling.

"I am the wife of an officer of Don Pedro, and having been separated nearly a year ago from my husband, who followed the prince into France, I am now trying to join him at Soria. But you know that the country round about is held by the soldiers of both parties, and it would fare ill with me if I fell into the hands of those of the pretender. And so I have assumed this disguise to escape them until such time as I meet my husband and his protection is assured me."

"In truth, 't was wisely done," said Agénor, now fully convinced of the truthfulness of the young woman. "And right joyous would I have been to offer you my service, but that it fits not with my duty, for I must haste with all the speed I may to fulfil my mission."

"Nay, listen," answered the fair traveller: "now that you know who I am, and that I know who you are, I am willing to go as quick as you desire, if you consent to take me under your protection and allow me to travel in your company."

"Ah! your opinion has changed, then, madame?" said Agénor.

"Yes. I have reflected that I might encounter persons quite as sharp-sighted as you are, but not as courteous."

"Then, madame, unless you accept my first proposal, how are we to manage?"

"Oh, judge not my ass by his appearance; all humble though be his looks, he is, like your horse, a thoroughbred.

He comes from the stables of Don Pedro and could support comparison with the swiftest courser."

"But your people, madame."

"Cannot your squire take my nurse behind him? The others will follow on foot."

"Better still would it be, madame, to leave your ass to your two servants who could ride turn about. Then might your nurse mount behind my squire, as you have just said, and you behind me, as I now propose. In this fashion, we should form a respectable company."

"Well, be it as you wish," said the lady.

And hardly were the words out of her mouth when, with the lightness of a bird, the lovely pilgrim leaped on the croup of Agénor's steed.

The two men next placed the old nurse behind Musaron, who laughed no longer.

One of the servants mounted the ass, the other held on to the crupper, and the whole party set out at a rapid trot.

VII.

HOW AGÉNOR AND THE UNKNOWN TRAVELLER RODE IN COMPANY, AND THE THINGS WHEREOF THEY COMMUNED DURING THE JOURNEY.

WHEN one young person holds another young person tightly embraced, and when both are handsome, lively, and high-spirited, and, above all, when they are seated on the same horse and compelled to endure in common the bumpings and lurchings entailed by a rough, uneven road, then it is surely hard for these two young persons to avoid becoming very intimate indeed.

The young woman began with questions. It was her right; was she not a woman?

"So, sir knight," said she, "I guessed correctly, and you are a Frenchman?"

"Yes, madame."

"And you go to Soria?"

"Oh! I told you that; you did not guess it."

"Granted. Doubtless, to offer your services to Don Pedro?"

Before giving a categorical answer to this question, Agénor reflected that he was simply escorting this woman as far as Soria, that he was sure to see the king before she could, and that, consequently, there was no danger of an indiscretion on his part.

"Madame," said he, "this time you are mistaken. I am not going to offer my services to Don Pedro, seeing that I belong to Don Henry of Trastamare, or rather to the constable Bertrand Du Guesclin, and I am going to the deposed monarch with proposals of peace."

"The deposed monarch, do you say?" exclaimed the young woman, uttering the first three words haughtily, but modifying the last, so that they expressed surprise only.

"Deposed, undoubtedly," answered Agénor, "since his rival is crowned king in his place."

"Oh, yes, no doubt you are right," said the young woman, carelessly; "and so you bear proposals of peace to the vanquished sovereign?"

"Which he would do well to accept, for his cause is lost."

"You think so?"

"I am sure of it."

"Why?"

"Because, being as badly surrounded and as badly advised as he is, he cannot resist."

"Badly surrounded?"

"Undoubtedly; he is pillaged and urged unto evil by every one: subjects, friends, and mistress."

"So his subjects?"

"Forsake him."

"His friends?"

"Pillage him."

"And his mistress?" said the young woman, hesitatingly.

"His mistress urges him to evil," answered Agénor.

The young woman frowned, and something like a cloud swept across her brow.

"You speak, I presume, of the Moorish damsel?" she asked.

"Of what Moorish damsel?"

"The new paramour of the king."

"What is that you say?" queried Agénor, his eyes now sparkling in turn.

"Have you not heard, then, that the king is madly in love with the daughter of the Moor Mothril?"

"With Aïssa!" cried the knight.

"You know her?" said the young woman.

"Know her? undoubtedly."

"Then how is it you are ignorant that this infamous unbeliever is in a fair way of pushing her into the bed of the king?"

"Stop!" shouted the knight, turning a face as pale as death to his companion; "speak not so of Aïssa, if you wish not that our friendship die ere ever it is born!"

"But how can I speak otherwise, señor, since I speak truth? This Moorish damsel is either now the king's acknowledged mistress or soon to become so; and the proof of it is that he attends her everywhere, walks beside her litter, gives concerts and festivals in her honor, and even goes to her residence, accompanied by his court."

"You are certain of what you say?" said Agénor, trembling, for he recalled the report made by the alcalde to Musaron; "it is true, then, that Don Pedro has visited Aïssa?"

"I am certain of many things, señor knight," said the fair traveller, "for we of the king's household learn new tidings quickly."

"Oh, madame, madame, you pierce my heart!" said Agénor, sadly, for in him youth unfolded its full and perfect flower, — a flower composed of the two most delicate substances of the soul, credulity when listening, artlessness when speaking.

"I pierce your heart?" asked the traveller, astonished. "Does it happen that you are acquainted with this woman?"

"Alas! I love her to distraction, madame!" said the knight, despairingly.

The young woman, with a gesture indicative of compassion, resumed,—

"But does she not love you, then?"

"She told me she loved me. Oh, that false traitor Mothril must needs have used force or sorcery with her!"

"He is a foul caitiff," said the young woman, coldly, "and has wrought much evil to the king. But can you imagine what is his purpose in acting thus?"

"It is very simple: he wishes to supplant Doña Maria Padilla."

"So you also hold that opinion?"

"Assuredly, madame."

"But," continued the traveller, "it is said that Doña Maria is much enamoured of the king; think you she will suffer Don Pedro to abandon her thus?"

"She is a woman, she is weak, and will succumb, just as Doña Bianca has succumbed. The only difference is that, while the death of the one was a murder, the death of the other will be an expiation."

"An expiation! So then, according to you, Doña Maria has something to expiate?"

"I do not give my own opinion, madame; I speak according to the world."

"And therefore, in your opinion, there will be no such lament for Maria Padilla as there was for Blanche de Bourbon?"

"Assuredly not; although, when both are dead, it will probably be discovered that the mistress was as unfortunate as the wife."

"Then you pity her?"

"Yes, even though she deserves less pity from me than from any one else."

"Why?" asked the young woman, her great jet-black eyes dilated and riveted on the knight.

"Because she is said to have advised the assassination of Don Frederic, and Don Frederic was my friend."

"Are you, perchance, the Frankish knight with whom Don Frederic made an appointment?"

"Yes, and he to whom the dog brought the head of his master."

"Sir knight, hear me well!" cried the young woman, seizing Agénor by the wrist. "Sir knight, by the salvation of my soul, by the share which Maria Padilla hopes to obtain of Paradise, I swear that it was not she who so advised, it was Mothril!"

"But she knew that the murder was to take place, and she offered no opposition."

The lady did not answer.

"She has done enough to merit the punishment of God, and her punishment will come from Don Pedro himself. Who can tell but that the reason why he loves her less already is because between him and this woman runs a brother's blood?"

"Perhaps you are right," said the unknown, in a thrilling voice; "but patience! patience!"

"You seem to hate Mothril, madame?"

"To the death."

"What has he done to you?"

"What he has done to every Spaniard: he has separated the king from his people."

"Women rarely feel such mortal hatred towards a man because of a political wrong as that which you profess to feel towards Mothril."

"I have also personal injuries to avenge: he has, during the last month, prevented me from meeting my husband."

"How has he contrived to do so?"

"He has established such strict surveillance around Don Pedro that neither message nor messenger can reach the king or those who serve him. I have sent two couriers to my husband, and they have not returned; the result is that I know not if I shall be permitted to enter Soria. Even you may not—"

"Oh! as for me, I shall enter, for I come as ambassador."

The young woman shook her head, ironically.

"You will enter, if it is his good pleasure," she said, in a voice rendered hoarse by some strong internal emotion.

Agénor extended his hand and showed the ring given him by Henry of Trastamare.

"This is my talisman," said he.

It was an emerald ring, the stone of which was held by two E's interlaced.

"Yes," said the young woman, "perhaps you may, after all, succeed in forcing your way through the guards."

"If I do, you shall also do so, for you belong to my suite, and that circumstance must insure you respect."

"Do you promise then, that, if you enter, I shall enter with you?"

"I swear it on my knightly faith!"

"Well! as guerdon of this oath, I charge you solemnly, sir knight, that you reveal to me what would most please you at the present moment!"

"Alas! what I most desire you cannot grant."

"Tell it me nevertheless, and we shall see."

"I wish to see Aïssa again and speak to her."

"If I enter the city, you shall see Aïssa and you shall speak to her."

"Thanks! Oh, for such a boon my gratitude shall be eternal!"

"How know you but that you will do for me far more than I can do for you?"

"But you are giving me back my life."

"And you are about to give me more than life," said the young woman, with a singular smile.

As they were drawing to the close of this interchange of vows and ratifying their treaty of alliance, they reached the village where it was intended to halt for a time. The fair traveller leaped nimbly from her steed, and, as the presence of Christians among a band of gypsies would look rather strange, to say the least of it, it was agreed that Christians and gypsies should separate for the time and come together again on the morrow at the distance of about a league from the village.

VIII.

THE VARLET.

The next day, although the knight was up very early, he found the gypsies breakfasting by a fountain, just a league from the village, as had been settled when they separated.

The arrangement was the same as on the day before, and the cavalcade started in the same order.

The time passed in conversation, in which Musaron and the old nurse took an active part. Still, although the discourse of these two important personages dwelt on many delectable and interesting subjects, we shall abstain from recording it, except to say that Musaron, in spite of his wonderful address, could not prevail on the old woman to tell him anything about her mistress he had not heard himself.

At length they came in sight of Soria.

It was a city of the second rank; but, at this warlike period, even cities of the second rank were surrounded by walls.

"Madame," said Agénor, "yonder is the city. If you believe the Moor to be as watchful as you told me, rest assured that he does not confine his visits to gates and battlements; he is certain to reconnoitre the plain also. I advise you, therefore, to be on your guard from this time forward."

"I have already thought of that," said the young woman, glancing around her, as if to become better acquainted with the neighborhood; "and, if you would kindly push on with your squire, yet not at too quick a pace, I shall have adopted every necessary precaution in less than a quarter of an hour."

Agénor obeyed. The young woman alighted, and, taking her nurse along with her, was soon lost in the depths of a coppice, while her two companions continued their journey.

"Ha! sir squire, you copy not the discretion of your master! Turn not your head thus!" cried the nurse to Musaron, for that sapient personage was taking pattern after those lost sinners in Dante, whose dislocated heads look backward while their trunks and legs are going forward.

But, in spite of this invitation, Musaron found it impossible to keep his eyes from wandering behind him, to such an uncontrollable pitch was his curiosity excited.

Now, the cause of this was that he had witnessed the disappearance of the two women into a clump of evergreen oaks and chestnut-trees, as we have already stated.

"Decidedly, sir knight," said he to Agénor, when convinced that his eyes could not penetrate the veil of verdure that enveloped the two women, "I am much afraid that, instead of being great ladies, as we at first surmised, our companions are nothing but gypsies after all!"

Unfortunately for Musaron, this was not the opinion of his master.

"Hold your tongue!" said Agénor; "you are grown an over-saucy babbler through fault of my complaisance."

Musaron held his tongue.

After some minutes during which they had scarcely gone a quarter of a league, so slowly did they ride, they heard a shrill, prolonged cry; it was the nurse calling to them.

They turned around and saw a young man coming towards them; he was apparelled after the Spanish fashion, and wore, hanging from his left shoulder, the little mantle usually borne by a stable varlet; he waved his hat as a sign that they should stop for him.

In a moment he was beside them.

"Here I am, seigneur," he said to Agénor, who, to his great astonishment, recognized his travelling companion; a blond wig entirely concealed her black hair, her shoulders, somewhat broadened under the mantle, looked like the shoulders of a healthy lad, her gait was bold, and even her complexion seemed browner since the color of her hair had changed.

"You see I have taken every necessary precaution, as I told you I would," continued the young man; "and your varlet will have no difficulty, I fancy, in entering the city along with you."

And he jumped, with the nimbleness of which Agénor had already experience, up behind Musaron.

"But your nurse?" asked the knight.

"She will stay at the neighboring village with my two squires, until I judge it the proper time to send for them."

"Then all is well; let us enter the city."

Musaron and the varlet preceded their master, who rode straight to the principal gate of Soria, which might now be seen behind an avenue of old trees.

Before, however, they had cleared more than two-thirds of this avenue, they were surrounded by a band of Moors, despatched against them by the sentinels on the ramparts, who had spied their approach.

Agénor was questioned as to the object of his journey.

As soon as he declared that his purpose was to have an interview with Don Pedro, the Moors placed the three travellers in the centre and conducted them to the governor of the gate, an officer selected by Mothril himself.

"I have come," said Agénor, when questioned a second time, "on the part of the constable Bertrand Du Guesclin, to confer with your prince."

On hearing a name which all Spain had learned to respect, the officer appeared troubled.

"And who are those in your company?" he asked.

"You can see for yourself: my squire and varlet."

"'T is well, remain here; I shall make known your request to Seigneur Mothril."

"Do as you like," answered Agénor; "but I warn you it is neither to Seigneur Mothril nor to any other than the King Don Pedro that I intend speaking first; and, moreover, you had best beware of questioning me further, as I may not brook it."

The officer bowed.

"You are a knight," he said, "and as such must know that the orders of a leader cannot be gainsaid; I must, therefore, execute the task appointed me."

Then, turning to his soldiers, —

"Let His Highness, the prime minister, be at once informed," said he, "that a stranger requests an audience of the king on the part of the constable Du Guesclin."

Agénor sought the eyes of his varlet, who, he noticed, looked very pale and very anxious. Musaron, more accustomed to adventures, was not at all put about by such a trifle.

"Comrade," said he to the young woman, "so much for the value of your precautions! You are sure to be recognized, in spite of your disguise, and we shall all be hanged along with you as your accomplices; but, of course, that does not matter, since it pleases my master."

The unknown smiled; she had recovered her presence of mind after a moment, which proved that she was not a stranger to perils either.

She sat down at some distance from Agénor, and seemed wholly indifferent to what was passing.

The travellers, after crossing two or three apartments filled with guards and soldiers, found themselves, at the time Musaron was making his lugubrious reflections, in one of those guard-houses which seem built within the wall of a tower; a single door opened on it.

All eyes were fixed upon this door, through which Mothril was expected to enter at any moment.

Agénor continued his conversation with the officer. Musaron discoursed with some Spaniards, who spoke to him of the constable and of their friends in the service of Don Henry of Trastamare.

The varlet, too, was monopolized by the governor's pages, who treated him as a child, and of no importance whatever.

The only person on whom a real watch was kept was Mauléon; still, his courteous bearing had entirely reassured the officer; and, in any case, what could a single man do against two hundred?

The Spanish officer invited the French officer to have some fruit and wine, and the governor's pages made their way through the hedge of guards for the purpose of waiting upon the visitor.

"It is not my master's custom to accept aught from any hand save mine," said the young varlet.

And he politely escorted the two pages into the next apartments.

At this moment, the sentinel was heard calling to arms, and the cry of "Mothril! Mothril!" re-echoed through the guard-house.

All arose immediately.

Agénor felt a shiver run through every one of his veins; he lowered his visor, and, through its iron bars, sought the eyes of the young varlet, in order that he might give her courage.

"What has become of our travelling companion?" he asked Musaron, in a low voice.

The latter replied in French, with the utmost calmness, —

"Monseigneur, she thanks you much for the service you have rendered her by enabling her to enter Soria; she has charged me to inform you that her gratitude is boundless, and that you shall soon have proof of it."

"Why, what is that you say?" said Agénor, astounded.

"That which she charged me to say to you when she left."

"Left?"

"By my faith, yes!" returned Musaron, "for left she has. An eel does not slip with such ease through the meshes of a net as she slipped through the guards. I saw from a distance her white plume gleaming for a time through the shadow, and, as I have seen nothing of it since, I presume she has escaped."

"God be praised!" said Agénor; "but hush!"

The warning was prudent, for the neighboring apartments were now resounding with the footsteps of a great number of cavaliers.

Mothril entered hurriedly.

"What is the matter?" asked the Moor.

"This knight," said the officer, "sent hither at the

behest of Messire Bertrand Du Guesclin, Constable of France, would speak with the King Don Pedro."

Mothril drew near Agénor, who, with lowered visor, looked not unlike a statue of iron.

The knight, drawing off his gauntlet, and exhibiting the emerald ring which the prince had given him as a token of recognition, said, —

" Look at this! "

" What am I to look at? " asked Mothril.

" The emerald ring given me by Doña Eleonora, the mother of the prince."

Mothril bowed.

"Pray, what would you?"

" I would speak to the king."

" You desire to see His Highness?"

" Yes."

" Your tone is somewhat haughty, sir knight."

" I speak in the name of my master, the King Don Henry of Trastamare."

" Then you must wait in this fortress."

" I am willing to wait. But I warn you I shall not wait long."

Mothril smiled ironically.

" As you will, sir knight," said he; "wait, then."

And he passed out, after saluting Agénor, whose eyes shot forth darts of flame through the iron grating of his helmet.

" Look to them well," whispered Mothril to the officer; "these are important prisoners, and you must answer for them on your head."

" What shall I do? "

"I will tell you to-morrow; meanwhile, see that he does not communicate with any one, *with any one*, — you understand?"

The officer saluted.

"Decidedly," said Musaron, with the greatest serenity, "I am convinced that we are done for, and that this closet of stone will be our coffin."

"What a glorious chance I had to strangle that miscreant!" cried Agénor; and then he murmured, "had I not been an ambassador!"

"One of the disadvantages of greatness," commented Musaron, philosophically.

IX.

THE BOUGH OF ORANGE.

AGÉNOR and his squire spent a very uncomfortable night in the prison wherein they were for the time locked up; the officer, obedient to the orders of Mothril, did not again appear.

It was Mothril's intention to return on the next morning. Having received warning of the approach of his visitors, at the very moment when he was about to accompany Don Pedro to a bull-fight, he had all the night to reflect upon what he ought to do; then, if he could not arrive at any fixed determination, he would again question Agénor, and on the result of the inquiry would depend the fate of the ambassador and his squire.

It was still possible that the envoy of the constable might be permitted to have an interview with Don Pedro; but certainly not until Mothril had succeeded in penetrating, by some means or other, the object of his mission.

The great secret of political improvisers is to know beforehand the matters with regard to which they will have to improvise.

So, after leaving the two prisoners, Mothril took the road to the amphitheatre, where, as we have said, the King Don Pedro amused his court with the spectacle of a bull-fight. This spectacle, ordinarily given by kings in the daytime, took place on the present occasion at night, and, as three thousand torches of perfumed wax lit up the arena, the customary magnificence of these entertainments was greatly enhanced on the present occasion.

Aïssa, seated on the right of the king, and surrounded by courtiers, who worshipped in her the rising star, looked on without seeing, and listened without hearing.

The king, gloomy and preoccupied, questioned the face of the young girl, hoping to read in the unchanging pallor of that brow and in the veiled brilliance of those flashing eyes the fond expectations which he never ceased to cherish.

Don Pedro, with his indomitable heart and fiery temper, resembled, at this moment, a race-horse held in check by the bit, whose impatience breaks forth in starts and plunges of which the spectators seek in vain the cause.

Then, suddenly, his brow grew dark.

He had just remembered, while gazing upon the features of this ice-cold maiden, the ardent mistress he had left at Seville, that Maria Padilla, who, according to Mothril, was as faithless and as fickle as fortune, and who, by her silence, gave countenance to Mothril's insinuations. The present coldness of Aïssa and the past love of Doña Maria afflicted him with a double sorrow.

Then, in thinking of this woman, for whom he felt such adoration that many attributed this adoration to magic, he heaved a sigh so bitter from the depths of his breast that the whole crowd of obsequious courtiers bent their heads as if in premonition of an approaching storm.

It was at one of these moments that Mothril entered the royal box, and, with an all-embracing glance, took note of the mental attitude of king and courtiers.

He perceived the tempest that was lowering in the

heart of Don Pedro; he guessed that the coldness of Aïssa was the cause of it, and he cast a look of menace and hatred upon the young girl, who remained perfectly unmoved, although she understood perfectly also.

"Ah! so you have come, Mothril!" said the king. "Your arrival is badly timed; I am bored."

The tone in which these words were uttered resembled the resonant bellow of a bull.

"I bring news to Your Highness," said Mothril.

"Important?"

"Undoubtedly; am I likely to disturb my sovereign on account of trifles?"

"Speak, then."

The minister whispered in the ear of Don Pedro, —

"An ambassador has arrived from the French, and seeks an audience."

"You see, Mothril," said the king, without appearing to listen to the Moor, "you see how little pleasure her presence in my court gives Aïssa. In good truth, I think you would do well to send this young woman back to her native Africa, which she regrets so much."

"Your Highness is mistaken," returned Mothril; "Aïssa was born at Granada, and, as she is not acquainted with a country she has never seen, she cannot regret it."

"Is there something else she regrets?" asked Don Pedro, turning pale.

"I do not believe so."

"But then, they who regret nothing act in a very different manner. Young girls of sixteen laugh and chatter; yet, in very truth, this young girl is dead."

"You know, sire, that no maidens are so serious,

none so chaste and reserved, as those of the Orient; and I have told you that Aïssa, although born at Granada, is of the purest blood of the Prophet. Aïssa's brows are encircled with a rough crown, — that of misfortune; you cannot, therefore, expect her to have those careless smiles and that noisy gayety which mark the women of Spain; never having been familiar with laughter or gossip, she cannot do as the Spanish señoritas do, — that is to say, toss back lightly the echo of jests she does not understand."

Don Pedro bit his lips and riveted his ardent gaze upon Aïssa.

"A woman does not change in a day," continued Mothril, "and those who guard their dignity longest guard their affection longest. Doña Maria almost offered herself to you, and Doña Maria has forgotten you."

The very moment Mothril uttered these words the branch of an orange-tree in flower, flung from one of the upper galleries, fell at the feet of Don Pedro, with the certainty of an arrow that reaches its goal.

The courtiers cried aloud, "Shame on such insolence!" some of them leaned forward to see whence the messenger had come.

Don Pedro picked up the bough; a note was tied to it. Mothril made a gesture as if he would seize the paper, but Don Pedro waved him aside.

"This note is addressed to me, and not to you," he said.

At the mere sight of the handwriting, he uttered a cry; at the first lines he read, his face cleared.

Mothril followed anxiously the effects produced by this reading.

Suddenly Don Pedro rose.

The courtiers rose also, ready to accompany the king.

"Remain!" said Don Pedro. "The spectacle is not yet finished; it is my will that you remain."

Mothril, who did not know what to make of this unlooked-for event, also rose, and stepped forward as if he would follow his master.

"Remain!" said the king. "It is my will."

The Moor returned to the box, utterly confounded, like the courtiers, by this strange incident.

He searched on every side for the author of the daring missive, but all his inquiries turned out useless.

Hundreds of women held orange flowers and orange boughs in their hands; none could tell him whence this note was hurled.

On returning to the palace, he questioned the Arab maiden; but Aïssa had seen nothing, had noticed nothing.

He tried to see Don Pedro; the door was closed against everybody.

The Moor passed a terrible night; for the first time an event of the highest importance had baffled his sagacity; although not able to base his fears on any probability, his presentiments told him that his influence had just encountered a serious shock.

Mothril had not yet closed an eye, when he was summoned to the apartments of Don Pedro.

The king left his chamber, carefully closing the door, and proceeded to meet the minister.

Don Pedro was paler than usual, but it was not sorrow that gave him this appearance of weariness; on the contrary, a smile of inward contentment flickered on his lips, and there was something more soft and gentle in his looks than usual.

He sat down, with a friendly nod to Mothril, and yet, the Moor thought he remarked an expression of firmness on his countenance that was foreign to their mutual relations.

"Mothril," he said, "you spoke yesterday of an embassy sent by the Frenchmen."

"Yes, may it please Your Highness; but as you made no reply, I did not believe it my duty to continue the subject."

"Besides, you were in no hurry to confess, Mothril," retorted Don Pedro, "that you had imprisoned the embassy, on the very night of its arrival, in the tower of the Lower Gate; is that not so, Mothril?"

Mothril shivered.

"How know you, seigneur?" he murmured.

"I know, and that is the main point. Who are those strangers?"

"Franks; at least, I think so."

"And why did you imprison them, when they told you they were ambassadors?"

"Yes, they told me so, I do not deny it," answered Mothril, who had recovered all his coolness in a moment.

"And you think they are not? Is that what you think?"

"Not exactly, sire, for I am really ignorant whether—"

"In that case, you should not have arrested them."

"Then it is the order of Your Highness—"

"That they be brought before me instantly."

The Moor started back.

"But that is impossible," said he.

"By the blood of our Lord! has aught happened to them?" asked Don Pedro.

"No, sire."

"Then make all the speed you can to repair your fault; for you have violated the law of nations."

Mothril smiled. He knew what reverence Don

Pedro showed for this same law of nations when it came into collision with his hatreds.

"I cannot permit my king," said he, "to surrender his royal person to the danger that menaces him, without, at least, taking measures for his defence."

"Fear not for me," cried Don Pedro, stamping the floor, "fear rather for yourself."

"I have naught to fear, seeing that I have nothing wherewith to reproach myself."

"Nothing wherewith to reproach yourself, Mothril? Examine your conscience."

"What means Your Highness?"

"I mean that you are not fond of ambassadors, whether they come from the east or whether they come from the west."

Mothril was beginning to feel somewhat troubled; this cross-examination was gradually assuming a threatening aspect; but as he did not know from what quarter the attack was likely to come, he was silent and waited.

The king continued, —

"Is this the first time you have arrested ambassadors who have been sent to me, Mothril?"

"The first time!" answered Mothril, staking all to win all; "there have come hundreds of such messengers, and I have never let a single one pass."

The king rose up in a fury.

"If I have erred," went on the Moor, "in driving from the palace of my king the assassins hired by Henry of Trastamare and Bertrand Du Guesclin to murder him, and if, in doing so, I have sacrificed a few who were innocent, among so many who were guilty, my head is there to pay the penalty."

The king sat down, and, after a moment, said, —

"'T is well, Mothril; I accept your excuse, which

may be true, and pardon you. But let this not happen again, and let every messenger who is sent to me be brought into my presence, do you hear? — whether he comes from Burgos or from Seville. As to these Frenchmen, they are really ambassadors, and I know it; it is our pleasure, therefore, that they be treated as ambassadors. Let them at once, then, be dismissed from your tower, and conducted with all the honors due to their position to the finest house in the city. To-morrow I shall receive them in solemn audience in the grand hall of the palace. Go!"

Mothril bent his head and passed out, utterly crushed with terror and astonishment.

X.

THE AUDIENCE.

Agénor and his faithful squire were lamenting, each after his own fashion.

Musaron adroitly insinuated to his master that he had predicted everything that happened.

Agénor replied that, as he knew what was about to happen, he had the less reason to complain of his fate.

To which Musaron answered that he also knew of ambassadors who had been hanged on gibbets; it was true that these gibbets were loftier than those used for ordinary malefactors, but he had been unable to discover that they were more comfortable on that account.

To which Mauléon had no reply ready.

The quickness with which Don Pedro dealt out justice was well known. Persons who hold the life of others in little esteem always do act quickly.

The two prisoners were absorbed in these melancholy thoughts, and Musaron was already examining the stones of the walls to see whether some of them might not be displaced, when Mothril stood upon the threshold, followed by an escort of captains, which he left outside the door.

Notwithstanding the suddenness of the Moor's entrance, Agénor had time to lower the visor of his helmet.

"Frenchman," said Mothril, "answer me, and do not lie, — that is, if you can speak without lying."

"Do you think others are like yourself, Mothril?" said Agénor, who, though he did not care to render his position worse by an angry outburst, had still an instinctive distaste to allowing himself to be insulted by the man he hated most in the world.

"What do you mean, dog?" retorted Mothril.

"You call me dog, because I am a Christian; but, in that case, your master is a dog also, is he not?"

This thrust reached the Moor and touched him.

"Who speaks of my master and of his religion?" said he. "Mingle not his name with yours, and believe not that you resemble each other because you both adore the same God."

Agénor sat down, shrugging his shoulders.

"Was it to tell me all this nonsense you came hither, Mothril?" asked the knight.

"No; there are certain important questions to which I desire an answer."

"Well, let us hear your questions."

"In the first place, I wish to know the measures you adopted to enter into correspondence with the king."

"With what king?" queried Agénor.

"I recognize but one, emissary of rebels, and that is the king, my master."

"Don Pedro? You would learn how I have been enabled to correspond with Don Pedro?"

"Yes."

"I do not understand you."

"Do you deny that you have asked an audience of the king?"

"No, for it was through you that I preferred that demand."

"Yes, but it was not I who transmitted that demand to the king — and yet — "

"And yet?" repeated Agénor.

"He knows that you are here."

"Ah!" muttered the knight, completely bewildered; and this "ah!" was echoed by another "ah!" that came with far greater emphasis from the lips of Musaron.

"So you will confess nothing?" said Mothril.

"What would you have me confess?"

"The means you employed to reach the king."

Agénor shrugged his shoulders a second time.

"Ask our guards," he said.

"Believe not, Christian, that you can obtain any grace from the king, except I consent thereto."

"Ha!" exclaimed Agénor; "then I am to see the king?"

"Hypocrite!" broke out Mothril, furiously.

"Good!" cried Musaron. "I think, from present appearances, there will be no need for me making a hole through the wall."

"Silence!" said Agénor. Then, turning to Mothril, "Well," he continued, "since I am to speak with the king, we shall see, Mothril, whether my words have as little weight as you imagine."

"Confess how you have made your arrival known to the king, tell me the conditions upon which you propose to make peace, and you may command all my influence."

"What avails an influence with which your very anger tells me I may dispense?" retorted Agénor, with a laugh.

"At least, let me see your face," cried Mothril, troubled equally by the laugh and by the tones of the voice.

"You will see me when we are both in the presence

of the king," rejoined Agénor. "To the king alone will I speak with heart and face unmasked."

Suddenly Mothril struck his forehead and looked around the chamber.

"You had a page?" said he.

"Yes."

"What has become of him?"

"Ask, question, search; it is your right."

"It is on this subject that I have now questioned you."

"Let us understand each other: to question is your right in regard to your officers, soldiers, slaves, but not in regard to me."

Mothril turned to his attendants.

"There was a page with this Frenchman," said he. "Let me know immediately what has become of him."

There was silence while the search was going on. Each of the three persons awaited the result with very different emotions, and these emotions might be read on their faces. Mothril, in a state of great agitation, walked up and down in front of the door, like a sentry before his box, or rather like a hyena in his cage. Agénor, tranquilly seated, had all the impassive stillness of a statue of iron. Musaron, though he let nothing escape him, remained as silent as his master, his eyes riveted on every movement of the Moor.

The answer was that the page had disappeared the evening before, and had not been seen since.

"Is this true?" asked Mothril of Agénor.

"By my faith, 'tis men of your creed who say so! Do infidels lie also, then?"

"But why has he fled?"

Agénor now understood everything.

"Doubtless to tell the king that his master was arrested," he replied.

"No one reaches the king when Mothril guards the king, without Mothril's knowledge," answered the Moor.

Then, suddenly striking his forehead, "Ah! the orange bough!" said he, — "the note!"

"Decidedly, this Moor is losing his wits!" muttered Musaron.

But in a moment Mothril appeared to recover his self-possession. Evidently, what he had discovered was less terrible than what he had feared at first.

"Well," said he, "you have won. I congratulate you on the adroitness of your page; the audience you have wished for is granted."

"And for what day?" demanded Agénor.

"For to-morrow."

"God be praised!" cried Musaron.

"But take care," continued the Moor, addressing the knight, "lest your interview with the king have not the happy ending you hope for."

"I hope for nothing," said Agénor. "I fulfil my mission, and that is the end of it."

"Would you not have a counsel from me?" asked Mothril, giving his voice an almost caressing tone.

"Thanks," replied Agénor, "I would have nothing from you."

"Why?"

"Because I accept nothing from an enemy."

The young man uttered these words in such tones of hatred that the Moor shuddered.

"'T is well," said he. "Adieu, Frenchman."

"Adieu, infidel," replied Agénor.

Mothril passed out; on the whole, he knew everything he wanted to know; the king had received his information from a source that was not at all dangerous. This was not what he had feared at first.

Two hours after this interview, an imposing guard of soldiers arrived at the tower, and conducted Agénor, with every mark of respect, to a house situated on the plaza of Soria.

Vast suites of apartments, furnished in the most sumptuous manner, had been prepared for the reception of the ambassador.

"You are now at home, seigneur ambassador of the King of France," said the captain commanding the escort.

"I am not the ambassador of the King of France, and deserve not to be treated as such. I am the ambassador of the constable Bertrand Du Guesclin."

But the captain contented himself with saluting, and retired.

Musaron made the tour of every chamber, inspecting the carpets, the furniture, and the stuffs, and saying, after every inspection, —

"Decidedly, we are better off here than at the tower."

While Musaron was making this careful review of the house and its contents, the grand governor of the palace entered, and inquired of the knight whether he would like to make any changes in his costume before appearing in the presence of the king.

"No," said Agénor. "I have my sword, my helmet, and my cuirass; they are the accoutrements of the soldier, and I am a soldier simply, sent hither by my captain."

The governor left, and ordered the trumpets to sound.

A moment after, a superb charger, magnificently caparisoned, was led to the door.

"I need no other horse but my own," said Agénor. "It was taken from me, let it be restored; that is all I desire."

In ten minutes the horse of Agénor was returned to him.

An immense crowd lined the space — which, for that matter, was very short — between the house of Agénor and the palace of the king. The young man's eyes sought among the women who thronged the balcony the face of the travelling companion he knew so well. But he soon gave up his quest in despair; evidently she was not there.

All the nobles faithful to Don Pedro formed a cavalry corps and were drawn up in the court of honor in front of the palace. A dazzling spectacle they presented, with their arms all covered with gold.

Agénor had scarcely dismounted when he began to feel just a little embarrassed. Events had succeeded one another with such rapidity that he had not had time, so far, to think of his mission, especially as he was persuaded that this mission would not be accomplished.

His tongue seemed glued to the roof of his mouth; he had not a single clear idea in his head. All his thoughts were confused, indistinct, beating against one another like clouds in the foggy days of autumn.

He entered the hall of audience like a blind man whose sight has been suddenly restored, and who is almost blinded again by the dazzling sheen of gold and purple and moving plumes lit up by the burning rays of a noontide sun.

Then a vibrating voice resounded in his ears, — a voice he remembered he had heard before at night in the garden of Bordeaux, by day under the tent of Caverley.

"Sir knight," said this voice, "you desired to speak with the king; you are in the presence of the king."

These words fixed the attention of Agénor on the

point from which they came. He recognized Don Pedro. At his right, sat a woman shrouded in a veil; at his left, stood Mothril.

Mothril was as pale as a corpse; he had just detected the lover of Aïssa in the knight before him.

The discovery flashed through his mind as soon as he set eyes upon him.

"Monseigneur," said Agénor, "I have never for a moment believed that I was arrested by the orders of Your Lordship."

Don Pedro bit his lips.

"Sir knight," he answered, "you are a Frenchman, and, are perhaps ignorant that, when the King of Spain is spoken to, he is addressed as Sire or Highness."

"Yes, I confess I am wrong," rejoined the knight, bowing; "you are king in Soria."

"Yes, king in Soria," returned Don Pedro, "and awaiting the hour when he who has usurped that title is no longer king anywhere."

"Sire," said Agénor, "fortunately, I have not come to discuss these high questions with you. I have come on the part of your brother, Don Henry of Trastamare, to propose to you a good and loyal peace, a peace of which your subjects stand in such great need, a peace at which your brotherly hearts will rejoice also."

"Sir knight," answered Don Pedro, "if you have come to discuss this matter with me, say why you rejected a week ago the proposal you make to-day?"

Agénor bowed.

"I am not judge, Your Highness," said he, "between your puissant seigniories; I repeat the words I have been told to repeat, and that is simply all. I follow the path that extends from Burgos to Soria, from the heart of brother to the heart of brother."

"Ah! you know not why I am offered peace to-day," said Don Pedro. "Well, I will tell you."

These words of the king produced a profound silence in the assembly. Agénor took advantage of the moment to turn his eyes a second time on the veiled woman and on the Moor. The veiled woman remained as dumb and as motionless as a statue. The Moor was pale and changed, as if he had concentrated in the tortures of a single night the sufferings of a lifetime.

"You offer peace in the name of my brother," said the king, "because my brother wishes me to refuse it, and knows that I shall refuse the conditions you are about to propose."

"Sire," answered Agénor, "you are as yet ignorant of those conditions."

"I know that you come to offer me the half of Spain; I know that you come to demand of me hostages, and that among these hostages are Mothril and his family."

Mothril, pale as he was before, now turned livid; his flaming eyes seemed to be trying to fathom the very depths of Don Pedro's soul, in order to be assured whether he would persevere in his refusal or not.

Agénor started; he had not disclosed the nature of the conditions to any one except to the gypsy, and he remembered that to her he had said only a few words.

"I see," he observed, "that Your Highness is remarkably well-informed, although by whom or how I am utterly unaware."

At the same moment the veiled woman, with a movement in which there was no affectation, raised her gold-embroidered veil and cast it back on her shoulders.

Agénor could scarcely refrain from uttering a cry of terror; in this woman who sat on Don Pedro's right he had to recognize his travelling companion.

There was a rush of blood to his face; he understood now where the king had got the information that spared him the trouble of expounding the conditions of peace.

"Sir knight," said Don Pedro, "learn this from my mouth, and repeat it to those who sent you: no matter what conditions are offered me, there is one I shall always reject; it is that of sharing my realm with any one. My realm is mine, and I shall dispose of it according to my good pleasure; when I am victorious, I, too, shall offer conditions."

"Then Your Highness wishes war?" asked Agénor.

"I do not wish it, I abide it," answered the king.

"And this is the immutable purpose of Your Highness?"

"Yes."

Agénor slowly drew off his steel gauntlet, and flung it at the feet of the king.

"In the name of Henry of Trastamare, King of Castile," said he, "I bring hither war."

The king rose, amid a great murmur and a frightful clashing of arms.

"You have faithfully fulfilled your mission, sir knight," said he; "it rests with us to do loyally our devoir as king. We offer you twenty-four hours of hospitality in our city, and, if it suits you, our palace shall be your abode, our table at your service."

Agénor, without answering, made a profound obeisance, and, raising his head, gazed steadily on the woman seated beside the king.

She returned his gaze, smiling softly the while. It even seemed to him that she laid a finger on her lips as if to say to him,—

"Patience! Hope!"

XI.

THE APPOINTMENT.

In spite of this tacit promise, the meaning of which, however, Agénor did not very well comprehend, he quitted the hall of audience in a state of anxiety that can be easily imagined. The only thing of which he had a certainty, or, at least, a strong probability, was that the unknown gypsy, with whom he had travelled so unceremoniously, was no other than the celebrated Maria Padilla.

The resolution of Don Pedro, which had been made known to the world even before he himself had uttered a word on the nature of his mission, was not what troubled him most; for, after all, Don Pedro had only learned in the evening what he would have been sure to learn on the morrow; that was of no consequence. But Agénor recalled the fact that he had delivered to the gypsy his secret of secrets, the nearest and dearest of all his secrets, — his love for Aïssa.

Once the jealousy of this terrible woman was aroused against Aïssa, who could tell where the frenzy that had already sacrificed so many innocent heads would stay its hand?

All these baleful thoughts, starting to life at once in the soul of Agénor, prevented him from remarking the evil looks of Mothril and the Moorish nobles, whom the proposal, made in the name of Henry of Trastamare, had wounded at once in their pride and in their interests.

The French knight was very brave and very quick-tempered; and it is probable, had he observed their provoking glances, he would not have maintained all the calmness and impassiveness that beseem an ambassador.

At the moment when he was, perhaps, about to note and answer them, his attention was distracted by another incident. Hardly was he outside the palace and beyond the hedge of guards that encompassed it, when a woman, muffled in a long veil, touched his arm, and, making a mysterious sign, beckoned him to follow her.

Agénor hesitated an instant. He knew with how many snares Don Pedro and his vindictive mistress were accustomed to surround their enemies, and what ingenuity they developed in accomplishing their schemes of vengeance; but, on the present occasion, the knight, good Christian though he was, felt inclined to believe in that fatality of the Orientals which takes from man his free will, and so takes from him also — is it not sometimes a blessing? — the power of foreseeing evil and guarding against it.

The knight, then, crushed down every emotion of fear: he told himself that he had struggled long enough; that it was good to make an end of the matter one way or another; and that, if fate had ordained this hour to be his last, fate was welcome.

He therefore followed the old woman, who made her way through a great concourse of people, — the same sort of a crowd that is to be found in all great cities, — and then, apparently sure of not being recognized, being so closely muffled up, went straight to the house that had been assigned to the knight as his lodging.

On the threshold of this house stood Musaron.

Once they were inside, it was Agénor who guided the old woman to the most remote of the apartments. The old woman followed him, and Musaron, suspecting that something new was going to happen, brought up the rear.

When they were inside the apartment they had chosen, the old woman raised her veil, and both Agénor and his squire recognized the nurse of the gypsy.

After all that had occurred in the palace, this apparition did not, by any means, surprise Agénor; but Musaron, in his ignorance, uttered a cry of wonder.

"Seigneur," said the old woman, "Doña Maria Padilla would converse with you, and therefore desires you to come this evening to the palace. The king will review the troops that have lately arrived, and during that time Doña Maria will be alone. Can she count upon you? Will you promise to visit her?"

"But," said Agénor, who could not make a pretence of entertaining a favorable opinion of Doña Maria which he did not feel, "why does Doña Maria want to see me?"

"Do you believe, sir knight, that to be invited to hold secret parley with such a woman as Doña Maria is so very great a misfortune?" said the nurse, with that complaisant smile belonging to old servants in the South.

"No," said Agénor; "but I confess I prefer those interviews that are held in the open, in places where there is no lack of space, and where a man can go with his lance and steed."

"And I with my arbalist," said Musaron.

The old woman smiled at these signs of uneasiness.

"I see," she said, "that I must fulfil my commission even unto the end."

And she drew a letter from her reticule.

Musaron, to whom in all such cases the rôle of lector belonged, took the paper and read: —

THE APPOINTMENT.

"This, sir knight, is a pledge of safety given by your travelling companion. Come to me at the hour and in the place which my nurse will tell you of, in order that we may speak of Aïssa.
"MARIA."

At these words Agénor started, and, as the name of his mistress is the religion of the lover, the name of Aïssa was at once accepted as a solemn safeguard; he bade the nurse lead the way, and he would follow, no matter where.

"In that case, sir knight," said she, "nothing could be simpler. I shall expect you this evening in the chapel of the castle. This chapel is used by the officers of our lord the king, but at eight in the evening the doors are closed. You will enter at half-past seven, and hide behind the altar."

"Behind the altar!" said Agénor, shaking his head, for he had all the prejudices of the men of the North; "I like not appointments made behind an altar."

"Oh, have no fear!" said the old woman, artlessly. "God has got so used to these little profanations in Spain that he no longer minds them. Besides, you will not have to stay there long. Behind this altar is a door through which the prince and those of his court can enter the chapel from their apartments. I will open this door, and you can vanish through it without being seen by any one."

"Without being seen? Take care, Sir Agénor!" said Musaron in French; "this smacks of throat-cutting. Don't you think so?"

"Be not afraid," answered the knight in the same language; "we have the letter of this woman, and, although signed only with her baptismal name, it is a guarantee. Should any evil befall me, you will return to the constable and Don Henry of Trastamare with this letter; you will tell them of my love, my misfortunes, and the treachery by which I was ensnared, and I know them not if they do not execute such vengeance on the traitors as shall send a thrill of horror throughout Spain."

"That is very well," rejoined Musaron; "but, in the mean time, it will not save you from having your throat cut, all the same."

"Yes; but if it is really for the purpose of speaking with me of Aïssa that Doña Maria sends for me?"

"Monseigneur, you are in love; that is the same as saying you are mad," answered Musaron, "and a madman is always right, especially when he is delirious. Forgive me, sir knight, but I speak the truth. I surrender; go, by all means."

And honest Musaron sighed deeply at the end of this peroration.

"But really," he exclaimed suddenly, "why should I not go with you?"

"Because an answer must be carried to Don Henry of Trastamare," said the knight, "and in case of my death, you alone can relate the result of my mission."

And Agénor gave his squire a succinct and clear account of Don Pedro's answer.

"But at least," said Musaron, who did not yet give up the point, "I can be on the watch around the palace."

"With what object?"

"To defend you, Count of Saint James!" cried the squire; "to defend you with my arbalist, which will lay low half a dozen of those yellow faces, whilst you are slaughtering another half dozen with your sword. There will be, at that rate, a dozen less infidels in the world, and that will surely be no hurt to our chances of salvation."

"My dear Musaron," said Agénor, "you will, on the contrary, do me the favor of not making an appearance at all. If I am slain, the walls of the Alcazar alone will know of the murder. But listen," he added, with that confidence which bespeaks the upright heart: "I believe that I have not insulted this Doña Maria Padilla; she cannot, therefore, bear me a grudge; nay, perhaps I have even rendered her a service."

"Yes, but then the Moor, this Mothril: you have insulted him often enough, have you not, both here and elsewhere? Now, unless I am mistaken, he is governor of the palace, and his kind intentions in your regard are shown by the fact that he wished to have you arrested at the gate, and thrown into a dungeon. I agree with you, it is not the female favorite we should fear; it is the male favorite we should guard against."

Agénor was just a little superstitious; and after the manner of lovers, he managed to harmonize his religion with his superstitions. He turned to the old woman, saying to himself, —

"If she smiles, I will go."

The old woman smiled.

"Go back to Doña Maria," he said to the nurse; "tell her I consent; this evening, after half-past seven, I shall be at the chapel."

"'T is well," replied the old woman; "you may expect me with the key of the door. Adieu, Señor Agénor; adieu, my gracious squire."

Musaron shook his head; the old woman disappeared.

"Now," said Agénor, turning to Musaron, "I cannot give you any letters for the constable; you might be arrested and the letters seized. You will tell him that Don Pedro is bent on war, and that he ought to begin hostilities at once. You have our money, and must make such use of it as will enable you to get to your journey's end as soon as possible."

"But what about yourself, Sir Agénor?—for it is necessary to take into consideration the chance that you may not be killed at all."

"I am in need of nothing. If I am betrayed, I have simply sacrificed a life of weariness and deceptions,—a life of which I am heartily tired. If, on the other hand, Doña Maria protect me, she will find me horses and guides. Depart, Musaron, depart on the instant even. The eyes that are riveted on me take no thought of you; it is known that I remain, and to that fact alone is any importance attached. Go! your horse is good and your courage great. As for me, I shall spend the rest of the day in prayer. Go!"

The plan adopted, adventurous though it was, was in harmony with the situation. And so Musaron did not persist in discussing it, not through courtesy to his master, but because he was convinced.

Musaron started a quarter of an hour after this decision had been made, and left the city without any difficulty. Agénor knelt in prayer, as he had said was his intention, and at half-past seven directed his steps to the chapel.

The old woman was waiting. She beckoned to him to hasten, and opened the little door, through which the knight followed her.

After defiling through several corridors and galleries, Agénor entered a low hall which was but half lit; a terrace, all covered with flowers, surrounded it.

Under a canopy was seated a woman, attended by a slave-maiden, whom she dismissed as soon as the knight appeared.

The old woman also discreetly retired when she had introduced the knight.

"Thanks for your punctuality, sir knight," said Doña Maria to Mauléon. "I knew already that you were gen-

THE APPOINTMENT. 93

erous and brave. I wished to thank you after having seemingly played you false."

Agénor did not answer. It was to speak of Aïssa that he had been summoned and that he had come.

"Approach," said Doña Maria. "I am so attached to Don Pedro that I had to think of his interests, even at the risk of injuring yours; but my love is my excuse, and you who love ought to understand me."

Maria was now drifting towards the object of this interview. Still, Agénor merely bowed and remained dumb.

"Meanwhile," continued Doña Maria, "as we have done with our own affairs, we wish to speak of yours, señor knight."

"Of which?" asked Agénor.

"Of those that interest you most keenly."

Agénor, at sight of that frank smile, that gracious gesture, and the cordial words that accompanied them, felt himself disarmed.

"Come, sit you there," said the enchantress, pointing to a chair beside her.

The knight did as he was ordered.

"You have believed me your enemy," she went on, "and yet I am nothing of the sort; and the proof of it is that I am ready to render you services at least fully equal to those you have rendered me."

Agénor looked at her with astonishment. Maria Padilla resumed, —

"Why not? Have you not been my loyal defender during that journey, and my prudent counsellor as well, without knowing it?"

"Certainly without knowing it," said Agénor, "for I was entirely unaware to whom I was speaking."

"For all that, you enabled me to be of service to the king, thanks to the information you gave me," added

Maria Padilla, smiling. "It is useless, then, for you to deny that you have been of service to me."

"Well, I suppose I must confess it, madame. But as for you —"

"You do not believe me capable of serving you. Oh, knight, you suspect my gratitude!"

"You may have the wish to be grateful; I do not deny it, madame."

"I have the wish and I have the power. Suppose — it is a mere supposition, of course — that you be detained at Soria."

Agénor started.

"I can make it easy for you to leave the city."

"Ah, madame!" said Agénor, "by doing so you serve the interests of Don Pedro as well as mine, for you will hinder the king from being charged with treason and cowardice."

"That would be true enough," answered the young woman, "if you were simply an ambassador and unknown except in that capacity, and if you came merely to fulfil a mission exclusively political, and if the king was the only one whose hatred or distrust you were likely to arouse; but, think well on it, have you not another enemy in Soria,— an enemy entirely personal?"

Agénor trembled visibly.

"Now, if such be the case," pursued Doña Maria, "can you not understand how such an enemy, supposing you have one, might glut his vengeance by laying a snare for you, and that, too, without consulting the king or taking thought of anything save his private resentment? Would it not be easy to prove that the king was no party to this act of revenge, should your fellow-countrymen demand an explanation? For, remember it well, knight, you are here for the purpose of watching over your own interests

quite as much as for the purpose of watching over those of
Don Henry of Trastamare."

Agénor sighed.

"Ah! I think you have understood me," said Maria.
"Well, should I save you from the danger that threatens
you —"

"You would save my life, madame, and my life is of
some importance to the interests of others at present; but
as far as I am concerned myself, I do not know that I
should be very grateful for your generosity."

"Why?"

"Because for life I care but little."

"You care but little for life?"

"Yes," said Agénor, shaking his head.

"Then you have some great sorrow?"

"Yes, madame."

"And supposing I were to know all about that great
sorrow?"

"You?"

"If I were to show you the cause of it?"

"You? you could tell me — you could show me —"

Maria Padilla went straight to the silken hangings that
shut the terrace from view.

"Look!" she said, as she drew them apart.

Thereupon was seen a lower terrace separated from the
upper one by clumps of orange-trees, pomegranates, and
laurels. Upon this terrace, in the midst of flowers, and
bathed in the golden light of a setting sun, a woman was
swinging in a purple hammock.

"Now?" said Doña Maria.

"Aïssa!" cried Mauléon, joining his hands in ecstasy.

"Mothril's daughter, I believe," said Doña Maria.

"O madame!" cried Mauléon, looking at the space
that divided him from Aïssa as if he would annihilate it.

"Yes, there! there! you are right, madame; there is the happiness of my life!"

"So near and yet so far!" said Doña Maria, smiling.

"Would you mock me, señora?" asked Agénor, anxiously.

"God forbid, sir knight! I am only saying that at this moment Doña Aïssa is an image of happiness. Often you think you have but to stretch your hand and touch it, and then again you are separated from it by some obstacle that is invisible, and yet insurmountable."

"Alas! I know it: she is watched, guarded."

"Imprisoned, sir Frenchman, imprisoned under the ward of stout bolt and bar."

"If I could only attract her attention!" cried Agénor: "if I could but see her and be seen by her!"

"So that would be a great boon to you?"

"The greatest boon on earth."

"Well, I will gain it for you. Doña Aïssa has not seen you as yet; she would wish to see you, though that would but increase your sorrow and hers, for it is a wretched resource when lovers can but stretch out arms to each other and confide their kisses to the air. You can do better, sir knight."

"Oh! what must I do? speak! speak! madame; command, or rather advise me."

"Do you see that door?" said Doña Maria, pointing to an outlet leading to the terrace itself. "This is the key of it, the largest of the three keys on the ring; you have to descend only a story; a long corridor, like the one that led you hither, ends at the garden of the next house, the trees of which you see above the terrace of Doña Aïssa. Ah! you begin to understand, I believe —"

"Yes, yes," said Mauléon, hanging on every word that issued from the lips of Doña Maria.

"This garden," she went on, "is shut in by a grating of which this is the key, the key next the first one. Once yonder, you might meet Doña Aïssa, for you could reach the foot of the terrace where she is swinging at this moment; but the wall of this terrace is perpendicular, it is impossible to scale it. Still, if you got there, you could call your mistress and speak to her."

"Thanks! thanks!" cried Mauléon.

"You are now somewhat more contented than you were? so much the better!" said Doña Maria, stopping him. "Still, there is a certain amount of danger in conversing thus at a distance; you might be heard. I say so, although Mothril is absent: he attends the king to the review of the troops that come to us from Africa, and he will not return until half-past nine or, perhaps, ten; it is now eight."

"An hour and a half! — Oh, madame, quick! quick! give me this key at once, I beg of you."

"Oh, we have plenty of time. Wait until the last rays of the sun that are now giving a reddish tinge to the landscape die away altogether; it will happen in a few minutes. Besides — do you wish that I should continue?" she added smiling.

"Continue."

"I do not exactly know how to separate this key from the third, for it was given to Don Pedro by Mothril himself, and I had a good deal of trouble in getting it."

"To Don Pedro!" said Agénor, with a shudder.

"Yes," answered Maria. "Now, just only imagine that this third key opens the door leading to a very convenient staircase, and that this very convenient staircase brings you to the terrace where Aïssa is, no doubt, dreaming about you at this very moment."

Agénor uttered a cry of joy.

"So that, once this door is shut upon you," continued Doña Maria, "you will be free to converse for an hour and a half with the daughter of Mothril, and that, too, without the fear of being disturbed. For, if any one come, and no one can come except through the house, you will have your retreat open and secured on this side."

Agénor fell on his knees and kissed the hand of his benefactress again and again.

"Madame," said he, "on whatsoever day my life may be useful to you, ask it: it shall be yours."

"Thanks; keep it for your mistress, Seigneur Agénor. The sun has disappeared, in a few moments it will be dark; you have but an hour. Go, and see that you do not compromise me with Mothril."

Agénor ran down the little stairs of the terrace and vanished.

"Sir Frenchman," cried Doña Maria to him, while he was flying, "in an hour your horse will await you at the door of the chapel; but let Mothril suspect nothing or we are both lost."

"In an hour I shall be there," answered the already distant voice of the knight; "I swear it."

XII.

THE INTERVIEW.

YES, it was Aïssa; pensive and alone, she was reclining in a hammock on the lower terrace adjoining her father's apartments and her own. Careless and dreamy, like a true child of the Orient, she was inhaling the evening breeze and following with her eyes the departing rays of the setting sun.

When the last beams of light had faded, her gaze wandered over the magnificent gardens of the Alcazar, seeking beyond the walls, beyond the trees, that which she had sought beyond the horizon, as long as the horizon existed. And what she sought was that imperishable idea, that deathless memory which takes thought neither of times nor places, and which is called love, that is to say, eternal hope.

She was thinking of the plains of France, greener and more velvety, if not more odorous; of those rich gardens of Bordeaux whose umbrageous bowers had sheltered the sweetest scenes of her life; and, as the human mind, when it dwells strongly on any subject, is ever in quest of some analogy, be it joyous or sad, in connection with that subject, her thoughts also recurred to the garden in Seville, where, for the first time, she had stood near Agénor, had spoken to him, had touched his hand, that hand she now burned to grasp once more.

There are abysses in the souls of lovers. Just as in the minds of madmen, extremes run across one another with the incoherent rapidity of dreams, so the smile of the young girl who loves, like that of Ophelia, sometimes dissolves in bitter tears and heart-rending sobs.

Aïssa, entirely overcome by her recollection of the past, smiled, sighed, wept.

She was in tears, tears that, perhaps, were to end in sobs, when a hurried step resounded on the stone staircase.

She thought it was Mothril, already returned, and speeding, as he sometimes did, to surprise her amid her most endearing dreams; for this man appeared to have an intuitive penetration that was akin to magic, an intelligence that, like some infernal torch, illumined everything around it, leaving nothing dark but itself, which remained immutable, profound, and omnipotent.

And yet it did not seem that that step could be Mothril's; the sound came from a quarter opposite that by which Mothril used to enter.

Then, with a shudder, her thoughts reverted to the king, that king whom she had ceased to fear, and consequently had forgotten, after the arrival of Doña Maria. The staircase from which the echo proceeded was the staircase Mothril had constructed as a secret passage for his sovereign.

She hastened, then, not to dry her tears, which would have smacked of vulgar dissimulation, and would, therefore, be utterly unbefitting her proud nature, but to banish a memory all too sweet, in presence of the enemy she must, perforce, encounter; if it was Mothril, she had dominion over her will; if it was Don Pedro, she had dominion over her poniard.

Then she affected to turn her back to the door, as if, Agénor absent, happiness or danger was indifferent to her, and prepared her ears to listen to the harsh words that would be in harmony with the sinister step which had already made her shudder.

Suddenly, she felt around her neck two mail-clad arms; she uttered a cry of anger and disgust, but her lips were closed by two greedy lips. Then, by the thrilling sensations that ran through her veins, even more than by the look she cast upon him, she recognized Agénor, kneeling on the marble at her feet.

She could hardly stifle the second cry, now one of joy, which almost burst from her mouth and swelled her heart. She rose, still encircled by her lover's arms, and, strong as the young panther that hurries with his prey into the thickets of the Atlas, she led, carried, so to speak, Agénor down the staircase, which hid in its mysterious shadow the joy of the two lovers.

The chamber of Aïssa, with its long window-curtains, opened on the passage at the foot of this staircase. She entered it on her lover's arm; and, as the light of the heavens was absorbed by the thick hangings, and, as no sound could make its way through the tapestried walls, for some moments nothing was heard but devouring kisses and sighs of flame lost in the long dark tresses of Aïssa, which had become loosened in the wild embrace, and now enveloped them both like a veil.

A stranger to our European customs, ignorant of the art of quickening desire by coy resistance, Aïssa gave herself up to her lover, as the first woman must have done, swayed by that impassioned instinct, that irresistible intoxication of happiness which is felt to be the supreme happiness here below.

"Thou! thou!" she murmured, in her transport; "thou in the palace of Don Pedro! thou restored at last to my longing love! Oh! the days have been too long in thy absence, and God has two measurements for time:

the minutes when I see thee that pass as shadows, and the days when I see thee not that have the length of centuries."

And then their voices were lost in one sweet and lingering kiss.

"Ah! thou art mine! mine!" cried Agénor. "The hatred of Mothril, what boots it! the love of the king, what boots it! I can die now."

"Die!" said Aïssa, with moist eyes and quivering lips; "die! Oh, no, you shall not die, my well-beloved! I saved you at Bordeaux, and shall I not save you a second time now? As for the king's love, feel my heart how little it be, how small the space it fills in the bosom that sinks and swells above it. Do you believe that this heart that is all filled with you, that beats but for you, has room for the shadow of another love?"

"Oh, God forbid that I should think for a moment that my Aïssa could forget me!" said Agénor. "But where persuasion fails, violence is often all-powerful. Have you not heard of the adventure of Leonora de Ximenes, to whom the brutality of the king left no other resource than the protection of a convent?"

"Leonora de Ximenes was not Aïssa, seigneur. The fate of the one could never be the fate of the other, and that, my love, I swear."

"You would defend yourself, I know full well, but that defence would entail, perhaps, your death!"

"And would you not love me better dead than belonging to another?"

"Oh, yes! yes!" cried the young man, pressing her to his heart. "Die, if it is necessary, but belong to none but me!"

And he infolded her anew in his arms with a movement of love that almost resembled terror.

The falling night, which was already darkening the outside walls, had robbed the objects in the room of form and outline. In this obscurity, all full of words of love and burning sighs, was it possible that they should not be consumed in that fire which devours without lighting, like those terrible flames that live under the waters?

For a long space of time the silence of death, or of love, reigned in the chamber where lately two voices had resounded, and two hearts had beat together madly.

Agénor was the first to break loose from this ineffable happiness; he girt on his sword, the steel scabbard of which clanked on the marble floor.

"What are you doing?" cried the young girl, seizing the knight by the arm.

"You have spoken truth, my love," answered Agénor; "time has two measurements: minutes for happiness, centuries for despair. I leave."

"You leave, but you take me with you; is it not so? We leave together?"

The young man, with a sigh, freed himself from the arms of his mistress.

"Impossible!" he said.

"Impossible! Why?"

"I have come hither with the sacred title of ambassador; I am under the safeguard of that title; I cannot violate it."

"But," cried Aïssa, "why should I quit you?"

"I have come hither, Aïssa," said the young man, "in the name of the good constable; I have come hither in the name of Henry of Trastamare, and having the implicit confidence of both. The one has confided to me the interests of French honor; the other, the interests of the Castilian throne. What should they say if they saw that, instead of fulfilling this twofold mission, I have been solely occupied with the interests of my love?"

"Who will tell them? What hinders you from concealing me from all eyes?"

"I must return to Burgos, and it is a three days' journey from Soria to Burgos."

"I am strong, and accustomed to fast riding."

"You are right; but the Arab cavaliers ride fast, far faster than you and I could at present. In an hour Mothril would perceive your escape; in an hour he would be on our track, Aïssa. I cannot return to Burgos as a fugitive."

"My God! my God!" cried Aïssa, "to part again!"

"This time, at least, the parting shall not be long. I call Heaven to witness to the truth of what I say, Aïssa! Let me be quit of my mission; let me once again be at the camp of Don Henry; let me surrender the trust with which he has honored me; let me once more become Agénor, the French knight, who loves you and you only, who lives but for you, and then I swear, Aïssa, I shall return here under some disguise or other, be it that even of an infidel, and then it shall be I who will carry you off by force, if you are not content to come of your own accord."

"No, no!" exclaimed Aïssa, "only to-day has begun my life; until to-day I did not live, for I did not belong to you; to-day I could not live away from your side. I could not now spend the time of absence in mere sorrow and silent weeping; no, I would shriek out my despair and woe. To-day I am your wife! Well, then, perish all those who would hinder the wife from following her spouse!"

"What! even our protectress, Aïssa! Even that generous woman who has led me to your side! Even that poor Maria Padilla on whom Mothril would wreak his revenge! And you know in what dire fashion Mothril avenges himself."

"Ah! I feel as if my life were ebbing away," murmured the young woman, for she saw that a superior force, the force of reason, was severing her from her lover. "But could I not join you on the way? I have two mules so fleet that they outspeed the swiftest horses. You will appoint a spot where I can await you or join you, and rest assured I shall be there."

"Aïssa, we come to the same point by a different path, — impossible! impossible!"

The young girl slipped down on her knees. The haughty Morisca was at the feet of Agénor praying, entreating.

At this moment the melancholy, plaintive sound of a guzla stirred the air above their heads, imitating the cry of an anxious lover calling her mate.

"Whence comes that sound?" said Aïssa.

"I guess," said Agénor; "let us haste."

Both mounted to the terrace.

The eyes of Agénor turned at once to the terrace of Maria.

Though the night was very dark, the sombre beams of the stars shed light enough to enable the two young people to distinguish a white-robed figure leaning over a parapet and turned in their direction.

Still, they might have doubted whether they were in presence of a phantom or a woman, had not the resonant vibrations of a musical instrument been heard from the same quarter.

"She calls me!" murmured Agénor, "she calls me! Do you hear?"

"Come, come!" cried the muffled voice of Doña Maria, in tones that seemed borne from a far distance.

"Do you hear, Aïssa, do you hear?" asked Agénor.

"Ah! I hear nothing, I see nothing," stammered the young girl.

At the same time, a flourish of trumpets, such as ordinarily gave notice of the return of the king to his palace, echoed along the terrace.

"Great God!" exclaimed Aïssa, all at once transformed into a weak and anxious woman, "they come! they come! Fly, my Agénor, fly!"

"A last farewell, my sweet one!" said Agénor.

"A last one it well may be!" murmured the young girl, gluing her lips upon the lips of her lover.

And she pushed the young man towards the staircase.

His footsteps had hardly died away when those of Mothril were heard; and the door which led to Maria Padilla's apartments was scarcely closed when that of Aïssa's chamber opened.

XIII.

THE PREPARATIONS FOR BATTLE.

THREE days after the events we have just related, Agénor, who returned by the road by which he had arrived, and had come up with Musaron, gave an account of the results of his mission to Henry of Trastamare.

No one attempted to minimize the dangers incurred by the knight in the performance of his duty. Accordingly, he received the thanks and praise of the constable, who ordered him to take his place at the side of the bravest division of the Bretons, under the banner of Sylvestre de Budes.

Preparations for war were going on everywhere. The Prince of Wales had obtained permission from the King of Navarre to pass through his territories, and had joined Don Pedro, leading with him a great army to co-operate with the fine African troops of the Spanish monarch.

On the other hand, the English adventurers, who had now all rallied to Don Pedro, were proposing to deal some doughty blows on the heads of the Bretons and Gascons, their inveterate and bitter enemies.

It is unnecessary to state that the most daring, but, if successful, the most lucrative designs fermented in the brain of our old friend, Sir Hugues de Caverley.

Henry of Trastamare was not backward in these warlike preparations. He had been joined by his two brothers, Don Tello and Don Sancho, and had intrusted a command to each. He was now proceeding by short stages to meet his brother Don Pedro.

Throughout all Spain was felt that feverish ardor which passes, so to speak, through the air, and is the herald of great events. Musaron, still as provident and, at the same time, as philosophical as ever, exhorted his master to eat the best game and drink the best wine, for thus would he be the stouter in battle, and advance himself in deeds of honorable adventure.

But Agénor, being now free from responsibility, and rendered by the possession of a moment more amorous than ever, was arranging in his mind all the combinations possible and impossible that might serve to bring him near to Aïssa. He wished to carry her off at once, and cared not to stake his chances on the issue of a battle, into which you may enter strong and brave, but from which you may depart sore wounded to the death or a fugitive.

To this intent, he had purchased two Arab steeds, which he could well do, owing to the liberality of Du Guesclin. These chargers were trained every day by Musaron to gallop long distances and to endure hunger and thirst.

At length it was learned that the Prince of Wales had emerged from the passes, and was entering the plain. He advanced, with the army he had brought with him from Guyenne, towards the city of Vittoria, a short distance from Navaretta.

He had thirty thousand horse and forty thousand foot, a force pretty nearly equal to that which Don Pedro commanded.

Henry of Trastamare, on his side, had under his orders sixty thousand infantry and forty thousand cavalry.

Bertrand, encamped among the rear-guard with his Bretons, was content to let the Spaniards indulge in their rodomontades, and celebrate in every direction the victory they had not yet gained.

But he had his spies, who brought him tidings every

day of what was done in the army of Don Pedro, and even in that of Don Henry; in fact, he knew all the plans of Caverley himself almost as soon as the fertile imagination of the adventurer produced them.

He knew, therefore, that the worthy captain, whose taste had grown fastidious from the capture of so many kings, had made a proposal to the Prince of Wales to end the war by one bold stroke.

His plan was the simplest that can be conceived; it was that of the bird of prey, who soars so high in the air that he is invisible, then suddenly swoops down on his quarry and bears it away in his claws at the very moment the victim least expects such a fate.

Sir Hugues de Caverley was to join forces with Sir John Chandos, the Duke of Lancaster, and a part of the English vanguard, burst suddenly on the quarters of Don Henry, carry off himself and his court, and thus, at one blow, hold for ransom a score of persons, any one of whom would have sufficed to make the fortunes of six adventurers.

The Prince of Wales accepted; he had everything to gain and nothing to lose by the bargain presented to him.

Unfortunately, Messire Bertrand Du Guesclin had, as we have stated already, spies who brought him news of all that was doing in the army of the enemy.

More unfortunately still, as a Breton, he had an old grudge against the English in general; and against Messire Hugues de Caverley in particular, he had a hatred that was quite fresh.

He recommended his spies, therefore, not to sleep a single instant, or, if they did happen to fall asleep, to sleep with one eye open.

Consequently, he was informed of the slightest movements of Sir Hugues de Caverley.

An hour before the worthy captain left the camp of

the Prince of Wales, the constable took six thousand Spanish and Breton horse, and sent, by a road opposite his own, Agénor and Le Bègue de Vilaine to take up a position in a wood through which ran a defile.

Each of them was to occupy a parallel portion of the wood; then, when the English had passed, they were to close up the defile behind them.

Henry of Trastamare, who had been warned, was, on his side, to hold all his men under arms.

Caverley would, therefore, knock against a wall of iron; then, when he tried to fall back, he would find himself surrounded by another wall of iron.

Men and horses were in ambush at nightfall. Each horseman lay on the ground, with his hand on the reins of his horse.

About ten, Caverley and his band entered the defile. The English felt so safe that they did not even try to reconnoitre the wood, which, however, the night rendered very difficult, if not impossible.

The Bretons and Spaniards united in the rear of the English, like the two broken pieces of a chain that are again welded together.

Towards midnight, a great uproar was heard. It was Caverley rushing on the quarters of Don Henry, and the latter meeting him with his war-cry of "Don Henry and Castile!"

Then Bertrand, with Agénor on his right, and Le Bègue de Vilaine on his left, dashed forward to the cry of "Notre Dame, Du Guesclin!"

At the same time, great fires were lit on the flanks and disclosed to view Caverley and his five or six thousand adventurers caught between two armies.

Caverley was not the sort of man to seek a useless death, however glorious it might be. Had he been in the place of Edward III. at Crécy, he would have fled; had he been in the place of the Black Prince at Poitiers, he would have surrendered.

But, as a person does not surrender unless at the last extremity, particularly when he runs a risk of being hanged after he has surrendered, he set spurs to his horse, and disappeared through an opening that was left unguarded, just as on the stage the traitor disappears through a badly closed side-scene.

All his baggage, a considerable sum in gold, and a casket of jewels and precious stones, the proceeds of three years of rapine, during which years the doughty captain had displayed more genius in escaping the hangman than would have made an Alexander, a Hannibal, or a Cæsar, fell into the hands of the Bastard of Mauléon.

Musaron made a strict reckoning of these valuables while the rest were stripping the dead or chaining the prisoners; at the end of his reckoning, he discovered that he was now in the service of one of the wealthiest knights in Christendom.

The change that had taken place was immense, and it had occurred in less than an hour.

The adventurers were cut in pieces; only two or three hundred escaped.

This success inspired the Spaniards with such daring that Don Tello, the young brother of Henry of Trastamare, pushing forward on his horse, wanted to march at once against the enemy, and that without making the slightest preparation.

"A moment, sir count," said Bertrand; "you are not going, I presume, to march all alone against the enemy and risk being taken prisoner ingloriously."

"But all the army will march with me, I suppose," answered Don Tello.

"No, seigneur, no," replied Bertrand.

"Let the Bretons remain, if they will," said the prince.

"I shall march with my Spaniards."

"For what purpose?"

"To beat the English."

"Excuse me," said Bertrand; "the English have been beaten by the Bretons, but they will not be beaten by the Spaniards."

"What do you mean?" cried Don Tello, impetuously, advancing towards the constable. "Why do you say so?"

"Because," said Bertrand, quite unruffled, "the Bretons are better soldiers than the English, but the English are better soldiers than the Spaniards."

The young prince flushed with anger.

"It is a strange thing," said he, "that the master here, in Spain, should be a Frenchman; but we shall soon learn if Don Tello is to obey instead of to command. Ho, there! all follow me."

"Not one of my eighteen thousand Bretons will budge an inch unless I make them a sign to do so," said Bertrand. "As to your Spaniards, I am not their master, except your master and mine, Don Henry of Trastamare, commands them to obey me."

"How prudent these Frenchmen are!" cried Don Tello, exasperated. "How cold they are, not only in presence of danger, but, even more so, in presence of an insult. I congratulate you, seigneur constable, on the possession of one of their characteristics."

"Yes, seigneur count, my blood is cold when it is at rest, but it is hot enough when in motion."

And the constable, quite ready to fire up, pressed his large clinched fist against his coat of mail.

"It is cold, I tell you," continued the young man,

" and that because you are old. Old age brings fear in its train."

"Fear!" cried Agénor, pushing forward his horse in front of Don Tello. "He who dares to mention fear once in the same breath with the constable shall not mention it twice!"

"Silence, my friend!" said the constable; "leave fools to their folly, and patience, patience!"

"Respect the blood royal!" cried Don Tello, "do you hear?"

"If you would be respected, respect yourself," said a voice suddenly, that made the young prince start, for it was that of his eldest brother, who had been informed of this dangerous altercation; "and, above all, do not insult our ally, our hero."

"Thanks, sire," said Bertrand; "your generous words have spared me a task always painful, that of chastising the insolent. But I do not allude to you, Don Tello: you understand already how wrong you have been."

"Wrong — I wrong! for saying that we should fight? Is it not true, sire, that we are about to march against the enemy?" said Don Tello.

"March against the enemy — at such a moment as this?" cried Du Guesclin; "why, it is impossible!"

"No, my dear constable," said Don Henry; "so far is it from being impossible that we join battle at daybreak."

"Sire, we shall be beaten."

"And why?"

"Because our position is bad."

"There is no position bad," cried Don Tello. "There are only brave men and cowards!"

"Sir constable," said the king, "my nobles insist on fighting, and I cannot refuse what they insist on. They have seen the Prince of Wales advancing into the field.

VOL. II. — 8

Were they to do nothing now, it would look as if they shrank from the conflict."

"For that matter," sneered Don Tello, "the constable will be free to stay where he is and look on while we are fighting."

"Seigneur," answered Du Guesclin, "I shall do whatever the Spaniards do, and more, I hope, besides; for, mark this well: you begin the attack in two hours, do you not?"

"Yes."

"Well, in four hours you shall be flying along the plain yonder before the Prince of Wales. And I and my Bretons, wherever we are, shall hold our ground there, without a single foot soldier falling back the length of his boot, or a single horseman falling back the length of a horse's shoe. Wait and you shall see."

"Come, sir constable," said Don Henry, "restrain yourself."

"I but speak the truth, sire. You wish to take the field, you say?"

"Yes, constable, I wish it because I must."

"Be it, then, as you order!"

And turning to his Bretons, —

"My children," said he, "a battle will soon be on. Prepare for it as best you may. — All these brave folk and myself as well," he continued, turning to the king, "are pretty likely to be killed or taken this evening, but your will be done above all. Still, remember that I shall lose in this battle only my life or my liberty, while you will surely lose a throne."

The king bent his head, and, turning to his friends, —

"The good constable is hard upon us this morning," he said; "nevertheless, make your preparations, my lords."

"Is it true, then, that we are to be killed to-day?"

said Musaron, in a tone loud enough to be heard by the constable.

The latter faced round.

"Good Heavens! yes, my worthy squire," said he, with a smile, " it is pure truth."

"It is annoying," said Musaron, slapping his hosen, the pockets of which were full of gold; "killed just at the moment we were going to be rich and enjoy life."

XIV.

THE BATTLE.

An hour after this mournful reflection of the wortny squire, as Bertrand styled Musaron, the sun rose above the plain of Navaretta, as pure, as calm, and as tranquil as if it were not soon to shine over one of the most famous battles that have stained with blood the annals of the world.

When the sun was above the horizon, the plain was occupied by the army of Don Henry, arranged in three divisions.

Don Tello, with his brother Sancho, commanded the left, at the head of twenty-five thousand men.

Du Guesclin, with six thousand men-at-arms, that is to say, with very nearly eighteen thousand horse, held the van.

Don Henry himself was stationed on the right, with twenty-one thousand horse and thirty thousand foot.

This army was disposed like the three steps of a staircase.

There was a reserve force of Aragonese, well-mounted and commanded by the Counts of Aigues and Roquebertin.

It was the 3d of April, 1368, and the evening and night before had been oppressive with heat and dust.

King Henry leaped on a strong Aragonese mule and rode from squadron to squadron, encouraging some, praising others, and representing especially the peril they would incur if they fell alive into the hands of the cruel Don Pedro.

Then he went to the constable, who was standing, cold and resolute, at his post, and, embracing him, said, —

"This arm is the arm that shall restore me my crown forever. Why is it not the crown of the universe? If it were, I should offer it to you, for it would be the only crown worthy of you."

Words like these are always the words used by kings in times of peril. It is true that when the peril passes, it sweeps them along with it as does the whirlwind the dust.

Then he knelt down, bareheaded, prayed to God, and every one imitated him.

At this moment, the rays of the rising sun spurted from behind the mountain of Navaretta, and the soldiers, as they looked upwards, perceived the first English lances covering the hill with a forest of spears, then slowly descending, their several divisions resting and forming on the ridges along the slopes.

Among the banners in the first rank, Agénor recognized that of Caverley, statelier and prouder now than it was at the night attack. Chandos and Lancaster who, as well as our captain, had escaped, were with him, and looked all the more resolute because they were intent on exacting a terrible revenge.

All three moved forward, and took up their position in front of Du Guesclin.

The Prince of Wales and the King Don Pedro placed themselves opposite Don Sancho and Don Tello.

Jean de Grailly, the Captal of Buch, commanded the division which was to encounter Don Henry of Trastamare.

The Black Prince, moved at the spectacle of so many men ready for mutual slaughter, instead of exhorting his troops, burst into tears, and asked of God, not victory, but that *right* which is the device of the English crown.[1]

Then the trumpets sounded.

Immediately the plain was felt to tremble under the hoofs of the chargers, and a deep, continued roar like the sound of two thunders, the one rolling before the other, rumbled and echoed in the air.

However, the two vanguards, composed of trained and resolute soldiers, advanced at a measured pace.

After the bowmen had shot their arrows, which darkened the air, the horsemen dashed on one another, fighting hand to hand and in silence; this, for the part of the army not yet engaged, was a terrible and exciting spectacle.

The Black Prince flung himself into the fray like a simple man-at-arms.

At the head of his whole squadron, he swept down on Don Tello.

It was the first pitched battle in which the young man had ever happened to be engaged, and when he saw the men who, with the Bretons, passed for the first soldiers in Europe, galloping upon him so furiously, he was frightened and fled.

His troops, seeing him recoil, turned rein, and, in an instant, the whole left wing of the army was thrown into confusion, under the influence of one of those panics whose inexplicable impulses sometimes entail shame on the bravest.

On passing again in front of the Bretons, who, although they at first formed the vanguard, were now

[1] *Dieu et mon droit.*— TR.

thrust to the rear by the advance of Don Tello, the Spanish prince quickened his pace, at the same time turning away his head.

As for Don Sancho, he encountered the contemptuous look of the constable, and, abashed by that overpowering gaze, he stopped short, turned back against the enemy, and was taken prisoner.

Don Pedro, who, with the Prince of Wales, was pursuing the enemy, eager to profit by this first success, when he saw the left wing in full retreat, spurred his charger at once against his brother Henry, who was struggling bravely against the Captal of Buch, but who was giving way before an attack on his flank by seven hundred fresh lances rendered more reckless by success.

Above the din of steel clashing against steel, of neighing horses, and combatants howling with fury, might be heard a voice that overpowered all this uproar: it was that of Don Pedro shouting, "No quarter for rebels! no quarter!"

He fought with a gilded axe, the gilding of which from edge to handle had disappeared under a sheath of blood.

During this time the reserve was entirely routed, its last ranks being reached by Olivier de Clisson and the Sire de Retz, who had outflanked the division. Only Du Guesclin and his Bretons remained, who, as they had promised, did not recoil a step. Formed into an impregnable square, they seemed a rock of iron, around which the conquering battalions rolled like long, greedy serpents.

Du Guesclin cast a quick glance towards the plain; he perceived clearly that the battle was lost; thirty thousand soldiers were flying in all directions, and in every spot where, not an hour before, none but friends and allies could be seen, now there were none but enemies. He understood that the only thing left was to die facing the foe, and doing him as much harm as possible.

He glanced towards the left, and descried an old wall, part of the ramparts of a ruined city. Two English companies separated him from this bulwark, which, once won, would save him from an attack in front. He gave an order in his full and resonant voice; the two English companies were crushed, and the Bretons stood with their backs to the wall.

There, Bertrand reformed his line and drew a moment's breath.

Le Bègue de Vilaine and the Maréchal d'Andreghem also took breath along with him.

Agénor, whose horse had been killed, was waiting behind a spur of the wall for a led-horse which Musaron was bringing him.

The constable, profiting by this interval of respite, raised the visor of his helmet, wiped his face, covered with dust and sweat, looked around and reckoned up quietly the number of men left him.

"The king?" he asked; "where is the king? has he been slain? has he fled?"

"No, messire," said Agénor, "he has not been slain, neither has he fled. Look yonder, he has fallen back and is coming hither."

Don Henry, covered with the blood of the enemy and with his own, the crown on his helmet broken by the dint of an axe, was making his way to the constable, all the time fighting like a worthy knight.

Harassed and breathless, yet never flying, but falling back on his charger, which ever fronted the enemy, the brave king was coming towards the Bretons, drawing on these faithful allies a cloud of English, who were keen as ravens for this rich quarry.

Bertrand ordered a hundred of his men to support Don Henry and deliver him.

These hundred men rushed upon ten thousand, opened a passage, and formed a circle around the prince, in the midst of which he could breathe.

But, as soon as he was free, Don Henry changed horses with a squire, flung away his battered helm, took another from the hands of a page, made sure that he had a firm grasp of the hilt of his sword, and, like another Antæus whose strength is restored by touching the earth, —

"Friends," he cried, "you have made me king; see if I be worthy of being so this day!"

And he rushed again into the fray.

His sword was seen to rise four times, and at every rise of that sword, an enemy fell.

"To the king! to the king!" said the constable; "let us save the king!"

And it was time; the English were closing in on Don Henry, as the sea closes in on the swimmer. He was on the point of being taken, when the constable reached his side.

Bertrand seized his arm, and, flinging some Bretons between the king and the enemy, —

"Enough," he said, "of such courage as that; more would be madness. The battle is lost, fly! It is for us to die here protecting your retreat."

The king refused; Bertrand made a sign; four Bretons laid hands on Henry of Trastamare.

"Now, 'Notre Dame, Guesclin!'" cried the constable, "we await the enemy!"

And, lowering his lance, he awaited the shock of thirty thousand horsemen, with all the men left to him, — an awful shock, which ought, seemingly, to have overturned the wall against which his little force was propped.

"We might as well bid each other good-bye here," quoth Musaron, as he shot the last shaft in his quiver among the enemy. "Ah, Seigneur Agénor, yonder are those ill-favored Moors, behind the English!"

"Well, adieu, my dear Musaron," answered Agénor, now again on horseback, and on his way to take his place beside the constable.

The host of men came on, rumbling like a thunder-cloud about to burst; all, however, that could be seen through the dust was a forest of lances advancing, the weapons lowered horizontally.

But suddenly there dashed into the space which was as yet empty, at the risk of being ground between the two masses, a horseman in black armor, black helmet with black crown, and holding in his hand a baton of command.

"Halt!" said the black knight, raising his arm; "he who advances a step is a dead man!"

At the sound of this powerful voice, the horses that were leaping forward might be seen reining back their heads under the pressure of the bit; some touched the earth with their quivering hams.

The prince, alone in the space which no one now ventured to enter, gazed with that peculiar sadness wherewith history has hallowed his brows, upon those fearless Bretons about to disappear under the onslaught of numbers.

"Good people and valiant knights," said he, "it does not please me that you should die thus; look well around you! A god could not resist what you see!"

Then, turning to Du Guesclin, and stepping a pace forward to salute him, —

"Good constable," he continued, "I am the Prince of Wales, and it is my wish that you live; your death would make too great a void among the brave. Your sword, I pray you."

Du Guesclin was a man able to understand true generosity; that of the prince touched him.

"It is a loyal knight who speaks," said he, "and I understand English spoken after that manner."

And he lowered his sword.

At their prince's voice, the English advanced with lowered lances, and without hurry or anger.

The constable took his sword by the blade.

He was on the point of surrendering it to the prince.

At that very moment, Don Pedro appeared on his foaming charger, all covered with blood, and with his armor dented in ten places.

"What!" he cried, swooping down on the constable; "what! you allow those people to live? But we shall never be master as long as they live. No quarter! death! death!"

"Ah! what a foul beast!" cried Du Guesclin; "and like a foul beast shall he die!"

Then, as the prince was rushing on him, he raised his sword by the blade, and, with the iron hilt, dealt on the head of Don Pedro a blow that would have felled an ox. Don Pedro bent under it and sank back on the crupper of his horse, stunned, almost dead.

Du Guesclin raised a second time his terrible weapon.

But when he ran forward to meet the prince, he left a vacant space behind him; two Englishmen slipped into it, and, while he was raising his arms, one of them seized him by the helmet, the other by the waist.

The soldier holding him by the helmet drew him backward, the soldier who held him by the waist tried to pull him from the saddle.

"Messire constable," they both cried together, "it is death or surrender."

Bertrand jerked his head out of the hands that held it, and, with the strength of a wild bull, he tore from the saddle-bows the Englishman who had seized his helmet, while, slipping the point of his sword through the gorget of the man who had seized him round the waist, he stifled the menace in blood.

But a hundred Englishmen leaped upon him at once, each wild to give the giant his death-stroke.

"Let me see," cried the Black Prince, in a voice of thunder, "let me see the one who will dare touch him with a finger!"

At once even the fiercest drew back, and Du Guesclin was safe.

"Enough, my prince," said he, "twice do I owe you my sword; in truth, more generous conqueror the world does not hold."

And he tendered his sword to the prince.

Agénor tendered his.

"Are you mad?" said Bertrand to him; "you have a good fresh horse between your legs. Fly, gain France, tell good King Charles I am a prisoner; and if he will do nothing for me, hie to my brother Olivier; he will do something, you may be sure."

"But, monseigneur," objected Agénor.

"No one is paying any attention to you; begone, it is my will."

"Whip and spur! whip and spur!" cried Musaron,

who desired nothing better than to be off; "let us profit by the circumstance that, at present, we are little; we shall return great!"

In fact, the English were occupied in disputing who should hold to ransom Le Bègue de Vilaine, the marshal, and the other great captains. Agénor slipped through them, Musaron slipped in behind his master, and both, setting spurs to their horses, dashed away under a hail of arrows, with which they were saluted, but too late, by Caverley and Mothril.

XV.

AFTER THE BATTLE.

THE number of prisoners made during the battle had been considerable.

The conquerors were counting and adding up their captives, just as if they were bags of crowns, docked and labelled.

The Green Knight and some French adventurers were distinguishing themselves, as well as Caverley, in this laudable occupation, which consisted in despoiling the prisoners, after carefully inscribing their names, surnames, titles, and grades.

The conquerors then divided their prizes among the several commanders. Du Guesclin found himself among the prizes assigned to the Prince of Wales, who gave him in charge to the Captal of Buch.

Jean de Grailly approached Du Guesclin, and, taking him by the hand, began politely to draw off his gauntlet, while his squires proceeded to strip him of the other portions of his armor.

Bertrand took the matter quietly; there was no violence used towards him. He was busy counting and recounting in his mind the names of his friends, sighing every moment at the thought that this one or that one would never respond to his silent roll-call.

"Valiant constable," said Grailly, "you made me prisoner at Cocherel; see how fickle fortune is: to-day you are mine."

"Oh, oh!" said Bertrand, "you are mistaken, my good lord. At Cocherel I took you; at Navaretta you guard me; you were my prisoner at Cocherel; at Navaretta you are my warden."

Jean de Grailly reddened; but such was the respect at this time bestowed on misfortune, that he preferred not to answer.

Du Guesclin was seated at the back of a ditch. He invited Le Bègue de Vilaine, Andreghem, and some others to approach him, for the Prince of Wales had just had the trumpets sounded, giving notice that his soldiers were to assemble.

"They are going to pray," said the constable; "His Highness is a right valiant prince, and pious withal. Let us pray also."

"You are going to thank God for saving you?" said Le Bègue de Vilaine.

"No; to ask of him revenge," retorted Bertrand.

The Prince of Wales, after kneeling and thanking the Lord for this great victory, called Don Pedro, who was casting savage glances around him, and who was too absorbed in sinister thoughts to bend a knee, even for an instant.

"We are, indeed, victorious, and yet you have lost a great battle," said the Black Prince.

"How?" returned Don Pedro.

"A king who recovers his crown only by shedding the blood of his subjects is really conquered."

"Rebels!" cried Don Pedro.

"Well, has not God punished them for abandoning you? Sire, tremble, lest God punish you, if you abandon those He has confided to your care."

"Sir prince," murmured Don Pedro, inclining, "I owe you my crown; but, of your grace, be not more unpitying than the Almighty. Strike not him who thanks you."

And he bent the knee. Prince Edward raised him.

"Thank God," he said; "to me you owe nothing."

Then the prince turned his back and went to his tent to take a little refreshment.

"My children," cried Don Pedro, giving rein to his ferocious desires, "strip the dead; the booty of the day is yours!"

And he was the first to leap upon a fresh horse and ride across the plain, examining with the keenness of hate every heap of corpses he met, but giving most attention to those on the banks of the stream where Don Henry had fought with the Captal of Buch.

Once there he dismounted, passed a long, sharp-edged dagger through his belt, and, with his feet lapped in blood, searched silently.

"You are quite sure," he said to Grailly, "that you saw him fall?"

"Quite sure," was the captal's answer; "his horse fell down; it was struck by an axe which my squire hurls with unerring aim."

"But he, but he?"

"He? he vanished under a cloud of arrows. I saw blood on his armor, and a whole mountain of overturned bodies rolled on top of him and buried him out of sight."

"Good, good!" cried Don Pedro, with ferocious joy; "but still let us search. Ah, yonder I see a crest of gold!"

And with the agility of a tiger, he leaped on the dead bodies, kicking aside those that covered the knight with the golden crest.

With trembling hand and dilated eye he raised the visor of the helm.

"His squire," he exclaimed, "nothing but his squire!"

"But these are the prince's arms," said Grailly; "it is true there is no crown upon his casque."

"Ah, the craft of him! the rascal craft of him! The coward gave his arms to his squire to make his escape the surer. But I foresaw everything; I caused the plain to be surrounded and watched; he could not cross the river. — And look! look! yonder are my faithful Moors leading some persons hither. He must surely be amongst them."

"Continue your search among the other dead bodies," said Grailly to the soldiers, who thereupon went to work with renewed ardor, "and five hundred piasters to the man who finds him alive!"

"And a thousand ducats to him who finds him dead!" added Don Pedro. "Let us go and meet those whom Mothril is bringing us."

Don Pedro again mounted his horse, and, followed by numerous cavaliers, who were eager to witness the spectacle likely to follow, he spurred to the end of the plain, where a band of white-robed Moors were seen driving before them a mob of fugitives they had picked up at a distance.

"I believe I see him, I believe I see him!" howled Don Pedro, quickening his pace.

He uttered those words as he was passing in front of the Breton prisoners. Du Guesclin heard, rose, and after embracing the plain in one piercing glance, —

"Ah! great God!" he cried, "what a misfortune!"

These words seemed to Don Pedro to confirm his happiest anticipations.

To give additional savor to his enjoyment, he determined that the constable should be a witness of it, and so he would be able to strike his two most powerful enemies, the one through the other.

"Remain here," he said. "You, seneschal, order Mothril to come hither with his prisoners, so that he and they may confront these Breton lords, leal friends of the usurper, — the vanquished usurper; champions of a cause wherewith they had no concern, and yet too powerless to make that cause triumph."

To these sarcasms, to this vindictive fury, the Breton hero did not even deign to offer a response; from his bearing, it might be supposed that he had not heard.

He was seated, and he continued seated, talking unconcernedly with the Maréchal d'Andreghem.

Meantime, Don Pedro had alighted. He was resting on a long axe, shaking the handle of his dagger, beating the ground with his foot as impatiently as if he could thus hasten the arrival of Mothril and the prisoners.

As soon as his voice had any chance of being heard, he shouted to the Morisco, —

"Ho, there! my doughty Saracen, my valiant white falcon, what game have you roused for me?"

"Right goodly game, my lord king," Mothril answered. "See you this banner?"

And, in fact, he held rolled about his arm a piece of cloth of gold, embroidered with the arms of Trastamare.

"It is he, then, — he!" exclaimed Don Pedro, transported with joy, "he!"

And, with a menacing gesture, he pointed to a knight armed at all points, with a crown on his helmet, but without either sword or lance, pinioned in the thousand coils of a silken cord, from each end of which hung a heavy leaden ball.

"He was flying," said Mothril. "I launched in his wake twenty coursers of the desert; the chief of my archers reached him, and received his death-wound, but another enmeshed him in the loop of the cord. He fell from his horse, and we had him; his banner was in his hand. Unfortunately, while he was making head against us, all alone, one of his friends escaped."

"Down with the crown! down with it!" cried Don Pedro, brandishing his axe.

An archer approached, and cutting the knots of the gorget, brutally knocked off the helmet with its golden crown.

A cry of mingled rage and terror escaped from the mouth of the king; a cry of boundless joy arose from the group of Bretons.

"The Bastard of Mauléon!" they exclaimed; "Noël! Noël!"

"The ambassador!—malediction!" murmured Don Pedro.

"The Frank!" stammered Mothril, furiously.

"I," said Agénor, quietly, saluting with a glance Bertrand and his friends.

"We," said Musaron, a little pale, but distributing kicks generously among the Moors on his right and left, for all that.

"He has escaped, then?" asked Don Pedro.

"Why, surely; yes, sire," replied Agénor. "I exchanged helmets with His Majesty behind a bush, and gave him my horse which was fresh."

"You shall die!" howled Don Pedro, blind with rage.

"Touch him, if you dare!" cried Bertrand. And, with a terrible bound, he threw himself between Agénor and Don Pedro. "Kill a disarmed prisoner! Oh! only a rascal coward like you could ever have had such a thought!"

"Then, wretched adventurer, 'tis thou who diest!" said Don Pedro, his mouth foaming, and every limb trembling.

He rushed with uplifted dagger upon the constable,

who stood, his fist clinched, looking mighty enough to overturn a bull with a single blow.

But a hand was placed on the shoulder of Don Pedro, a hand like unto the hand wherewith in Homer Minerva seizes Achilles by his yellow locks.

"Hold!" said the Prince of Wales. "You would dishonor yourself, King of Castile! Hold, and fling away your dagger. I wish it!"

His nervous arms had nailed Don Pedro to the spot; the steel fell from the hands of the assassin.

"Sell him to me, at least!" vociferated the madman; "you shall have his weight in gold."

"You insult me!—Beware!" answered the Black Prince. "If Du Guesclin were yours, right gladly would I buy him of you for his weight in precious stones, and right sure am I, too, you would sell him. But he is mine. Do you hear me?— mine. Back!"

"King!" murmured Du Guesclin, who could hardly be restrained, "king most foul! King who would murder prisoners! we shall meet again!"

"I believe it," said Don Pedro.

"And I am sure of it," rejoined Bertrand.

"Lead the constable of France at once to my tent," said the Black Prince.

"Wait a moment, my gracious prince; the king would remain with the Bastard of Mauléon, and butcher him."

"Oh, I do not say no!" retorted Don Pedro, with his hideous smile; "but the bastard, at least, belongs to me."

Du Guesclin groaned; he looked at the Prince of Wales.

"Sire," said the latter, "a single prisoner shall not be slain to-day."

"Not to-day. I am well content;" and Don Pedro darted a look of intelligence at Mothril.

"Sire, our victory has rendered this day right glorious, has it not?" continued the Prince of Wales.

"Beyond doubt, seigneur."

"Then you will grant me a gift and request, sir king?" Don Pedro bowed.

"I ask you to make me a present of this young man," said the prince.

A deep silence followed these words, to which Don Pedro, pale with fury, did not at once reply.

"Oh!" he said, "Your Highness makes me feel that you are indeed my master. To lose my vengeance!"

"Then, if I am your master," cried the Black Prince, indignantly, "I order that this knight be freed from his bonds, and that his arms and horse be restored to him."

"Noël, Noël! to the good Prince of Wales!" shouted the Breton knights.

"Ransom, at least," said Mothril, to gain time.

The prince looked askance at the Moor.

"How much?" he asked, disgusted.

The Moor did not answer.

The prince unfastened a diamond cross from his breast and offered it to Mothril.

"Take it, infidel!" said he.

Mothril bent his head and murmured, quite low, the name of the Prophet.

"You are free, sir knight," said the prince to Mauléon. "Free to return to France and announce that the Prince of Wales, content with possessing for a season the most redoubtable knight in the world, will dismiss Bertrand Du Guesclin after the campaign, and will dismiss him without ransom."

"Alms to those French beggars!" murmured Don Pedro.

Bertrand heard him.

"If it please you, sire," he said to the prince, "you will not be so generous to me; I should blush before your friends to accept your gracious offer. I belong to a master who would pay my ransom ten times over, if I let myself be taken so often, though each time I ranked my value as high as that of a king."

"Then fix your ransom yourself," said the prince, courteously.

Bertrand reflected a moment.

"Prince," said he, "I am worth seventy thousand florins of gold."

"Praised be God!" ejaculated Don Pedro, "his pride ruins him. No one in France has the half of that sum, not even King Charles himself."

"It is possible," replied Bertrand; "but, since the knight of Mauléon speeds to France, I would pray him, of his gentleness, to ride with a squire through every highway and village in Bretagne, and on every highway and in every village cry these words: 'Bertrand Du Guesclin is prisoner to the English! — Spin, women of Bretagne, spin; from you awaits he his ransom!'"

"I will do it, by God!" cried Mauléon.

"And you will bring the sum to monseigneur, ere I have time to grow weary here," said Bertrand, "which, for that matter, I think can never happen, though my duress last my life, being in the company of so sweet and generous a prince."

The Prince of Wales offered his hand to Bertrand. "Knight," said he to Agénor, now free and delighted to have his sword again, "you have borne yourself on this day like a right loyal soldier. By saving Henry of Trastamare, you have deprived us of the great vantage of our battle. Yet we bear you not ill-will, in that you have thus opened for us other paths wherein we may earn glory.

Take this gold chain, and also this cross, which the infidel would not have."

He saw Don Pedro whispering to Mothril and the answering smile of the latter, at the meaning of which the constable was showing evident signs of uneasiness.

"Let no person stir," cried the prince. "I will punish with death whosoever dares to cross the limits of my camp, — yes, though he be prince or king!

"Chandos," he added, "you are constable of England, and, like a brave knight, you will conduct the Sire de Mauléon to the nearest town, and give him the necessary safe-conduct."

Mothril, again discouraged by this clear-sighted and persevering interpretation of his hideous plots, turned a desponding glance on his master.

Don Pedro's triumphant joy was no more, he was cast down in the dust; he had no longer hope of revenge.

Agénor knelt before the Prince of Wales, then kissed the hand of Du Guesclin, who clasped him in his arms, and whispered in his ear, —

"Announce to the king that our devourers are gorged, and now will sleep for a little; tell him, if he send me my ransom, I shall lead them where I promised. Bid my wife sell our last bit of land; I have many Bretons to ransom."

Agénor, deeply affected, mounted his good steed, bade adieu to his companions, and rode away.

Musaron growled, —

"Who could ever have told me that, some day, I should prefer an Englishman to a Moor?"

XVI.

A TREATY OF ALLIANCE.

At the very time victory was perching on the banner of Don Pedro, and Du Guesclin was falling into the hands of the enemy, and Mauléon, on the order of the constable, was quitting the field of battle, whither he was to be led back with the helm and mantle of King Henry, a courier was quitting the same field of battle and speeding towards the village of Cuello.

There, two women, placed a hundred yards from each other, the one in a litter with an escort of Arabs, the other on an Andalusian mule, with a train of Castilian cavaliers, were awaiting events with all the anguish of fear and hope.

Doña Maria dreaded a battle, the loss of which would ruin Don Pedro's prospects and deprive him of his liberty.

Aïssa recked little of victory or defeat, except either issue brought her back her lover. Little to her booted the fall of Don Pedro or the rise of Don Henry, except in the funeral procession of the one or in the train of the other's triumphal chariot she could again see Agénor.

Thus, both women had terrible misgivings on one and the same evening. Maria was more than anxious; she was jealous. She knew that, once a victor, Mothril would no longer have to busy himself with the pleasures of the king. She had guessed all his policy, and Aïssa, in her simplicity, had confirmed her instinctive suspicions.

So, although the young girl was guarded by twenty trusty slaves of Mothril, and although the Moor, according to his usual custom, had shut her up in her litter, Maria did not lose sight of her.

The Moor, not wishing to expose his precious treasure to the risks of battle, and the brutality of the English auxiliaries, had left the litter at the village of Cuello, which consisted of some twenty huts, and was very nearly two leagues from the field of battle at Navaretta.

He had given his slaves formal orders.

They were, in the first place, to wait for him, and to open the litter to none save himself.

If he did not return, or was slain, he had given other injunctions, as will be seen later.

Aïssa, then, was awaiting the issue of the battle at the village of Cuello.

As to Maria, Don Pedro, when he quitted Burgos, had left her well guarded. She was to stay there until she had news of him; she had a large sum in money, besides precious stones, and Don Pedro had sufficient confidence in that devoted love to be assured that, should reverse betide him, Maria would be more loyally attached to him in evil than even in good fortune.

But Maria did not wish to suffer that torture of vulgar women, — jealousy. Her principle was that it is better to risk a misfortune than to ignore a treason. She distrusted the weakness of Don Pedro; she knew that Cuello was at too short a distance from Navaretta.

So, taking with her six squires and twenty men-at-arms, friends rather than servitors, she mounted a fine Aragonese mule, and, without exciting suspicion, proceeded to encamp at the foot of a hill behind which rise the huts of Cuello.

Ascending the hill, she beheld the advance of the battalions of the two armies. She might have viewed the combat, but her heart failed her, on account of the importance of the events to be decided.

It was there that she had come so close to Aïssa.

She had sent an intelligent courier to the very field of battle, and she was awaiting him, placed, as we have said, at a very short distance from Aïssa, whom slaves, lying on the grass, were guarding.

The courier arrived. He announced that the battle was won. A man-at-arms himself, indeed a knight and one of the chamberlains of Don Pedro's court, he knew the principal knights in the hostile army. He had seen Mauléon at the time of his reception in solemn audience at Soria. Besides, Maria had pointed Agénor out particularly to him, and the bar, quartered on his shield with the lion issuant gules, made him easily recognizable.

He was come with the tidings that Henry of Trastamare was conquered, Mauléon a fugitive, and Du Guesclin a prisoner.

This news, while more than gratifying all Maria Padilla's ambition and pride, awoke in her soul all her jealous fears.

To see Don Pedro conqueror, and once again on his throne, was the dream of her love as well as of her pride; but Don Pedro, happy, envied, exposed to the temptations of Mothril! — that was the spectre that troubled a love even so anxious and devoted.

Maria determined on her course, and that with all the daring which characterized her.

She ordered the men-at-arms to follow her, and descended the mountain, conversing with her messenger.

"You say the Bastard of Mauléon has fled?" she asked.

"As flies the lion, yes, madame, with a cloud of arrows hurtling around him."

It was of Agénor's first flight that the messenger was speaking, for he had already left when the bastard was brought back wearing the mantle and helmet of Don Henry.

"Where is he thought to have gone?"

"To France; the bird that escapes flies towards its nest."

"'T is very likely," she thought.

"How many days does it take to reach France from here?" she said aloud.

"For a lady like you, madame, twelve."

"And after how many days would a person be safe from pursuit, — a person like the Bastard of Mauléon, for example?"

"Oh, madame, in three days a man might defy his most blood-thirsty enemy. Besides, this young knight has not been pursued. They were content to hold the constable."

"By the way, what has become of Mothril?"

"He received orders to watch the plain and prevent the escape of fugitives, above all, of Henry of Trastamare, if he still live."

"He will no longer trouble himself about Mauléon," she thought again. Then, turning to the courier, she said, "Follow me, knight."

She approached the litter of Aïssa; but, as she drew near, the Moorish guardians rose from the grass which they had been pressing in careless drowsiness.

"Ho there!" said she, "who commands here?"

"I, señora," answered the Moorish chief, who was recognizable by the purple of his turban and his floating girdle.

"I wish to speak to the young woman concealed in that litter."

"Impossible, señora," said the chief, shortly.

"Perhaps you do not know me?"

"Oh, yes, very well," answered the Moor, with a half smile; "you are Doña Maria Padilla."

"You must know, then, that I have all power, by order of the King Don Pedro."

"Over Don Pedro's people," said the Moor, gravely, "not over those of Mothril the Saracen."

Such resistance rendered Doña Maria uneasy.

"Have you orders to the contrary?" she said mildly.

"I have, señora."

"At least, tell me what they are."

"To any one else I should refuse to tell them, señora; to you, who are all-powerful, I will say that, if the battle be lost and the Señor Mothril come not immediately after, I must conduct Doña Aïssa to where he is; in that case, I am to withdraw from here with my men."

"But the battle is won," said Doña Maria.

"Then Mothril will come."

"Supposing he is dead?"

"Then," continued the Moor, imperturbably, "I must conduct Doña Aïssa to the King Don Pedro; at the very least, Don Pedro will become the guardian of the daughter of a man who has died for him."

Maria shuddered.

"But he lives, he will come, and, in the mean time, I may surely say two words to Doña Aïssa. Do you hear me, señora?" said she.

"Madame," said the chief, quickly approaching the litter, "force not the señora to speak to you, for, in such a case, I have an order far more terrible."

"An order of what nature?"

"To kill her with my own hand, if any communication between her and a stranger should stain the honor of my master and thwart his will."

Doña Maria recoiled in terror. She knew the manners of the country and the people, the fierce and untractable manners of men who silently executed the commands of their superiors, with all the fury engendered by their blood, and all the brutality engendered by their climate.

She turned back to her courier knight, who, along with his other men-at-arms, was standing with lance in hand, all as motionless as statues of iron.

"I need that litter," said she, "but it is well defended, and the Moorish leader threatens to kill the woman inside, if any one approach her."

The knight was a Castilian, that is to say, full of imagination and gallantry; moreover, he had the capacity to invent, and the courage and strength to execute.

"Señora," said he, "that yellow-faced rascal makes me laugh, and it angers me that he should have frightened Your Grace. He does not, then, reflect that, if I nailed him to the shaft of his litter, he could hardly kill the lady it hides."

"What! kill a man who has his orders!"

"See what a fine watch he keeps! he has actually to send some of his men to fetch the arms of his companions."

These words were uttered in pure Castilian. The Moors looked on with big, astonished eyes, for, though they had understood the Arabic spoken to them by Doña Maria, and though they understood the rather alarming gestures of the knights, they did not understand Spanish, faithful in this to the customary usages of the Mohammedan religion, which concentrate in the Arabian language and in the Koran all power and all superiority.

"Look, madame, they will be the first to attack, if we do not retire. Blood-thirsty dogs are these Moors," said the knight, feeling a strong desire to couch a lance under the eyes of a fair and noble dame.

"Stay!" said Doña Maria, "stay! You think they do not understand Castilian?"

"I am sure of it. Try to speak it to them, señora."

"I have another idea," answered Maria Padilla.

"Doña Aïssa," said she in Spanish, and in a loud voice, but addressing the knight as it were, "do you hear me? If you do, shake the curtains of your litter."

At these words, the silken curtains of the litter were seen to tremble repeatedly.

The Moors did not stir, entirely taken up as they were with their task of watching.

"You see that not one of them has turned round," said the knight.

"It may be only a trick," said Doña Maria; "let us wait a while."

After a time, she continued her address to the young woman in the same manner.

"You are watched only on one side of the litter; the Moors, whose attention is wholly directed to this side, leave you free on the side opposite to that upon which we are stationed. If the litter is closed, cut the curtains with your knife, and slip down. Yonder, about two hundred yards from here, is a large tree, behind which you may hide. Act promptly, for your chance of meeting again one whom you know is at stake; I will secure you the means of doing so."

No sooner had Maria Padilla, with an air of the greatest indifference, uttered these words, than the litter was seen to oscillate, rocking almost imperceptibly. The knights advanced a step towards the Moors, apparently with hostile intent. The Moors, on their side, also advanced, bending their bows and unfastening their maces.

However, the Castilians, whose faces were turned towards the Moors, had seen, on the other side of the litter, the fair Aïssa flying like a dove across the vacant space between the litter and the wide-branching tree.

When she had got there, —

"Be it as you wish," said Doña Maria to the Moors; "keep your treasure, we do not care to touch it; but have the goodness to fall back and open us a passage."

The chief, whose face cleared immediately, did as requested; his companions imitated him.

So the result was that the escort of Doña Maria passed through quickly and safely, and took up a position between Aïssa and those who, a moment before, were her guardians.

Aïssa had understood everything when she saw before her this protecting wall of iron. She threw herself into the arms of Doña Maria, kissing her hands passionately.

The chief of the Moorish archers perceived that the litter was empty, understood the stratagem, and uttered a cry of rage; he saw that he was tricked, ruined! For a moment he had the thought of rushing headlong on Maria's men-at-arms; but, frightened by the inequality of the struggle, he preferred jumping on a horse, held by one of Mothril's squires, and galloped at a rattling pace for the field of battle.

"There is no time to lose," said Doña Maria to the knight; "señor, you shall have all my gratitude if you succeed in saving this young woman from Mothril, and putting her on the road taken by the Bastard of Mauléon."

"Madame," answered the knight, "Mothril is the favorite of the king, this young woman is his daughter; consequently, you are asking me to rob him of her."

"But you are in my service, sir knight."

"To ask me to do so is more than is needed, madame, and if I must perish, at least it will be my consolation that I have given my life for you. Yet, should Don Pedro meet me absent from my post, what answer shall I make him? The fault will be very grave; I shall have disobeyed my king."

"You are right, señor; it shall not be said that the life and honor of a brave knight like you have been compromised by the caprice of a woman! But you will show us our way, Doña Aïssa will take horse, you will attend me as far as the road followed by the Bastard of Mauléon, and there — oh, why there we shall leave her, and you will return with me."

This, however, was by no means the intention of Doña Maria. She was merely counting on gaining time by saving the scruples of the knight. She was a woman accustomed to will and to have her will, and she had supreme confidence in her star.

The knight set his horse to the pace of Doña Maria's hackney. Aïssa was mounted on a white mule of rare vigor and beauty; the escort started at full gallop, and, cutting the plain to the left of the battlefield, were off like a shot in the direction leading to the French highway, traced upon the horizon by the huge birches that waved backwards and forwards, responsive to the western wind.

None spoke, none thought of aught except increasing the pace of their foaming horses. Already were the two

leagues passed over with lightning speed, already was
that battlefield, with its bloody burthen, its corpses,
and its ruined harvests, left so far behind that it looked
like some gigantic winding-sheet filled with the dead
and the dying, when, on turning a hedge, Maria descried a horseman, who was evidently galloping towards
her.

She recognized him by his sword-belt and his plume.

"Don Ayalos!" she cried to this prudent courier,
who, to avoid a party that had a suspicious look, was
already making a detour, "is that you?"

"Yes, noble lady, it is I," answered the Castilian,
who recognized the mistress of the king.

"What tidings?" said Maria, bringing her sinewy
hackney to a sudden halt.

"Extraordinary! It was believed that Henry of
Trastamare was a prisoner, taken by Mothril, who was
in pursuit of the fugitives; but, when the visor of the
supposed king was raised, the captive was none other
than the Bastard of Mauléon, lately the French ambassador! After flying, he had let himself be taken to
save Don Henry."

Aïssa uttered a cry.

"He is taken!" said she.

"He is taken, and, when I was leaving, the king,
transported with anger, was threatening him with his
vengeance."

Aïssa raised her eyes to heaven in despair.

"Would he kill him?" she exclaimed. "Impossible!"

"He has been very near killing the constable."

"But he must not die!" cried the young woman,
spurring her mule towards the field of battle.

"Aïssa! Aïssa! would you ruin me, and would you
ruin yourself also?" said Doña Maria.

"He must not die," repeated the young girl, frantically, and she continued her course.

Doña Maria, irresolute, gasping with emotion, was trying to recover her self-control, when the earth was heard groaning under the weight of a troop of swift horsemen.

"We are lost," said the knight, rising in his stirrups; "it is a squad of Moors who are advancing with a fleetness that outstrips the wind, and yonder is their chief in front of them."

And, in fact, before Aïssa could have swerved from her path, this furious cavalcade, opening like some wave hurled on the corner of a rounded cliff, encircled and clutched her in its embrace, then infolded her companions and Doña Maria herself, who, in spite of all her resolution, turned pale and almost fainted; she was on the left of the knight, who, on this occasion, did not belie his courage.

Then Mothril galloped on his Arab steed from out the centre of the group, seized Aïssa's bridle, and, in a voice stifled with emotion, said, —

"Where were you going?"

"I was seeking Don Agénor whom you would kill," she said.

Mothril next perceived Doña Maria.

"Ah! in company with Doña Maria!" he cried, grinding his teeth ferociously. "I divine it all! I divine!"

The expression of his face grew so frightful that the knight set his lance in rest.

"Twenty against a hundred and twenty; we are lost," thought the Castilian.

XVII.

THE TRUCE.

But an affray was not what Mothril desired.

He turned his eyes slowly towards the plain, cast a last look on the field of battle, and, addressing Maria Padilla, —

"I believe, madame," said he, "that our lord the king had appointed a certain place for your retreat; might I ask has he changed his intentions, and are you obeying a new order?"

"Order!" answered the haughty Castilian; "do you forget, Saracen, that you speak to one who is accustomed to give orders, not receive them?"

Mothril bowed.

"But, madame," said he, "though you may have the privilege of acting as you will, you do not suppose that you have also the privilege of disposing of Doña Aïssa according to your good pleasure. Doña Aïssa is my daughter."

Aïssa was preparing to answer with some furious exclamation, but Maria interrupted her.

"Señor Mothril," said she, "God forbid I should bring trouble into your family! Those who would be respected, respect others. I saw Doña Aïssa alone and in tears, dying with anxiety, and I took her with me."

Aïssa could no longer restrain herself.

"Agénor!" she cried, "what have you done with my knight, Agénor de Mauléon?"

"Ah!" returned Mothril, "so that is the lord about whom my daughter is so anxious?"

And a fatal smile lit up for a moment his shrivelled features.

Maria did not answer.

"So that was the lord to whom you were conducting my weeping daughter?" continued the Moor, addressing Doña Maria. "Answer, madame, answer."

"Yes," said Aïssa, "and I am determined to find him. Oh, you need not bend your brows on me, my good father, you frighten me not. When Aïssa wills, she wills. I am resolved to find Don Agénor de Mauléon; lead me to him."

"To an infidel?" rejoined Mothril, whose face turned now actually ghastly.

"To an infidel, for that infidel is —"

Maria interrupted her.

"The king! the king!" she cried; "he is coming this way."

At once, the Moor made a sign to his slaves. Aïssa was surrounded and separated from Maria Padilla.

"You have killed him!" she exclaimed; "well, I, too, can die!"

And she drew from its golden sheath a little blade as keen-edged as a viper's tongue, and which flashed back its sheen to the sunlight of the plain.

Mothril rushed towards her; all his fury was gone, all his ferocity gave place to the most torturing anxiety.

"No," he cried, "no, he lives! he lives!"

"Who will assure me of it?" answered the young girl, questioning the Moor with her flaming eyes.

"Ask the king himself; will you believe the king?"

"'T is well! do you ask, and let him answer."

Don Pedro had approached.

Maria Padilla had thrown herself into his arms.

"Seigneur," suddenly said Mothril, whose head seemed to be almost wandering, "is it true that this Frenchman, this Mauléon is dead?"

"No, by hell!" said the king, in a gloomy voice. "I have not even been able to strike that traitor, that demon; no, he flies, the wretch, sent away to France by the Black Prince, he flies, free, happy, scoffing, like the sparrow escaped from the vulture."

"He flies," repeated Doña Aïssa, "he flies! is it really true?"

And her eyes questioned all the by-standers.

But in the interval, Maria Padilla, who had gathered positive information, and who knew that the safety of Mauléon was assured, made a sign to the young girl that she might remain and that her lover was safe and sound.

Suddenly, all the delirium of the Moorish maiden was calmed, as the tempests are calmed on the return of the sun.

She allowed Mothril to lead her, following him with downcast eyes, not perceiving that the King Don Pedro fixed upon her an inflamed look, altogether absorbed in this one thought that Agénor was living, in this one hope that she could see him again.

Maria Padilla surprised that look of the king, and guessed its meaning; but, at the same time, she read on the face of the young Morisca the profound disgust which the cruel phrases of the king had raised within her.

"No matter," said she, "Aïssa shall not remain at court; she shall leave; I will unite her again with Mauléon. It must be so. Mothril will oppose it with all his power. But the die is cast; Mothril or I must succumb in the struggle."

And, just as she had made up her mind on the course she was to pursue, she heard the king sigh in the ear of the Moor, —

"The fact is that she is very beautiful! I never saw her so beautiful as to-day."

Mothril smiled.

"Yes," continued Maria, pale with jealousy, "that is the whole cause of the war!"

The return of Don Pedro to Burgos was made with all the splendor that a decisive victory gives to legitimate power.

The rebels had no longer any hope, they submitted; and their enthusiastic repentance was as potent a factor in changing the ordinary cruelty of Don Pedro to clemency as had been the exhortations of the Prince of Wales.

The king, then, was satisfied with the hanging of a dozen burghers, the cudgelling of a hundred of the most notorious mutineers at the hands of his soldiers, and the confiscating for the use of his treasury of the property of some of the richest citizens of one of the richest cities in Spain.

And next, as he was weary of these mad struggles, as he saw fortune smile upon him, and as he felt a longing to warm again his heart and soul in the joyous sunshine of festivals, he made Burgos a royal city. Balls and tournaments succeeded each other without interruption. Dignities and rewards were distributed, war was forgotten, and hatred was almost forgotten also.

Mothril was watching, but, instead of busying himself, like a prudent minister, with events, with a probable renewal of the war, he lulled the king into deep security.

Don Pedro had dismissed the English, who were discontented; some strong fortresses, still in their power, were a poor and dangerous indemnity for the enormous expenses of the war.

The Prince of Wales had drawn up and presented his account to his ally. The sum was frightful. Don Pedro, feeling that it was perilous to levy taxes at the moment of his restoration, demanded time for payment.

But the English prince knew his ally; he would not wait. There were, then, beyond any doubt, germs of misfortune around Don Pedro, even in his prosperity, of such a nature, that the most unfortunate prince in the world, the most utterly ruined prince among vanquished princes, would have preferred his state to that of this sovereign.

But this was the moment Mothril was waiting for, and, perhaps, had foreseen. Without affecting to be moved, he smiled at the pretensions of the Englishman, suggesting to the Spanish prince that a hundred thousand Saracens would be quite as useful as ten thousand Englishmen, would cost less, would open a path for the supremacy of Spain in Africa, and that a double crown would be the result of this policy.

Then he hinted that the only means of uniting the two crowns on the same head was an alliance; that a daughter of the ancient Arab princes who had the venerated blood of the caliphs in her veins, sitting beside Don Pedro on the throne of Castile, would, in a single year, rally all Africa, nay, all the Orient to that throne.

And this daughter of the caliphs, it was well understood, was Aïssa.

Henceforth, the path of the Moor was smooth. He touched on the realization of his dreams. Mauléon was no longer an obstacle, since he was gone. Moreover was this obstacle really an obstacle? Who was this Mauléon? A knight, a dreamer, frank, loyal, and credulous! Was such an antagonist as he to be an object of fear to the sombre and crafty Mothril?

The serious obstacle came, therefore, from Aïssa, and from Aïssa alone.

But force conquers all resistance. All that was wanted was to prove to the young girl that Mauléon was unfaithful. It was easy. Was there ever a time when the Arabs did not practise, either espionage to discover truth, or false testimony to establish falsehood?

A still graver impediment, and one that made the Moor bend his brows, was this haughty and beautiful woman, this woman still omnipotent over the mind of Don Pedro by custom and the tyranny of pleasure.

Maria Padilla, ever since she had become aware of the plans of Mothril, had labored to countermine them with an ability worthy, in every respect, of her rare and keen-sighted intellect.

She knew every desire of Don Pedro, even the slightest, she captivated his attention, she extinguished every fire, even the faintest, which she had not herself lit.

Docile when she was alone with Don Pedro, imperious in presence of all others, she continued to keep up with Aïssa, whom she had made her friend, a secret understanding.

Talking to her unceasingly of Mauléon, she held her back from thinking of Don Pedro; and besides, there was no need for any one to fan the love of the ardent and faithful young girl. Her love, it could be easily seen, would end only with her life.

Mothril had not yet been able to surprise these mysterious interviews; his distrust was slumbering. He saw only one of the threads of the intrigue, the one he held in his hand; the other escaped him, lost in a darkness that was full of artifice.

Aïssa no longer appeared at court; she was waiting silently for the realization of the promise made by Maria to give her trustworthy tidings of her lover.

And, in fact, Maria had despatched an emissary to France with instructions to find Mauléon, inform him of the situation of affairs, and return with some token of remembrance for the poor Moorish girl fretting her life out while waiting until they should meet again.

This emissary, a sharp mountaineer upon whom she could count, was no other than the son of the old nurse with whom Mauléon had met her in her gypsy disguise.

Such was the condition of affairs in Spain as well as in France; such were the two vital interests that were in antagonism, — furious enemies, waiting but for the moment when, having acquired by repose and study all the fulness of their strength, they might rush headlong, the one upon the other.

We may now return to the Bastard of Mauléon, who, except for the enduring love that was to lead him back to Spain, was returning to his country, light-hearted, joyous, and proud of his liberty, like that sparrow of which spoke the King of Spain.

XVIII.

THE JOURNEY.

AGÉNOR understood all the difficulty of his position.

To be free, by the generosity of the Prince of Wales, was a privilege of which many might envy him the continuance.

Agénor pushed forward as fast as he could, thanks to the pressing exhortations of Musaron, who, shaking his ears at the joyful thought that he still possessed them, used all his eloquence in painting the dangers of a pursuit and the charms of a return to one's native land.

But honest Musaron was losing his time. Separated from Aïssa, Agénor was master of his body only. His soul was in Spain, anxious, suffering, dismayed.

However, such was, at this period, the sense of duty, that Mauléon, whose heart waxed wroth at the thought of leaving his mistress and palpitated with joy at the thought of secretly going back to find her, — that Mauléon, we say, continued bravely his route at the risk of losing forever his beautiful Morisco, in order to accomplish the mission with which the constable had charged him.

The poor horse had been shown too little mercy. The noble animal, which had supported the fatigues of war and obeyed the amorous caprices of his master, became exhausted at Bordeaux, where Mauléon left it until he should return.

Then, after changing horses, according to the system long afterwards invented by Louis XIV. of ingenious memory, our traveller at last, utterly worn out, utterly unexpected, and, therefore, inspiring fear, fell at the feet of the good King Charles, who was paling up his peach-trees in the fine garden of the Hôtel Saint-Paul.

"Oh! oh! what is the matter, and what tidings do you bring me, Sire de Mauléon?" said King Charles, to whom nature had given this privilege: when he once saw a man, he recognized him ever after.

"Sire king," replied Agénor, putting one knee on the ground, "the tidings I have come to announce are sad: your army has been conquered in Spain."

"The will of God be done!" replied the prince, turning pale. "But the army will rally again."

"There is no longer an army, sire!"

"God is merciful," said the king, in a lower tone. "How is the constable?"

"Sire, the constable is the prisoner of the English."

The king heaved a stifled sigh, but did not utter a word. Then, almost immediately, his face cleared.

"Tell me of the battle," he said, after a moment. "Where did it take place?"

"At Navaretta, sire."

"I am listening."

Agénor related the disaster, the annihilation of the army, the capture of the constable, and how he had been saved, almost miraculously, by the Black Prince.

"I must ransom Bertrand," said Charles V., "if, however, they will put him to ransom."

"Sire, they have consented to the ransom."

"For how much?"

"Seventy thousand florins of gold."

"And who has fixed it?" said the king, startled by the largeness of the amount.

"The constable himself."

"The constable! he seems to me to be very generous."

"Do you think, sire, he has estimated himself above his value?"

"If he had estimated himself at what he is worth, all the treasures of Christendom could not restore him to us."

But while rendering this justice to Bertrand, the king fell into a gloomy reverie, the meaning of which Agénor could not misunderstand.

"Sire," said he, immediately, "let not Your Majesty put yourself to the trouble of ransoming the constable. Sire, Bertrand has bade me see his wife, Madame Tiphaine Raguenel, who has a hundred thousand crowns belonging to him, and will give them for the ransom of her husband."

"Ah! the good knight!" said Charles, brightening up, "he is, then, as good a treasurer as he is a warrior. I should not have believed it. A hundred thousand crowns! Why, he is richer than I! Let him lend me, then, these seventy thousand florins. I will pay them back soon. But do you really believe he possesses them? If he were to find he had them no longer?"

"Why, sire?"

"Because Madame Tiphaine Raguenel is very jealous of the glory of her husband, and her behavior yonder is that of a magnificent and charitable lady."

"Then, sire, in case she no longer had any money, the good constable gave me another commission."

"What is it?"

"To traverse Bretagne, crying, 'The constable is the prisoner of the English; pay his ransom, men of Bretagne! and you, women of Bretagne, spin!'"

"And," said the king, quickly, "you will take one of my banners, with three of my men-at-arms, to shout that

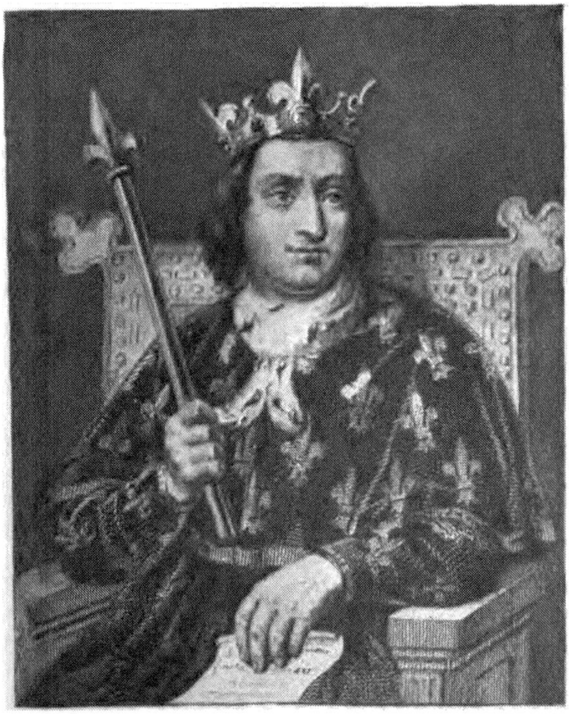

cry throughout all France! But," added Charles, "do not do this except in the last extremity. It is possible that we may rectify here the misfortune of Navaretta. Odious name! that word Navarre always brings woe to France."

"Impossible, sire; you will, doubtless, soon see the fugitive prince, Henry of Trastamare. Every trumpet in Gascony will peal forth the triumph of the English, and afterwards, poor Bretons, wounded and begging their way, will return to their country, relating to all their lamentable history."

"It is true! Start, therefore, Mauléon, and if you again see the constable —"

"I shall see him again."

"Tell him that nothing is lost if he is restored to me."

"Sire, I had another message from him for you."

"What is it, pray?"

"'Tell the king,' he whispered in my ear, 'that our plan goes well, that many of the rats of France have died of the burning heat of Spain, not being able to get accustomed to the climate.'"

"Our brave Bertrand! So he could laugh, then, even at that cruel moment?"

"Always invincible, sire; as fine in defeat as he is great in victory."

In this fashion did Agénor take leave of King Charles V., who ordered three hundred livres to be given to him, — a magnificent gift, enabling Agénor to purchase two good war-horses for fifty livres each. He gave ten livres to Musaron, who renewed his habiliments in the Rue de la Draperie. Agénor also bought in the Rue de la Heaumerie one of those newly invented helmets that closed with a spring, and presented it to his squire, whose head gave way so easily to the blows of the Saracens.

This useful and agreeable present raised still higher the spirits of Musaron, and he began to have, near his master, the soothing and proud feeling that he was a gentleman squire.

They started.

France is so beautiful! It is so sweet to be young, strong, valiant, to love and to be loved, to have a hundred and fifty livres at your saddle-bows, and to wear an entirely new sallet, that Mauléon inhaled the pure air in great gulps, that Musaron capered on his saddle and curvetted like a man-at-arms on horseback, and that both acted as if the one would have said, "Look at me, I love the fairest girl in Spain;" the other, "I have seen the Moors and the battle of Navaretta, and I have a helmet that cost eight livres, purchased at Poinerot's, Rue de la Heaumerie."

In this joyousness and in this fine array, Agénor arrived at the frontiers of Bretagne, where he had to demand of the reigning prince, Duke Jean de Montfort, permission to visit Dame Raguenel on her lands, and to raise the money necessary for the ransom of the constable.

This commission, intrusted to Musaron, Agénor's ordinary negotiator, was a delicate one. The Comte de Montfort, son of the old Comte de Montfort, who had made war against France with the Duke of Lancaster, although his feelings towards Bertrand, who was chiefly instrumental in raising the siege of Dinan, were rancorous, — but, as we have said, it was the time of fine deeds and noble hearts, — the Comte de Montfort, on learning the misfortune of Bertrand, forgot all his enmity.

"Permit it!" said he, "why, I demand it. Raise on my lands all the contributions you require. Not only do I wish to see him free, but I wish to see him my friend, if he returns to Bretagne. Our land is honored in being his birthplace."

Having thus spoken, the count received Agénor with distinction, gave him the present due to every royal ambassador, and, having done him the honor to furnish him with an escort, ordered him to be conducted to Dame Tiphaine Raguenel, who was then at La Roche-Derrien, one of the domains of the family.

XIX.

MADAME TIPHAINE RAGUENEL.

TIPHAINE RAGUENEL, daughter of Robert Raguenel, Seigneur de La Bellière, a viscount and a man of the first rank, was one of those accomplished women heroes but seldom met, whether it be that God does not concentrate on the same family all his precious gifts, or that the merit of one spouse ordinarily absorbs that of the other.

Tiphaine, in her youth, was surnamed Tiphaine the Fay. She was skilled in medicine and astrology. It was she who had foretold the triumph of Bertrand in his two celebrated combats, to the gaping wonder of the anxious Bretons; it was she who, when Bertrand was weary of service and wished to return to his lands, sent him back, by her counsels and predictions, to the glorious life from which he acquired fortune and imperishable renown. In fact, until the war made by Charles of Blois on Jean de Montfort,— a war in which Bertrand was called to the command of the army,— the Breton hero had only had an opportunity of displaying the unrivalled strength, adroitness, and courage of the champion duellist and partisan leader.

Accordingly, the influence enjoyed by Tiphaine Raguenel over her husband and over the country was that of a great queen.

She had been beautiful; she was of high lineage. Her cultivated mind gave her superiority over many sages in council, and she had added to her other precious qualities the matchless disinterestedness of her husband.

When she learned that a messenger from Bertrand was coming to her, she went forth to meet him with her ladies and pages.

Anxiety was depicted on her countenance. She had, almost involuntarily, apparelled herself in weeds of mourning; and this, in the present state of things, — for the disaster of Navaretta was generally unknown, — had struck the guests and serfs of the manor of La Roche Derrien with superstitious terror.

Tiphaine came, then, to meet Mauléon, and received him at the drawbridge.

Mauléon had forgotten all his gayety, and his face assumed the ceremonial aspect of a messenger of ill tidings.

He bowed first, then sank on one knee, subjugated by the imposing presence of the noble lady, and still more by the gravity of the news he was bringing.

There was a mournful silence around the knight, and on those manly Breton faces was painted the most gloomy anxiety.

It was remarked, however, that the knight had not any crape attached to his banner or to his sword, as was usual in case of death.

Agénor collected his thoughts and began the sad recital, which Dame Raguenel listened to without giving the least sign of surprise. Still, the shadow that clouded her noble features grew ever darker and heavier. Dame Tiphaine listened, we repeat, to the painful story.

"Well," said she, after all the Bretons had uttered their cries of distress and ejaculated their prayers, "you come on the part of my husband, sir knight?"

"Yes, dame," replied Mauléon.

"And, being a prisoner in Castile, he has been put to ransom?"

"He has put himself to ransom."

"At how much?"

"At seventy thousand florins of gold."

"It is not too high for so great a captain. But where does he expect to find this sum?"

"He expects it from you."

"From me?"

"Yes; have you not a hundred thousand crowns of gold which the constable brought back from his last expedition and confided to the care of the monks of Mont-Michel?"

"It is true the sum was a hundred thousand crowns, sir messenger, but it is spent."

"Spent!" cried Mauléon, involuntarily, who recalled the words of the king, — "spent!"

"As it was right it should be, I think," continued the lady. "I took the sum from the monks to equip a hundred men-at-arms, to succor twelve knights of our country, to bring up nine orphans, and, as nothing was left to marry the two daughters of one of our friends and neighbors, I pledged my plate and jewels. There is nothing in the house except what is strictly necessary. However, poverty-stricken though we be, I hope I have acted as Messire Bertrand would wish me to, and I believe he would approve and thank me if he were here."

These words, "if he were here," uttered with such emotion by such noble lips, and in such noble language, drew tears from all eyes.

"It only remains for the constable to thank you, as, indeed, you deserve, and to await the help of God."

"And of his friends," said some, enthusiastically.

"And, as I have the honor to be the faithful servant

of Messire le Connétable," said Mauléon, "I shall now proceed to accomplish the task imposed on me by Messire Du Guesclin in anticipation of what has happened. I have the trumpeter of the king, a banner with the arms of France, and I am going to travel through the country, announcing the tidings. Those who would see Messire le Connétable free and safe will rise and contribute."

"I would have done it myself," said Tiphaine Raguenel; "but it is better that you should do it, with the permission of Monseigneur le Duc de Bretagne, first of all."

"I have that permission, madame."

"Now, dear sires, you hear," continued Tiphaine Raguenel, looking around confidently on the increasing crowd; "those who wish to show to the knight here present the interest they take in the name of Du Guesclin will surely regard his messenger as a friend."

"And, in the first place," cried a knight who had just stopped behind the group, "I, Robert, Comte de Laval, will give forty thousand livres for the ransom of my friend Bertrand. And this money follows me; my pages are bringing it."

"May the nobles of Bretagne imitate you, generous friend, in proportion to their wealth, and the constable will be free this evening," said Tiphaine Raguenel, greatly moved by this liberality.

"Come, sir knight," said the Comte de Laval, "I offer you the hospitality of my house. From to-day you will begin your collection, and, on my faith, it will be ample! Let us leave Dame Tiphaine to her sorrow."

Mauléon kissed respectfully the noble lady's hand, and followed the count, amid the benedictions of a great concourse of people, attracted by the news.

Musaron did not feel at all happy. He had been in

danger of being stifled by the populace, who clasped his thigh and kissed his stirrup, neither more nor less than if he had been a knight banneret.

The hospitality of Comte de Laval promised some rare days to our most sober and vigilant squire, and then, Musaron, let us confess it, had a weakness: he liked to see, if it were only for its color, a great quantity of gold.

The collections were already going on from parish to parish, constantly increasing in size. The humble hut gave a day's labor, the castle gave the value of ten oxen, or a hundred livres, the bourgeois, not less generous or less national, curtailed his table of a dish or his wife's gown of an ornament. In a week, Agénor picked up a hundred and sixty thousand livres at Rennes, and, that vein being exhausted, he resolved to begin the working of another.

Moreover, it is certain, as says the legend, that the women of Bretagne spun their distaffs more industriously for the liberty of Du Guesclin than they had ever done to feed their children and clothe their husbands.

XX.

THE MESSENGER.

MAULÉON had been a week the guest of the Comte de Laval near Rennes, when, one evening, at the very time he was returning laden with a bag of gold, duly registered by the ducal scribe and the agent of Dame Tiphaine Raguenel, the good knight, finding himself between the town and the castle, in a ravine lined with hedges, perceived two men whose aspect was strange and whose attitude was alarming.

"Who are those people?" asked Agénor of the squire.

"Upon my soul! they are not unlike Castilians," cried Musaron, looking askance at a knight followed by a page, who were each mounted on a little Andalusian horse with long tail and flowing mane, and, with helm on head and shield on breast, had backed against the hedge, in order to observe the Frenchmen and question them on passing.

"Undoubtedly, the armor is Spanish; and the long, thin, flat swords are not unlike those worn by Castilians."

"And does n't that tell you anything, messire?" asked Musaron.

"Yes, certes — But this cavalier would speak with me, I think."

"Or take your bag, seigneur. Luckily, I have my arbalist."

"Let your arbalist alone; see, neither of them has touched his arms."

"Seigneur!" cried the stranger, in Spanish.

"Are you speaking to me?" said Agénor, in the same language.

"Yes."

"What do you want with me?"

"Point me out the road to the castle of Laval, if you please," said the cavalier, with that politeness which distinguishes the man of rank everywhere, and the humblest Castilian in all circumstances.

"I am going there, seigneur," said Agénor, "and can serve as your guide, but I warn you that the lord of the place is absent; he set out this morning to make an excursion in the neighborhood."

"Is there no one at the castle?" said the stranger, with evident disappointment. "Must I, then, seek still further?" he murmured.

"But I did not say there was nobody there, seigneur."

"Perhaps you are on your guard," said the stranger, raising his visor; for this visor, as well as that of Musaron, was lowered, — a prudent custom adopted by all travellers who, in those days of mistrust and brigandage, were ever on their guard against attack and treason.

No sooner, however, did the Castilian disclose his face than Musaron cried out, —

"Oh! Jesus!"

"What is the matter?" asked Agénor, in surprise.

The stranger also looked astonished at this exclamation.

"Gildaz!" whispered Musaron in the ear of his master.

"Who is Gildaz?" demanded Mauléon, in the same tone.

"The man we met on our journey in company with Madame Maria, — the son of that good old gypsy who made an appointment with you in the chapel."

"Good heavens!" said Agénor, seized with anxiety, "what can they be doing here?"

"Pursuing us, perhaps."

"Prudence!"

"Oh! you know well there is no need of your advice on that point."

During this conference the Castilian was examining the two speakers, gradually falling back in evident fear.

"Bah! what harm can Spain do us in the middle of France?" said Agénor, reassured, after a moment's reflection.

"You are right; some news for us, perhaps," said Musaron.

"Oh! that is what makes me tremble. I fear events more than men. No matter! Let us question them."

"On the contrary, let us be prudent. What if they were emissaries of Mothril!"

"But you remember seeing this man with Maria Padilla."

"And have you not seen Mothril with Don Frederic?"

"'T is true."

"Then, let us be on our guard," said Musaron, bringing to his breast the arbalist which was swinging from his bandoleer.

The Castilian saw the movement.

"Why do you suspect us?" said he. "Have we introduced ourselves in discourteous fashion, or does the sight of my face displease you?"

"No," said Agénor, stammering, "but — what is your business at the castle of the Sire de Laval?"

"I am perfectly willing to tell it, seigneur. I want to meet a knight who lodges with the count."

Musaron, through the holes of his visor, darted a speaking glance at his master.

"A knight — named?—"

"Oh, seigneur, ask me not to be guilty of an indiscretion in repayment of the service you may render me. I should prefer waiting until some less inquisitive traveller pass along this road."

"You are right, seigneur, you are right; I will not question you further."

"I was very hopeful when I heard you speak in the language of my country."

"Hopeful of what?"

"Of the speedy success of my mission."

"To this knight?"

"Yes, seigneur."

"What harm will it do you to name him, since I am sure to know it when we arrive at the castle?"

"Because then, seigneur, I shall be under the roof of a lord who will not allow me to be ill-treated."

Musaron had a happy inspiration. He was always brave when a danger threatened his master.

He raised his visor resolutely, and approached the Castilian.

"*Valga me Dios!*" cried the latter.

"Well, Gildaz, good-day!" said the squire.

"You are the man I seek!" exclaimed the Castilian.

"Here I am, then," returned Musaron, unsheathing his heavy cutlass.

"Oh! there is no need of that. Is this lord your master?"

"What lord, and what master?"

"Is this knight Don Agénor de Mauléon?"

"I am," said Agénor. "Come, let me know my fate; whether it be good or evil, I am in haste to know it."

Gildaz regarded the knight with a sort of mistrust.

"But if you are deceiving me?" said he.

Agénor made a brusque movement.

"Hear me!" said the Castilian; "a good messenger ought to be on his guard."

"But you recognize my squire, rascal."

"Yes, but I do not recognize his master."

"You distrust me, then, scoundrel?" cried Musaron, in a fury.

"I distrust everybody when my duty is at stake."

"Take care, yellow face, that I do not serve you out for this! My knife is sharp-edged."

"Indeed!" said the Castilian, "and my rapier also. You are not reasonable. Will my commission be executed, if I am slain? Or, if you are, will it be executed better? Let us go quietly to the manor of Laval; when there, let some one name the Seigneur de Mauléon, without any previous warning, and the orders of my mistress will be immediately fulfilled."

This word made Agénor bound. He cried, —

"Good squire, you are right, and we were wrong! You come to me from Doña Maria, perhaps?"

"You shall know immediately, if you are, indeed, Don Agénor de Mauléon," said the obstinate Castilian.

"Come, then!" cried the young man, with feverish impatience. "Come, — yonder are the towers of the castle, — come quick! You shall have every satisfaction, good squire. Spur, Musaron, spur!"

"I pray you let me ride in front, then," said Gildaz.

"As you will; go, but go quick."

And the four cavaliers clapped spurs to their horses.

XXI.

AÏSSA.

AGÉNOR had scarcely entered the manor of Laval, when the Castilian, who did not lose sight of a gesture or a word, heard the warden of the tower say, —

"Welcome, Sire de Mauléon!"

These words, joined to the reproachful looks Musaron hurled at him from time to time, were enough for the messenger.

"May I say a few words to you privately, monseigneur?" asked he at once of the young man.

"Will yon court, planted with trees, suit you?" inquired Agénor.

"Perfectly, monseigneur."

"You know," continued Mauléon, "that I do not distrust Musaron, who is more a friend than a servant; as for your companion — "

"Seigneur, you see what he is; he is a young Moor I found nearly two months ago, on the road leading from Burgos to Soria. He was dying with hunger; he had been beaten almost to death by the servants of Mothril and by Mothril himself, who had threatened to stab the poor boy because he showed a leaning towards the religion of Jesus Christ. I found him then, all pale and bleeding. I brought him to my mother, whom, perhaps, you know," added the squire, smiling, "and we dressed his wounds and gave him something to eat. Since then, he has been as devoted to us as a dog, devoted even to death.

So, when, two weeks ago, my illustrious mistress Doña Maria —"

The squire lowered his voice.

"Doña Maria!" murmured Mauléon.

"The same, seigneur; when my illustrious mistress, Doña Maria, summoned me and intrusted me with an important and dangerous mission, — 'Gildaz,' said she, 'you will take horse and start for France; put plenty of gold in your valise, and see you have a good sword; you will search on the road to Paris for a gentleman' (and my mistress gave me a description of yourself, seigneur) 'who is certainly on his way to the court of the great King Charles the Wise; take a faithful companion with you, for your mission, I tell you, is a dangerous one.'

"I thought at once of Hafiz, and I said to him, 'Hafiz, get on horseback and take your poniard.'

"'Immediately,' answered Hafiz; 'give me time just to go to the mosque.' For you know, seigneur," said Gildaz, sighing, "that, among us Spaniards, there are to-day churches for the Christians and mosques for the infidels, as if God had two abodes.

"I let the boy go to the mosque; I got ready his horse as well as mine; I hung to the saddle-bow the long poniard which you may see fastened to it by a silken chain, and, when he returned, half an hour after, we started. Doña Maria had written the letter I am about to give you."

Gildaz lifted up his cuirass, opened his doublet, and said to Hafiz, —

"Your poniard, Hafiz!"

Hafiz, with his tawny complexion, his white eyes, and his impassive mien, had remained, during the entire narrative of Gildaz, as silent and motionless as a stone.

While the good squire was recounting his rank, fidelity,

and discretion, the young Moor did not once wink; but when he spoke of his half hour's absence at the mosque, a kind of redness, a sort of pale, sinister fire invaded his cheeks, and a glare of something like anxiety or remorse flashed from his eyes.

When he was asked for the poniard, he stretched out his arm slowly, drew the weapon from its sheath, and handed it to Gildaz.

Mauléon called on Musaron for aid.

The latter was, most assuredly, expecting to have something to do in the winding up of the scene.

He took the envelope, tore it, and began reading to Mauléon the contents of the epistle, while Gildaz and Hafiz kept at a respectful distance.

"Seigneur Don Agénor," wrote Maria Padilla, "I am well watched, surrounded with spies and perils; but the person you know of is so still more than I. I have a sincere regard for you; but the person in whose behalf I write loves you still more than I. We have both thought that it would please you to have in your possession, now that you are in France, that which you regret.

"Be then at Rianzares, near the frontier, a month after the reception of the present notice. I shall know the precise date of your arrival at Rianzares by the faithful messenger I am sending you. Wait patiently there and say nothing. You will witness the approach, not of a litter you are acquainted with, but of a fleet mule bringing you the object of all your desires.

"Then, Seigneur de Mauléon, fly; then, renounce your trade of arms, or, at least, never again set foot upon Castile; this do on your faith as a Christian and knight. Then, enriched by the dowry your wife will bring you, happy in her love and beauty, guard your treasure, like a vigilant knight, and sometimes bless Doña Maria Padilla, a very unhappy poor woman of whom this letter is a last farewell."

Mauléon felt moved, transported, intoxicated.

He bounded, and, snatching the letter from Musaron, imprinted on it an ardent kiss.

"Come," said he to the squire, "come, let me embrace you, — you who have, perchance, touched the garments of her who is my protecting angel."

And he wildly embraced Gildaz.

Hafiz did not lose sight of a single detail in the scene, but he did not stir.

"Tell Doña Maria —" cried Mauléon.

"Silence, seigneur!" interrupted Gildaz; "that name — so loud."

"You are right," returned Agénor, in a lower tone. "Tell, then, Doña Maria that in a fortnight —"

"No, seigneur," replied Gildaz, "the secrets of my mistress do not concern me; I am a courier, not a confidant."

"You are a model of fidelity and noble devotion, Gildaz, and, poor as I am, you shall receive from me a handful of florins."

"No, seigneur, nothing; my mistress pays me liberally."

"Then, your page, your faithful Moor —"

Hafiz opened his eyes wide, and the sight of the gold sent a thrill through his breast.

"I forbid you to take anything, Hafiz," said Gildaz.

An imperceptible movement revealed to the perspicacious Musaron the fierce self-restraint of Hafiz.

"The Moors are generally greedy," said he to Gildaz, "and that one there is more so than a Moor and a Jew together, and I saw him dart a very ugly look at you, Gildaz."

"Bah! all Moors are ugly, Musaron, and the devil

alone can make anything out of their grimaces," replied Gildaz, smiling.

And he gave back the poniard to Hafiz, who grasped it almost convulsively.

Musaron, at a sign from his master, prepared at once to write a reply to Doña Maria.

The scribe of the Sire de Laval happened to be passing through the court.

Musaron stopped him, borrowed a parchment and pen, and wrote, —

"Noble lady, you overwhelm me with happiness. In a month, that is to say, on the seventh of the next month, I shall be at Rianzares, ready to receive the dear object you are sending me. I cannot renounce the trade of arms, because I wish to be a great warrior to do honor to my well-beloved lady; but Spain shall never see me again, I swear it by the Christ! unless you summon me thither, or some misfortune prevent Aïssa from joining me, in which case I would run even to hell to find her. Adieu, noble lady! pray for me."

The knight made a cross at the foot of the parchment, and Musaron wrote under the cross, —

"This is the signature:
"Sire Agénor de Mauléon."

While Gildaz was concealing the letter of Mauléon under his breastplate, Hafiz was watching from his horse every movement of the squire, more like a tiger than a faithful hound. Once he saw the place where the deposit rested, he appeared indifferent to the rest of the scene, as if there was no longer anything to see, and his eyes were of no more use to him.

"And what do you now, good squire?" said Agénor.

"I must set out again on my unflagging steed, seigneur,

and reach my mistress in twelve days. Such is her order; it behooves me, then, to be on the alert. It is true I am not so very far from her. There is, I am told, a short cut by way of Poitiers."

"You are right. Farewell till we meet again, Gildaz; good-bye, Hafiz. *Vrai Dieu!* it shall not be said that, though you refuse a gratuity from a master, you decline a gift from a friend."

And Agénor took off his gold chain, worth a hundred livres, and threw it round the neck of Gildaz.

Hafiz smiled, and his tawny face was strangely illumined by that infernal smile.

Gildaz, amazed, accepted, kissed the hand of Agénor, and departed.

Hafiz rode behind, as if attracted by the glitter of the gold that danced on the broad shoulders of the squire his master.

XXII.

THE RETURN.

MAULÉON made all his arrangements immediately. It was not joy that he felt now, it was peace. Henceforth, a perfect union with his mistress, security in love. Rich, beautiful, and loving, Aïssa came to him as one of those dreams that God sends to men, before the morning dawns, to show them that this earthly life is not everything.

Musaron shared the enthusiasm of his master. To have the management of a great house in that rich country of Gascony, for example, where the land feeds the idle, enriches the industrious, and becomes a paradise for the wealthy, to command varlets and serfs, to raise cattle and horses, have the ordering of the chase, — such were the sweet visions that assailed in crowds the very active imagination of Agénor's worthy squire.

Already Mauléon was thinking that he could not trouble himself about wars for a year, as Aïssa would occupy all his attention; for he owed to her, and he owed to himself, a year of tranquil happiness in return for so many painful hours.

Mauléon awaited impatiently the return of the Sire de Laval.

This lord had, on his side, gathered considerable sums among several noble Bretons, destined to pay the ransom of the constable. The scribes of the king and the Duke of Bretagne collated their accounts and the result showed that the half of the seventy thousand florins of gold was already found.

It was satisfactory to Mauléon, who hoped the king would do the rest; and he knew enough of the Prince of Wales to be certain that, in case the first half of the ransom arrived, the English would set the constable at liberty, if their policy did not counsel them to retain him though the whole sum was paid.

But, to relieve his punctilious conscience, Mauléon travelled through the rest of Bretagne with the royal standard, and made his appeal to the Breton people.

Every time he rode through a market-town, he was preceded by this doleful cry: —

"The good constable is the prisoner of the English; people of Bretagne, will you leave him in captivity?"

Every time, we say, that he encountered, in this pilgrimage, those Bretons so brave, pious, and melancholy, he excited the same groans and the same indignation, and the poor said to one another: "Quick, to work! we must eat less of our black wheat and pile sou upon sou for the ransom of Messire Du Guesclin."

In this fashion, Agénor collected six thousand more florins, which he intrusted to the men-at-arms of the Sire de Laval and to the vassals of Dame Tiphaine Raguenel, to whom he returned to say farewell before leaving.

And then a scruple came to him. He could leave, he ought to go in search of his mistress, but his mission as ambassador was not yet ended. Agénor, who had promised Doña Maria never again to enter Spain, was, nevertheless, bound to carry to Bertrand Du Guesclin the money collected by his exertions in Bretagne, — that precious money for whose arrival doubtless the captive of the Prince of Wales was sighing.

Placed between these two duties, Agénor hesitated for a

long time. An oath, and he had taken that oath to Doña Maria, was a sacred thing; his affection, his respect for the constable appeared to him sacred also.

He imparted his troubles to Musaron.

"Nothing easier," said the ingenious squire. "Ask Dame Tiphaine for an escort of a dozen armed vassals to guard the money; the Sire de Laval will add four lances, the king of France will give, provided it cost him nothing, a dozen men-at-arms; with this troop, which you will command as far as the frontier, the money will be safe. Once you are at Rianzares, you write to the Prince of Wales, who sends you a safe-conduct; in this fashion, the money is sure to reach the constable."

"But then, I myself — my absence?"

"The pretext of a vow."

"A falsehood!"

"It is not, in fact, a falsehood, since you have made a vow to Doña Maria. Then, even if it were a falsehood, your happiness is well worth a sin."

"Musaron!"

"Oh, sir knight, you need n't play the monk; you are marrying a Saracen. That, in my mind, is a mortal sin of another feather."

"'T is true, alas!" sighed Mauléon.

"And then," continued Musaron, "the lord constable would be very hard to please if he insisted on having you as well as the money. But, believe me, I know men; as soon as he sees the florins twinkle, the collector will be forgotten. Besides, if the constable of France will see you, he will see you; you don't intend burying yourself, I suppose?"

Agénor acted as usual; he surrendered. Moreover, the result proved that Musaron was perfectly right. The Sire de Laval furnished some soldiers, Dame Tiphaine

THE RETURN. 179

Raguenel armed twenty of her vassals, the Seneschal of Maine supplied twelve men-at-arms in the name of the king; and Agénor, in company with one of the young brothers of Du Guesclin, started for the frontier, making as long stages as possible, for he was in a hurry to reach the place of appointment at least two or three days before the date fixed by Doña Maria Padilla.

It was a triumphal progress, this march of the thirty-six thousand florins destined for the ransom of the constable. The few companions remaining in France after the departure of the companies were very humble in their aspirations, and, however longingly these brigands might look upon the prey, and a very fine one it was, it was hopeless to think of devouring it. They preferred, then, when they saw it pass before their lairs, to applaud chivalrously, to bless the name of the glorious prisoner, and to assume an air of the deepest respect, seeing that to be disrespectful would insure them the chance of laying their bones on the field of battle.

Mauléon directed the expedition with such ability that, in fact, on the fourth day of the month, he reached Rianzares, a little market-town long in ruins, but which, at the time, enjoyed a certain consideration, as one of the places through which travellers between France and Spain usually passed.

XXIII.

RIANZARES.

The market-town lay upon the slope of a hill, and Agénor could easily observe, from the lodgings he had selected, the white road that went winding upwards between two steep walls of rock.

Meanwhile, his soldiers took the rest, of which every one was badly in need.

Musaron had indited, in his finest style, an epistle for the constable, and another for the Prince of Wales, informing both of them of the arrival of the thirty-six thousand florins of gold.

A man-at-arms, escorted by a Breton squire chosen from among the vassals of Dame Tiphaine, had been despatched to Burgos, where the prince was said to be at present, because of fresh rumors of war that were circulated through the country.

Each day Mauléon, who had a perfect knowledge of the localities, reckoned up the distance made by Gildaz and Hafiz.

According to his calculations the two messengers must have crossed the frontier a fortnight ago, at the least.

During this fortnight they would have had time to find Doña Maria, who must have been able to make preparations for the flight of Aïssa. A good mule travels twenty leagues a day. There was nothing, then, to hinder the fair Morisca from reaching Rianzares in five or six days.

Mauléon made some discreet inquiries as to the passage of the Squire Gildaz. There was, in fact, no reason for supposing that the two men had not gone through the defile at Rianzares, for it was easy, safe, and well known.

However, the mountaineers answered that, during the time mentioned by Agénor, they had seen only one horseman pass, — a young and rather savage-looking Moor.

"A Moor, young!"

"Twenty, at most," replied a countryman.

"Clad in red, was he?"

"And with a Saracen morion, yes, seigneur."

"Armed?"

"With a long poniard. It hung by a silken chain from his saddle-bow."

"And you state that he arrived at Rianzares alone?"

"Quite alone."

"What did he say?"

"He cast about for a few Spanish words, which he pronounced badly and rapidly, asked if the passage in the rock was safe for horses, and if the little river at the foot of the hill was fordable. When we said it was, he pushed forward on his swift black horse and disappeared."

"Alone! it is strange," said Mauléon.

"Hum!" added Musaron, "alone, it is singular."

"Supposing Gildaz crossed the frontier at some other point, so as to awaken as little suspicion as possible? Eh, Musaron, what do you think of it?"

"I think Hafiz was a very ill-favored fellow."

"Besides," continued Mauléon, thoughtfully, "who can say that it was really Hafiz who passed by Rianzares?"

"In fact, it is better to believe that he did n't."

"And, then, I have noticed that the man who is just within reach of supreme happiness is distrustful of everything, and sees an obstacle in everything."

"Ah, yes! you are, indeed, within reach of happiness, for it was to-day, if we have not made a mistake, that Doña Aïssa was to arrive. We ought to keep a good watch during the whole night in the neighborhood of the river."

"Yes; I would not care to have our companions see her arrive. They are a little narrow-minded, and I am afraid of the effect this escape might have on them. The sight of a Christian in love with a Moorish damsel is enough to daunt the bravest, and any misfortune that happened would be imputed to me as a chastisement coming from God. But, do what I can, this solitary Moor, clad in red, with a poniard at his saddle-bow, and his likeness to Hafiz, take up all my thoughts."

"Well, in a few moments, or a few hours, or, at most, in a few days, we shall know what to look forward to," answered the philosopher. "Till then, monsieur, we have no ground for sadness; so let us be of good cheer, if you please."

It was really the best thing Agénor could do. He was cheerful and waited.

But the first day, the seventh of the month, passed, and nothing appeared on the highway, except a few dealers in wool and a number of wounded soldiers, or some fugitive knights from Navaretta, on foot and ruined, travelling by short stages through the woods, making long circuits in the mountains, and thus managing to reach their native land after a thousand privations and dangers.

Agénor learned from these poor people that the war had already been renewed in several places, that the tyranny of Don Pedro, rendered more heavy by that of Mothril, was becoming an intolerable burden to the Castiles, and that many emissaries of the vanquished pretender were travelling through the cities, urging the leading burghers to resist the tyranny of the restored dynasty.

These fugitives asserted that they had already witnessed the organization of several bodies who hoped for the speedy return of Henry of Trastamare. They added that a considerable number of their companions had seen letters from the prince in which he promised to return soon with a body of soldiers levied in France.

All these warlike reports inflamed the martial ardor of Agénor, and, as Aïssa did not arrive, love could not calm the fever that fires the blood of young men when they hear of the clash of arms.

Musaron was beginning to despair. He frowned oftener than usual. He was very sore on the subject of Hafiz, to whom, as to some malignant demon, he attributed the delay of Aïssa, "and a good deal more, too," he added, when his ill-humor was at its height.

As for Mauléon, he wandered incessantly along the road, like a body seeking its soul, until his eyes grew familiar with every turn and bush and stone and shadow, and he could tell a mule's steps two leagues away.

Aïssa did not arrive; nothing came from Spain.

But, on the other hand, there arrived from France, at intervals as regular as those measured by the hand of a clock, bands of armed men, who took up their positions in the neighborhood, and seemed to be awaiting the signal to enter simultaneously.

The chiefs of these bands conferred together on the arrival of every fresh contingent, and exchanged pass-words and instructions that seemed mutually satisfactory, for, without any other precautions, men of all arms and of all countries fraternized and lived together on the best possible terms.

One day, Mauléon, less engrossed than usual by Aïssa, inquired more at length as to the cause of the arrival of so many men and horses. He learned that these different bands were awaiting a supreme leader and new re-enforcements, and that then they were to return to Spain.

"And the name of the leader?" he asked.

"We don't know; he will tell it to us himself."

"So everybody is going to enter Spain except me!" cried Agénor in despair. "Oh, my oath! my oath!"

"Why, monseigneur," replied Musaron, "your grief is making you lose your senses. There is no oath if Aïssa does n't arrive; and if she does n't arrive let us push on."

"It is not time yet, Musaron; hope remains to me. I have still hope, and shall always have it, for I shall always love."

"If I could just only talk a half an hour with that little blackamoor Hafiz," growled Musaron. "I should like — merely to look at him — face to face."

"And what could Hafiz do against the all-powerful will of Doña Maria? It is she we ought to accuse, Musaron, she — or rather my ill fortune!"

A week passed and no news from Spain. Agénor was nearly mad with impatience, and Musaron with anger.

At the end of this week there were five thousand armed men scattered along the frontier.

Wagons, some loaded with provisions and others with money, escorted, it was said, these imposing forces.

The men of the Sire de Laval and the Bretons of Tiphaine Raguenel were also waiting impatiently for the return of their messenger, in order to learn whether the Prince of Wales would consent to the liberation of the constable.

At length the messenger returned, and Agénor ran eagerly as far as the river to meet him.

The man-at-arms had seen the constable, embraced him, been welcomed by the English prince, and had received a magnificent present from the Princess of Wales. This princess had deigned to say that she looked forward to the coming of the Chevalier de Mauléon and intended rewarding his devotion, for virtue honored all men, to whatever nation they belonged.

The messenger added that the prince had accepted the thirty-six thousand florins on account, and that the princess, seeing him hesitate, had said, —

"Sire, my husband, I wish the good constable to be liberated by me, for I admire him as much as his own countrymen. We are, to some extent, Bretons also, we of Great Britain. I will pay thirty thousand florins of gold for the ransom of Messire Bertrand."

Consequently, the constable was going to be free, even if he were not already free before the payment.

At these tidings, all the Bretons who were escorting the ransom leaped for joy, and, as joy is more catching than grief, all the troops gathered near Rianzares, when they learned the result of the embassy, raised such a hurrah of joy that the old mountains were shaken to the very depths of their granite foundations.

"Let us enter Spain," cried the Bretons, "and bring back our constable!"

"The very thing we must do," said Musaron, in a low tone to Agénor. "No Aïssa, no oath; we are losing time; forward, monsieur!"

And Mauléon, yielding to his ardent anxiety, answered, —

"Forward!"

The little band, followed by the prayers and blessings

of every one, cleared the defile nine days after the date fixed by Maria Padilla for the arrival of the Morisca.

"We are pretty sure to meet her on the way," said Musaron, as a last argument to decide his master.

As for ourselves, we shall go ahead of them to the court of the King Don Pedro, and, perhaps, find out and impart to the reader the cause of this ill-omened delay.

XXIV.

GILDAZ.

DOÑA MARIA was standing on her terrace, reckoning the days and hours, for she foreboded, or, rather, felt sure, that the persevering calmness of the Moor meant mischief to herself and to Aïssa.

Mothril was not a man to fall asleep in this fashion; never had he been able to so dissemble his thirst for vengeance that his enemies should have no warning of it for a whole fortnight.

To exhibit the utmost zeal in providing festivals for the king, to be always manœuvring for the introduction of the Saracen auxiliaries into Spain, and so prepare the way for the union of the two promised crowns on the head of his master, — such were his apparent occupations. He neglected Aïssa; he saw her only once in the evening, and almost always in company with Don Pedro, who sent to the young girl the rarest and most magnificent presents.

Aïssa, counselled at first by her love for Mauléon, then by her friendship for Doña Maria, accepted the presents which she was free to spurn when once received. Treating the prince with her usual coldness, and not suspecting that this very coldness served but to inflame his ardor, she sought in Doña Maria's eyes, whenever she met her, the thanks due to her loyal conduct.

And, in similar fashion, the eyes of Doña Maria said, —

"Hope! The plan we have conceived ripens every day in its obscurity. My messenger will soon return, bringing to you both the love of your fair knight and the liberty without which there is no real love."

At last the day, so eagerly longed for by Doña Maria, arose.

It was one of those mornings that burst forth in summer only under the beautiful skies of Spain; the dew trembled on every leaf on the flower-clad terraces of Aïssa, when Doña Maria saw the old woman, whom we are acquainted with, enter her room.

"Señora!" said she, with a long-drawn sigh,— "señora!"

"Well, what is the matter?"

"Señora, Hafiz is here."

"Hafiz! Who is Hafiz?"

"The companion of Gildaz, señora."

"What! Hafiz and no Gildaz?"

"Hafiz and no Gildaz,—yes, señora."

"Good Heavens! let him enter. Have you any other news?"

"No other news, señora. Hafiz would tell me nothing, nothing; and I am weeping, as you see, señora, because the silence of Hafiz is more depressing than would be the most alarming words from any one else."

"Come, come, take heart!" said Doña Maria, although she was shuddering herself; "it is nothing, a delay, merely, and that is all."

"But why did not Hafiz delay also?"

"Oh, on the contrary, the very thing that reassures me is the return of Hafiz. You see, Gildaz, knowing how anxious I was, did not care to keep him with him, and so he sends him to me; you may be certain we have good news."

But the nurse was not so easily consoled: the consolations of her mistress were just a little too precipitate.

Hafiz entered.

He was calm and humble. His eyes expressed respect, just as the eyes of cats and tigers become dilated in presence of those who fear them, but contract and almost close in presence of those who regard them angrily, or from the vantage ground of a dominant will.

"What! alone?" said Maria Padilla.

"Alone,— yes, madame," answered Hafiz, timidly.

"And Gildaz?"

"Gildaz, mistress," replied the Saracen, looking round him, "Gildaz is dead."

"Dead!" cried Doña Padilla, clasping her two hands in anguish. "Poor boy! is it possible?"

"Madame, he had an attack of fever on the way."

"And he so robust!"

"He was robust, indeed; but the will of God is stronger than that of man," replied Hafiz, sententiously.

"A fever! And why did he not warn me?"

"Madame," said Hafiz, "we were both traversing a defile in Gascony, and were attacked by mountaineers, whom the sound of gold attracted."

"The sound of gold! How imprudent!"

"The French seigneur gave us gold, he was so joyful! Gildaz thought he was alone in these mountains, and the fancy took him to count our treasure; then he was suddenly struck by an arrow, and we saw several armed men approach. Gildaz was brave; we defended ourselves."

"My God!"

"As we were about to yield,— for Gildaz was wounded, — his blood flowed — "

"Poor Gildaz! — and you?"

"I also, mistress," said Hafiz, slowly tucking up his wide sleeve and baring his arm, which was slashed by the blade of a poniard; "as we were wounded, the robbers took our gold and fled immediately."

"And what followed, great God, what followed?"

"And then, mistress, Gildaz had an attack of fever, and felt that death was near—"

"Did he say nothing?"

"Yes, mistress, when his eyes grew heavy: 'Stay,' said he, 'you are sure to escape; be faithful, as I have been; run to our mistress and place in her hands this packet which the French seigneur has confided to me.' Here is the packet."

Hafiz drew from his bosom a silken envelope, all pierced with dagger thrusts and stained with blood.

Doña Maria, shuddering with horror, touched the envelope and examined it.

"This letter has been opened," said she.

"Opened!" said the Saracen, his big eyes looking astonished.

"Yes, the seal is broken."

"I do not know," said Hafiz.

"You have opened it, have you not?"

"I! why I do not know how to read, mistress."

"Some one else, then?"

"No, mistress; look well, you see the opening at the place of the seal: the arrow of a mountaineer pierced the wax and parchment."

"It is true! it is true!" said Doña Maria, yet still distrustful.

"And the blood of Gildaz is all around the rents, mistress."

"It is true! poor Gildaz."

And the young woman, fixing a last look upon the Saracen, found that childlike face so bland and stupid and expressionless that she could not suspect any longer.

"Relate to me the end, Hafiz."

"The end was, mistress, that scarcely had Hafiz handed me the letter when he expired. I at once resumed my journey, as he had told me to do, and, poor, hungry, but never relaxing my speed, I have brought you the message."

"And you shall be well rewarded, my child!" said Doña Maria, moved to tears; "yes, you will remain with me, and if you are faithful — intelligent — "

The forehead of the Moor lit up for a moment, and then darkened again instantaneously.

Maria read the letter we know already, compared the dates, and, giving way to the natural impetuosity of her character, said to herself, —

"To work! now to work!"

She gave the Saracen a handful of gold, saying, —

"You can rest for the present, my good Hafiz; be ready in a few days, for I am going to employ you."

The young man passed out radiant. When he touched the threshold, bearing away his gold and his joy, the groans of the nurse broke forth more forcibly. She had just learned the fatal news.

XXV.

OF THE MISSION OF HAFIZ AND HOW HE HAD FULFILLED IT.

On the evening of the day when Hafiz brought to Doña Maria the letter from France, a shepherd had presented himself at one of the gates of the city and asked to speak to Seigneur Mothril.

Mothril, who was then occupied in saying his prayers in the mosque, gave up everything to wait upon this singular messenger, who certainly did not look like the herald of a most high and puissant ambassador.

Very soon after Mothril and his guide passed out of the city, he perceived a little Andalusian horse browsing on the heath on a moor, and, stretched on the scanty grass among the pebbles, the Saracen Hafiz, who was watching with his big eyes everything that came from the town.

The shepherd, after being paid by Mothril, ran gayly to join his lean goats on the hillside. Mothril, entirely forgetful of etiquette, sat down — though he was a prime minister — beside the gloomy child with the immutable face.

"God be with you, Hafiz! you are back, then?"

"Yes, seigneur, you see me."

"And you left your companion far away enough to suspect nothing?"

"Very far away, seigneur, and, beyond doubt, he suspects nothing."

Mothril understood his messenger. He knew that with all Arabs euphemism is a necessity, and that to them it is a matter of the highest moment to avoid pronouncing, as long as possible, the word "death."

"You have the letter?" said he.

"Yes, seigneur."

"How did you get it?"

"If I had asked Gildaz for it, he would have refused me. If I had tried to take it by force, he would have beaten and, doubtless, killed me, for he was stronger than I."

"You employed address?"

"I waited till we arrived at the heart of the mountain that divides Spain and France. The horses were very tired; Gildaz let them rest, and fell asleep himself on the moss at the foot of a high rock.

"This was the moment I was looking for. I crawled towards Gildaz and struck my poniard into his breast; he raised his arms, uttering a hoarse cry, and his hands were all wet with blood.

"But he was not dead, I knew it well. He was able to draw his cutlass and strike me on the left arm. I drove my dagger into his heart, and he expired immediately.

"The letter was in his doublet; I drew it out. I then rode all night on my little pony in the direction of the wind, abandoning the corpse and the other horse to the wolves and ravens. I crossed the frontier, and without being disturbed, finished my journey. Here is the letter I promised you."

Mothril took the parchment, the seal of which was whole, although it had been pierced through by the poniard Hafiz had plunged into the heart of Gildaz.

Taking an arrow from the quiver of a sentinel, he

drilled the wax until the silk of the seal was broken, then greedily ran over the letter.

"Good!" said he; "we shall all be at the place of meeting."

And he began to muse. Hafiz was waiting.

"What shall I do, master?"

"You will take horse again and receive this letter; then, early to-morrow morning, knock at the door of Doña Maria. Tell her the mountaineers attacked Gildaz, and wounded him with arrows and daggers; but that, when dying, he gave you this letter. That will be all."

Very well, master."

"Go, ride about all night; let your clothes be wet with dew, your horse with sweat, just as if you had only arrived in the morning. Then await my orders, and do not come near my house for a week."

"The Prophet is pleased with me?"

"Yes, Hafiz."

"Thanks, master."

Such was the manner in which the letter had been unsealed; such was the nature of the tempest that was rumbling over the head of Doña Maria.

However, Mothril did not stop at what he had done.

He waited for morning, and, robing himself in magnificent apparel, went to find Don Pedro.

When the Moor entered the royal apartment, the king, seated in a large velvet-covered arm-chair, was toying mechanically with the ears of a young wolf he was fond of taming.

At his left, in a chair of the same kind, sat Doña Maria, pale and angry, for, ever since she had taken her place so close to Don Pedro, the king had not, being doubtless busy with other thoughts, addressed her a single word.

Doña Maria, proud like all the women of her country, endured this insult impatiently. She did not speak, and, as she had no friendly wolf to tease, she had to be contented with piling up in her heart distrust upon distrust, anger upon anger, schemes on top of schemes.

Mothril entered; it gave Maria Padilla an opportunity for an outburst as she was passing from the room.

"You leave, madame," said Don Pedro, disturbed in spite of himself by the furious exit which he had provoked by his indolent reception of his mistress.

"Yes, I leave," said she. "I do not wish you to waste on me any of that gracious condescension which you are doubtless storing up for the benefit of the Saracen Mothril."

Mothril heard, but did not seem irritated. If Doña Maria had been less furious, she would have guessed that this calmness of the Moor sprang from some secret assurance of a very speedy triumph.

But anger does not calculate; its own self-satisfaction is enough for it. It is really a passion. He who slakes his thirst therein revels in enjoyment.

"Sire," said Mothril, affecting profound sorrow, "I see that my king is not happy."

"No," replied Don Pedro, with a sigh.

"We have much gold," added Mothril. "Cordova has contributed."

"So much the better," said the king, carelessly.

"Seville is arming twelve thousand men, and we gain two provinces," continued Mothril.

"Ah!" said the king, in the same tone.

"If the usurper return to Spain, I think that, before

a week, we shall have him a prisoner and shut up in some castle."

Never had the word usurper failed to arouse the king to a violent rage; this time, Don Pedro said, without any anger, —

"Let him come; you have gold and soldiers; we shall take him, try him, and have his head sliced off."

At this moment, Mothril drew near the king.

"Yes, my king is very unfortunate," he resumed.

"And why, my friend?"

"Because gold no longer pleases you and power disgusts you, and you see nothing sweet in vengeance; because, in a word, you no longer have for your mistress a look of love."

"Yes, Mothril, I no longer love her, and, because of this void in my heart, nothing appears to me any longer desirable."

"When your heart seems so empty, king, is it not because it is full of desires? desire, you know, is like air shut up in skins."

"Yes, I know my heart is full of desires."

"Then you love?"

"Yes, I think I love."

"You love Aïssa, the daughter of a powerful monarch. Oh! I pity and I envy you at the same time, for you can be very happy or much to be pitied, seigneur."

"It is true, Mothril, I am very much to be pitied."

"She does not love you, you mean?"

"No, she does not love me."

"Do you think, seigneur, that her blood, pure as that of a goddess, is ruffled by the passions to which another woman would yield? Aïssa is worthless for the harem of a voluptuous prince; Aïssa is a queen, and will smile only on a throne. There are certain flowers, you see, my prince, that only blossom on the summits of mountains."

" A throne — I — marry Aïssa, Mothril? what would the Christians say? "

" How do you know, seigneur, that Doña Aïssa, loving you because you will be her spouse, will not sacrifice her God for your sake, when she has given you her soul? "

An almost voluptuous sigh escaped from the breast of the king.

" She would love me! "

" She will love you."

" No, Mothril."

" Well, then, seigneur, plunge into sorrow, for you deserve not to be happy, you despair with the goal before you."

" Aïssa avoids me."

" I believed Christians more ingenious in divining the hearts of women. With us the passions are concentrated, and, apparently, effaced under the thick layer of slavery, but our women are free to say everything and, consequently, to conceal everything; so they force us to be more clear-sighted in reading their hearts. How is it you would have the proud Aïssa love openly him who always moves under the escort of a woman who is the rival of all women that might love Don Pedro? "

" Would Aïssa be jealous? "

A smile was the sole response of the Moor; then he added, —

" Amongst us the turtle is jealous of her companion, and the noble tigress suffers herself to be torn with tooth and claw by her rival in presence of the tiger about to select the one or the other."

" Ah, Mothril, I love Aïssa! "

"Marry her."

"And Doña Maria?"

"The man who has slain his wife to gratify his mistress, hesitates to dismiss the mistress he no longer loves, though he would thereby gain five million subjects and a love more precious than the entire earth!"

"You are right, but Doña Maria would die of it."

The Moor smiled again.

"You are sure she loves you, then?"

"Loves me? Do you doubt it?"

"Yes, seigneur."

Don Pedro turned pale.

"He loves her still," thought Mothril; "I must not arouse his jealousy or he would prefer her to all others."

"I doubt it," he resumed, "not because she is unfaithful to you, which I do not believe, but because, seeing that she is less loved, she persists in living with you."

"I would call that love, Mothril."

"And I would call that ambition."

"You would banish Maria?"

"Yes, to obtain Aïssa."

"Oh! no — no!"

"Suffer, then."

"I believe," said Don Pedro, riveting on Mothril his flaming eyes, "that if you saw your king suffer, you would not have the courage to say to him, 'Suffer!' — I believe that you would not fail to cry out, 'I will relieve you, my lord.'"

"At the expense of the honor of a great king of my country; no, rather death!"

Don Pedro remained plunged in a gloomy reverie.

"I shall die then," said he, "for I love this girl, or

father — " cried he, with a sinister flash, " no, I shall not die."

Mothril knew his king well enough to be aware that no barrier was able to resist the fury of that indomitable man's passions.

"He would use violence," he thought; "we must prevent such a result."

"Seigneur," said Mothril, "Aïssa has a fine soul, and would believe in oaths. If you swore to marry her after having solemnly abandoned Doña Maria, I think Aïssa would confide her destiny to your love."

"Would you pledge yourself to that?"

"I would."

"Well, then," cried Don Pedro, "I will break with Doña Maria, I swear it!"

"That is another thing; make your conditions, my lord."

"I will break with Doña Maria, and give her a million crowns. There will not be in the country she selects for her residence a princess more wealthy or more honored."

"Be it so; your generosity is worthy of a magnificent prince; but that country must not be Spain!"

"Is that necessary?"

"Aïssa will never be reassured unless the sea, ay, an impassable sea, separate your old love from your new."

"We shall put the sea between Aïssa and Doña Maria, Mothril."

"'T is well, my lord."

"But I am the king; you know that I do not accept conditions from any one."

"It is true, sire."

"Therefore the bargain, somewhat like a bargain

amongst the Jews, must be arranged between us without binding any one except you."

" How can that be done ? "

" Doña Aïssa must be delivered to me as a hostage."

" Only that ? " said Mothril, ironically.

" Madman ! do you not see that love is burning, devouring me, that, at this moment, I am showing an excess of delicacy which makes me laugh, as if the lion has scruples when he is hungry ? Do you not see that if you stand haggling with me about Aïssa, I shall take her ? Do you not see that, if you roll your angry eyes, I shall have you arrested and hanged, and that all the Christian knights will be there to see your body on the gibbet and pay court to the new mistress ? "

" It is true," thought Mothril. " But Doña Maria ? " he said aloud.

" I tell you I am hungry for love, and Doña Maria shall see how Blanche de Bourbon died."

" Your wrath is terrible, my master," answered Mothril, humbly, " and a maniac would be he who refused to bend the knee before you."

" You will deliver Aïssa to me ? "

" If you order me, yes, sire; but, if you do not follow my advice, if you do not get rid of Doña Maria and crush her friends, who are your enemies, if you do not remove all the scruples of Aïssa — ponder on it well — you will not possess this woman, she will kill herself ! "

It was the king's turn to shudder and meditate.

" What do you want, then ? " said he.

" I desire you to wait for a week. Do not interrupt me ! Then let Doña Maria carry things with a high hand for the time. Aïssa will set out for a royal castle, and no one will guess her flight or the goal of her journey; you will win over this young girl; she will be yours and will love you."

"But Doña Maria?"

"If she is lulled for a time, she will awake conquered. Let her fume and fret. You will have exchanged a mistress for a lover; Maria will never forgive you your infidelity, and she will be the first to leave you."

"Yes, it is true she is proud; and you think Aïssa will come?"

"I do not think it, I know it."

"On that day, Mothril, ask of me the half of my kingdom and it is yours."

"You can never reward more justly services more loyal."

"So, then, in a week?"

"At the last hour of daylight, yes, my lord. Aïssa will depart from the city, escorted by a Moor, and I shall conduct her."

"You give me new life, Mothril."

"Until then, do not arouse the suspicions of Doña Maria."

"Fear nothing. I have well concealed my love and grief; do you believe I shall not conceal my joy?"

"Announce, then, my lord, that you intend setting out for one of your country castles."

"I shall do so," said the king.

XXVI.

HOW HAFIZ MISLED HIS TRAVELLING COMPANIONS.

Meanwhile, Doña Maria had, since the return of Hafiz, renewed her understanding with Aïssa.

The latter did not know how to read, but the sight of the parchment which her lover's hand had touched, and particularly the cross, the emblem of his loyal constancy, had filled the heart of the young girl with joy, and twenty times had her lips rested on the sacred emblem in a very intoxication of love.

"Dear Aïssa," said Maria, "you are about to depart. In a week you will be far from here, but you will be very near him whom you love; and I do not think you will regret this country."

"Oh, no, no; it will be life to breathe the air he breathes."

"Then you will be once more united. Hafiz is a prudent boy, very faithful and very intelligent. He knows the road, and, then, you will not fear this child as you might if he were a man, and I am sure you will have the more confidence, travelling in his company. He belongs to your country; you will both speak the language you love.

"This casket contains all the jewels; remember that, in France, even a very rich lord does not possess the half of what you are bringing to your lover. Besides, my bounty will follow the young man, though he were to go with you to the end of the world. Once in

France, you have no longer anything to fear. I am contemplating a great reform here. The king must banish the Moors from Spain. They are the enemies of our religion, and they serve as a pretext for the envious to tarnish the glory of Don Pedro. When you are gone, I shall set to work resolutely."

"On what day am I to see Mauléon?" said Aïssa, who had heard nothing but the name of her lover.

"You may be in his arms five days after you leave this city."

"I shall ride twice as fast as the swiftest horseman, madame."

It was after this conversation that Doña Maria summoned Hafiz and asked him if he should not like to return to France as the escort of the poor sister of Gildaz.

"Poor child, she is inconsolable for the death of her brother," she added, "and would wish to give his unfortunate remains Christian burial."

"I am well pleased," said Hafiz; "fix the day for my departure, mistress."

"To-morrow you will mount a mule I shall give you. The sister of Gildaz will also have a mule, and another one will bear my nurse, who is her mother, as well as some effects for the ceremony she wishes to accomplish."

"Very well, señora, to-morrow I shall start. At what hour?"

"In the evening, after the gates are closed and the fires extinguished."

Hafiz had no sooner received this order than he transmitted it to Mothril.

The Moor went immediately to see Don Pedro.

"Seigneur," said he, "this is now the seventh day; you can set out for your pleasure-house."

"I was waiting," replied the king.

"Start, then, my king, it is time."

"All the preparations have been made," added Don Pedro. "I shall set out the more willingly that the Prince of Wales is sending me a herald of arms to demand money."

"And the treasury is to-day empty, seigneur; for you know we hold ready the sum destined to appease the fury of Doña Maria."

"Good! that is enough."

Don Pedro gave all the orders his departure rendered expedient. He affected to invite several ladies of the court to accompany him on the journey, and made no mention of Doña Maria.

Mothril watched the effect of this insult on the haughty Spaniard, but Doña Maria did not complain.

She passed the day with her companions in playing the lute and listening to the singing of her birds.

When it was evening and all the court had departed, Doña Maria gave out that she was dreadfully bored, and ordered a mule to be got ready for her.

At a signal given by Aïssa, who had the freedom of her house, now that Mothril had accompanied the king, Doña Maria descended and mounted her mule, after muffling herself up in a large mantle such as duennas used.

In this guise, she went for Aïssa herself by the secret passage, and, as she had expected, she found Hafiz, who had been in the saddle for more than an hour, and was searching through the darkness with his piercing eyes.

Doña Maria showed the guards her pass and gave them the watchword. The gates were opened, and, a quarter of an hour afterwards, the mules were racing rapidly over the plain.

Hafiz rode in front. Doña Maria remarked that he diverged to the left instead of following the straight road.

"I cannot speak to him, for he would recognize my voice," she whispered to her companion; "but do you, whom he does not know, ask him why he changes his course."

Aïssa questioned him in Arabic, and Hafiz, apparently quite surprised, answered, —

"Because it is shorter by the left, señora."

"Very well," said Aïssa, "but take care not to go astray."

"Oh," said the Saracen, "I know where I am going."

"Do not be alarmed," said Maria, "he is faithful; besides, I am with you, and my sole object in accompanying you is to set you free in case you should be stopped by any troops in the neighborhood. In the morning you will have made fifteen leagues, and you need have no further fear of soldiers. Mothril is watching, but over an area limited by his own and his master's indolence. After we get beyond that, I shall leave you to pursue your route alone. Then, I shall cross the country and knock at the doors of the palace where the king dwells at present. I know Don Pedro; he regrets my absence and will receive me with open arms."

"The castle is near here, then?" said Aïssa.

"It is seven leagues from the city we have quitted, but farther to the left; it is situated on a mountain we could see yonder on the horizon, if the moon rose."

Suddenly, the moon, as if obeying the voice of Doña Maria, rushed forth from a black cloud whose borders she edged with silver. Soon, a soft, pure light was shed over woods and fields, so that the travellers found themselves all at once enveloped in brightness.

Hafiz turned to his companions and then looked around him; the road had given place to a wide moor bounded by a lofty mountain on which arose a round, bluish-looking castle.

"The castle!" cried Doña Maria; "we have gone astray!"

Hafiz started; he had thought he recognized the voice.

"You have gone astray, have you not?" said Aïssa to the Moor; "answer."

"Alas! can it be possible?" said Hafiz, artlessly.

He had scarcely finished, when, from the bottom of a ravine, lined with green oaks and chestnuts, four horsemen hurried forth, whose fiery steeds, with their quivering nostrils and flowing manes, speedily pushed on over the declivity.

"What does this mean?" said Doña Maria, in a hollow voice. "Are we discovered?"

And, without adding a word, she muffled herself up in her mantle.

Hafiz began to utter shrill cries, as if he were afraid; but one of the horsemen pressed a handkerchief on his lips, and led away his mule.

Two of the ravishers goaded the mules of the women until the animals galloped wildly in the direction of the castle.

Aïssa wished to cry out, to defend herself.

"Silence!" said Doña Maria; "with me you have nothing to fear from Don Pedro, with you I have nothing to fear from Mothril. Hush!"

The four horsemen, just as if they were driving a flock to the pen, headed their captives for the castle.

"It looks as if they were expecting us," thought Doña Maria. "The gates have been thrown open, and yet no trumpet has sounded."

And, in fact, the four horses and the three mules made a very noisy entrance into the court of this palace.

One window was lit, and at it a man was standing. He shouted with joy when he saw the mules.

"It is Don Pedro and he was expecting some one," murmured Doña Maria, who recognized the king's voice; "what does all this mean?"

The horsemen ordered the two women to dismount, and then conducted them to the hall of the castle.

Doña Maria supported Aïssa, who was all trembling.

Don Pedro entered the hall, leaning on Mothril, whose eyes sparkled with joy.

"Dear Aïssa," said he, hurrying towards the young girl, who was quivering with indignation, and whose flashing eyes and restless lips seemed to be asking her companion to tell her if this were not a betrayal.

"Dear Aïssa," repeated the king, "forgive me for having thus frightened you and this good woman; permit me to bid you welcome."

"And what about me?" said Doña Maria, throwing back the hood of her mantle; "you do not salute me, seigneur?"

Don Pedro uttered a cry, and recoiled in terror.

Mothril, pale and trembling, almost fainted under the crushing look of his enemy.

"Come, order an apartment to be got ready for us, our host," continued Doña Maria, "for you are our host, are you not, Don Pedro?"

Don Pedro, staggering, utterly disheartened, bent his head and returned to the gallery.

Mothril fled. But fury had already taken the place of fear in his soul.

The two women clasped each other tightly, and waited in silence.

A moment after, they heard the doors closing.

The major-domo, bowing to the ground, begged Doña Maria to be good enough to enter her apartments.

"Do not leave me!" cried Aïssa.

"Fear nothing, I tell you, child; see! I have but shown myself, and a look of mine has sufficed to tame these ferocious beasts. Come, follow me. I am watching over you, I tell you."

"But you! Oh, fear for yourself also!"

"I!" returned Maria Padilla, smiling haughtily; "who would dare? it is not for me to be afraid in this castle."

XXVII.

THE PATIO OF THE SUMMER PALACE.

THE apartments to which Doña Maria was conducted were well known to her. She used to live in them in the days of her power and prosperity. Then all the court knew the road to those galleries, with their wooden pillars, painted and gilded, that ran round a patio or garden of oranges, in the centre of which was a marble basin.

At that period, only pages were to be seen stationed in front of the rich brocaded hangings, and lackeys, eager to perform their services under those magnificently lighted galleries.

In the patio below, under the thick branches of the trees in flower, Moorish symphonies would be hidden, so sweetly sad and melting that they seemed like perfumes slowly breathed towards the heavens, when they mounted from singer's lips or musician's fingers.

To-day all was silence. Being separated from the rest of the palace, this gallery looked gloomy and empty. The trees had still their foliage, but it had a forbidding aspect; the marble fountain poured forth in floods its foaming waters, but with a noise like the roar of an angry sea.

At the extremity of one of the longest sides of this parallelogram, a little arched and pointed door led into a passage connecting the gallery of Aïssa with the gallery occupied by the king.

This passage was long and narrow. Formerly, Don Pedro had ordered that it should be always hung with precious stuffs, and that the floor should be strewn with flowers. But, during the long interval that had elapsed between his two visits, the hangings had grown faded and ragged, and the withered flowers rustled under the feet.

When love is dead, all that aided love moulders away. It is thus with those impassioned creepers that flower and twine luxuriant around the tree they love, but dry up and fall lifeless when they can no longer inhale the sap and life of their companion.

No sooner was Doña Maria installed in her apartments than she asked for her servants.

"Señora," replied the major-domo, "the king has not come to stay, but only for a hunting-party. He has not brought a train of servants with him."

"Still, the hospitality of the king cannot allow his guests to want what they need here."

"Señora, I am at your orders, and whatever you require — "

"Give us refreshments, then, and a parchment for writing."

The major-domo inclined and passed out.

Night came on. The stars shone in the heavens. In the farthest depths of the patio a screech-owl was shrieking, silencing with his sepulchral hooting the nightingale perched under Doña Maria's windows.

Aïssa, in this darkness and under the influence of her sombre surroundings, frightened by the still fury of her companion, stood trembling in the remotest corner of the apartment.

She saw Doña Maria pass and repass, like a pale shadow, her eyes wandering, but lit up with many a project.

She did not dare to speak for fear of disturbing this anger and changing the direction of this sorrow.

Suddenly, the major-domo reappeared, bearing waxen flambeaux, which he set upon a table.

A slave followed with a silver-gilt basin upon which were two wrought silver cups, preserved fruit, and a large flask of sherry wine.

"Señora," said the major-domo, "you are served."

"I do not see the ink and parchment I asked for," said Doña Maria.

"Señora," replied the major-domo, embarrassed, "we have made a long search, but the chancellor is not here, and the parchment is in the king's coffer."

Doña Maria frowned.

"I understand," said she, "very well; thanks, leave us."

The major-domo passed out.

"I am parched with thirst," said Doña Maria; "my dear child, will you give me something to drink?"

Aïssa hastened to fill one of the cups with wine, and offered it to her companion, who drank greedily.

"Is there no water?" she added; "this wine increases my thirst instead of quenching it."

Aïssa searched around her and perceived an earthen jar painted with flowers, one of the kind used in the East to keep water fresh, even under the sun.

She filled from it a cup of pure water, with which Doña Maria mixed the wine left in the other cup.

But her mind had already forgotten to attend to the wants of the body; her thoughts were concentrated elsewhere and had gone back to their gloomy abiding-places.

"What am I doing here?" she said to herself. "Why am I losing time? I must either convict the traitor of his treason or I must try to reclaim him once more."

She turned abruptly to Aïssa, who was following every one of her movements.

"Come, young girl, you whose eyes are so pure that your very soul seems to look forth through them, come, answer a woman who is the most unfortunate of women: Are you proud? would you sometimes, perchance, envy the splendor of my prosperity? Have you listened, during the sinister hours of night, to the evil angel that would turn you away from love and impel you towards ambition? Oh, answer me! Oh, remember that all my fate lies in the words you are about to utter. Answer me as you would answer to your God: Know you anything of this plan for carrying you off? Did you suspect it? Did you hope it?"

"Madame," replied Aïssa, with an air at once sad and gentle, "my kind protectress, you who have seen me flying to meet my lover with a joy so ardent, you ask me did I hope to draw near to another!"

"You are right," said Doña Maria, impatiently; "but your answer, though it contain within it, perhaps, all the candor of your soul, still appears to me a subterfuge; it is because my soul, look you, is not pure like yours, and because every earthy passion clouds and upsets it. I reiterate my question then: Are you ambitious? and would the hope of a high estate — even a throne — console you for your love?"

"Madame," said Aïssa, the very thought of such a future sending a shudder through every fibre of her being, "I know not if I may convince you in your distress; but, by the living God! be He mine or be He yours, I swear that if Don Pedro hold me in his power, and attempt to impose upon me his love, I swear that I shall have a poniard to pierce my heart, or a ring like yours, to inhale from it a deadly poison."

"A ring like mine!" cried Doña Maria, recoiling and hiding her hand under her mantle. "You know—"

"I know, because every one in the palace has said with bated breath that, being devoted to Don Pedro, and dreading to fall into the hands of his enemies, after the loss of some battle, you were in the habit of carrying in that ring a subtle poison which, at need, would give you your freedom. It is, for that matter, a custom with the people of my country. I shall not be less valiant and faithful for my Agénor's sake than you are for Don Pedro's. I am resolved to die when I see him in danger of losing what belongs to him.

Doña Maria wrung the hands of Aïssa, and even kissed her on the brow with a kind of savage tenderness.

"You are a noble child," she said, "and your words would show me my duty, had I not something more sacred to guard in this world than my love. Yes, I ought to die, having lost my future and my glory; but who will watch over this ingrate and coward whom I still love? Who will save him from a shameful death, and a downfall more shameful still? He has not a friend; he has thousands of furious enemies. You do not love him, you will never yield to any suggestion. It is all that I desire, because the contrary is the only thing I dreaded. The line I am about to follow is now fully traced. Before to-morrow's dawn, there will be a change in Spain of which the whole universe shall speak."

"Madame," said Aïssa, "beware of the impulses of your dauntless soul. Take care lest I be alone in the world, I who have no hope of happiness save in you and through you."

"I am thinking of all that: misfortune is purifying my

soul. I am selfish no longer, having cast from me all selfish love.

"Listen, Aïssa. I am about to take a decisive step. I am going to find Don Pedro. Search in a casket, inlaid with gold, which ought to be in the next chamber, and you will find a key. It is the key of a secret door leading to the apartments of Don Pedro."

Aïssa ran, and returned with the key, which Doña Maria took possession of.

"Must I remain alone in this gloomy abode, madame?" said the young girl.

"I know a spot wherein you may be in absolute security. Here, perhaps, you might be molested; but come with me. Next to the chamber from which you have just taken the key is another, the last one, inclosed by walls through which there is no issue. Shut in there, you will have nothing to fear."

"Alone! oh, not alone! I should be frightened."

"Child! — yet you cannot accompany me. I go to the king, and it is the king you fear."

"It is true," said Aïssa. "Yes, madame, I am resigned, I will wait; but not in that dark and remote chamber, oh, no, but here, on the cushions which you have pressed, yonder where everything will remind me of your presence and your protection."

"But you are much in need of rest, however."

"I am not in any need of it, madame."

"As you wish, Aïssa. Spend the time of my absence in praying to your God that I may triumph, for then shall you, to-morrow, without fear and in full daylight, take the road that leads to Rianzares; to-morrow you will bid me farewell, saying to yourself, 'I go to my husband, and no power on earth is strong enough to keep me apart from him.'"

"Thanks, madame, thanks!" cried the young girl, showering kisses on the hands of her generous friend. "Oh, yes, yes! I will pray and God will hear me!"

At the moment the two young women were exchanging this tender farewell, a head might have been observed rising gradually from the depths of the patio under the branches of the orange-trees, until at length this inquisitive head was on a level with the gallery, and shrouded in the thickest darkness.

Once it was indistinguishable from the objects around it, it remained motionless.

Doña Maria left the young girl and took briskly the road leading to the secret door.

The head, without stirring, turned its big white eyes upon Doña Maria, saw her enter the mysterious corridor, and listened.

And, in fact, the noise of a door grating on its rusty hinges was heard at the other extremity of this lobby. Immediately the head disappeared from the middle of the tree, descending like that of a serpent, with all possible speed.

It was the Saracen Hafiz who glided in this fashion down the polished trunk of a lemon-tree.

At the bottom he found awaiting him a gloomy figure.

"What! you are down already, Hafiz?" said this personage.

"Yes, master, for there is nothing further to see in the apartment. Doña Maria has just passed out."

"Where is she going?"

"She went to the end of the gallery on the right, and then disappeared."

"Disappeared! Oh, by the holy name of the Prophet! she has gone through the secret door, and to speak with the king. We are lost."

"You know I am at your orders, Seigneur Mothril," said Hafiz, turning pale.

"Well, follow me to the royal apartments. At this hour all are asleep. There are neither guards nor courtiers. You will go to the king's patio, climb up to his window, as you have done here, and listen there as you have listened here."

"There is a simpler way, Seigneur Mothril, and you could listen yourself."

"What is it? Great God, make haste!"

"Follow me, then. I shall climb a column in the patio, reach a window, make my way through it, and slip along to a door in the rear which I shall open for you. In this way you can hear at your ease all that Don Pedro and Maria Padilla are saying or about to say."

"You are right, Hafiz, and the Prophet inspires you. I will do as you say. Lead on."

XXVIII.

AN EXPLANATION.

DOÑA MARIA was under no illusion: the danger was extreme.

Rendered indifferent by a possession of several years, rendered apathetic by success, and corrupted by that very adversity which purifies good natures that happen to have gone wrong, Don Pedro required incitements for what is evil, not counsels for what is good.

The question was to effect a change in the bent of this soul, and with love nothing would have been impossible; but it was to be feared that Don Pedro no longer loved Doña Maria.

She was going, then, blindly along that road whose every corner was illuminated for her enemy Mothril.

No doubt if she had met the Moor on the way, and she had held a poniard in her hand, she would have stricken him without mercy, for she felt that this accursed influence had been weighing on her life for a year, and was beginning to dominate it.

Maria was thinking of all this when she opened the secret door and found herself in the apartment of the king.

Don Pedro, frightened, uncertain, was wandering like a shadow up and down his gallery.

The silence of Doña Maria and her dangerous anger had filled him with the most lively apprehension and the most threatening resentment.

"She comes," he said, "to brave me in my very court; she shows me that I am not the master, and, really, I am not, when the arrival of a woman upsets all my plans and destroys the hope of all my pleasures. 'T is a yoke I must break. I am not strong enough to act alone, I must have help."

Just as he spoke these words, Maria glided like a fairy over the floor of polished porcelain, and, taking him by the arm, said, —

"And who will help you, seigneur?"

"Doña Maria!" cried the king, as if he had seen a spectre.

"Yes, Doña Maria, who has come to ask you, to ask the king, in what is the counsel or, if you prefer it, the yoke of a high-born Spaniard, a woman who loves you, more dishonoring and more oppressive than the yoke imposed upon Don Pedro by Mothril, on a Christian king by a Moor?"

Don Pedro wrung his hands in fury.

"No impatience," said Doña Maria, "no anger. This is not the hour nor the place for either. You are here, sire, at home, and I come not, as you are well aware, to dictate to you your decisions. So, as you are the master, seigneur, do not take the trouble to get enraged. The lion does not quarrel with the ant."

Don Pedro was not accustomed to this humble attitude of his mistress. He stopped in amazement.

"What do you want, madame?" said he.

"Very little, seigneur. You love, it seems, another woman; it is your right. I shall not discuss the good or the ill of it; it is your right. I am not your wife; and, if I were, I would remember that, for my sake, you have inflicted sorrows and tortures on those who have been your wives."

AN EXPLANATION.

"Do you reproach me with that?" said Don Pedro, haughtily, for he was in search of an excuse to get angry.

Doña Maria sustained his look with firmness.

"I am not God," she said, "to reproach kings with their crimes! I am a woman, alive to-day, dead to-morrow, an atom, a breath, a nothing; but I have a voice, and I make use of it to tell you that which you can hear only from me.

"You love, Don Pedro, and every time that you have loved, a shadow has swept across your eyes and hidden from you the universe. But you turn around your head. What do you hear? What preoccupies you?"

"I thought," said Don Pedro, "I heard steps in the neighboring chamber. But no, it is impossible."

"Why impossible?— everything is possible here. See to it, sire, I entreat. What if we were heard?"

"No, there is no door to that chamber, and I have not a servant near me. It is some of the tapestry raised by the evening breeze and beating against a panel."

"I told you," resumed Doña Maria, "that, as you no longer love me, I have come to the determination to retire."

Don Pedro started.

"That delights you, I am very glad of it," said Doña Maria, coldly; "it is why I am acting as I do. I shall retire, then, and you will nevermore hear of me. From this moment, seigneur, Doña Maria Padilla is no longer your mistress; she is a humble servant who is about to make you know the truth as to your position.

"You have won a battle, but you will be told that others have won it for you; in such a case, your ally becomes your master and is sure to prove it sooner or later. The Prince of Wales has even already demanded considerable sums that are due to him. This money you have not; his twelve thousand lances that have fought for you are now going to fight against you.

"Moreover, the prince your brother has found help in France, and the constable, who is the idol of every one bearing a French name, is about to return, thirsting for revenge. You have two armies to fight; what have you to oppose to them?

"An army of Saracens — O Christian king! But one path lies open before you by which you may return to the confederation of the princes of the Church, and that path you refuse to follow. You wish to draw down upon your head not only the force of temporal arms, but the wrath of the Pope and his excommunication! Think of it, sire: the Spaniards are religious, they will abandon you; already even the mere presence of the Moors among them frightens and disgusts them.

"That is not all. The man who is urging you to destruction is not satisfied that that destruction should be compassed by your misery and degradation, that is to say, by your exile and dethronement; he would also impose upon you an infamous alliance, he would make of you a renegade. As God hears me! I do not hate, I love Aïssa, I protect and defend her as a sister, for I know her heart and I know her life. But Aïssa, were she the daughter of a king, which she is not, as I will prove, is not more worthy to be your wife than I, the daughter of the ancient knights of Castile, I, the noble heiress of twenty ancestors, each the equal of a Christian king. And yet, did I ever ask you to have our love consecrated by a marriage? Surely, I might have done so, surely, Don Pedro, you have loved me?"

Don Pedro sighed.

"That is not all. Mothril speaks to you of the love of Doña Aïssa, nay, perhaps, he promises it to you."

Don Pedro looked restless, and keenly interested, as if he would catch the words of Maria before they left her lips.

"He promises that she will love you, does he not?"

"Supposing he does, madame?"

"That may be, sire, and you deserve more than love. There are certain persons of your realm, and these persons the equals of Aïssa, I believe, who have for you more than adoration."

The brow of Don Pedro cleared; Doña Maria was skilfully setting every sensitive chord in his soul in vibration.

"But, nevertheless," continued the young woman, "Doña Aïssa will not love you, because she loves another."

"Is that true?" cried Don Pedro, furiously; "is it not a calumny?"

"So little of a calumny that, if you question her before she has been able to communicate with me, she will tell you word for word what I am now about to tell you."

"Go on, madame, go on; by doing so, you will render me a real service. Aïssa loves some one. Whom does she love?"

"A French knight, named Agénor de Mauléon."

"That ambassador, sent to me at Soria; and Mothril knows this?"

"He knows it."

"You assert this?"

"I swear it."

"And her heart is so entirely captive that for Mothril to promise me her love has been a shameless falsehood, an odious treason?"

"A shameless falsehood, an odious treason."

"You will prove it, señora?"

"As soon as you bid me, seigneur."

"Say what you have said over again, so that I may be persuaded of its truth."

Doña Maria towered above the king. She held him by his pride and his jealousy.

"'By the living God!' said Aïssa to me just now, and her words are still resounding in my ears, 'I swear that if Don Pedro hold me in his power, and attempt to impose upon me his love, I swear that I shall have a poniard to pierce my heart, or a ring like yours, to inhale from it a deadly poison.'

"And she pointed to this ring I have on my finger, señor."

"That ring —" said Don Pedro, terrified. "Pray what does that ring contain, señora?"

"A subtle poison, seigneur. I have been wearing it for two years to make sure of my liberty of soul and body in case I should some day encounter one of those evil chances in your fortunes, which I have so faithfully followed, and fall into the hands of your enemies."

Don Pedro was struck with remorse at the sight of heroism so simple and touching.

"You have a noble heart, Maria," said he, "and I have never loved woman as I have loved you. But the evil chances are far away, — you can live!"

"*As he has loved me!*" thought Maria, turning pale. "He no longer says, 'as he loves me!'"

"And so that is the resolve of Aïssa?" resumed Don Pedro, after a silence.

"Her firm resolve, seigneur."

"It is idolatry, on her part, for this French knight."

"It is a love equal to that which I have had for you," answered Doña Maria.

"Which you have had?" said Don Pedro, weaker

than his mistress, and showing his wound at the first touch of pain.

"Yes, seigneur."

Don Pedro frowned.

"May I question Aïssa?"

"When you please."

"Will she speak in presence of Mothril?"

"In presence of Mothril? yes, seigneur."

"And she will tell all the details of her love?"

"She will even confess to that which puts a woman to shame."

"Maria!" cried Don Pedro, with terrible excitement, "Maria! what have you said?"

"The truth," she replied simply.

"Aïssa dishonored — "

"Aïssa, whom certain persons would seat beside you on your throne and place in your bed, is betrothed to the Seigneur de Mauléon by ties that God alone can now rend asunder, for they are the ties of a marriage consummated — "

"Maria! Maria!" exclaimed the king, drunk with fury.

"I owed you this last confession. It was I who, at her entreaty, introduced the Frenchman into the chamber in which Mothril held her imprisoned; it was I who, as the guardian of their loves, was to reunite them on the soil of France."

"Mothril! Mothril! no chastisement will be too intense, no torture too harrowing to make you expiate this cowardly outrage. Bring Aïssa hither, madame, I pray you."

"Seigneur, I go to her. But reflect, I beseech you. I have betrayed the honor of this young girl to serve the interest and honor of my king. Is it not better for you to trust to my word? Can you not believe me without demanding a proof that bereaves this poor child of her honor?"

"Ah! you hesitate; you are deceiving me."

"Sire, I do not hesitate; I but try to restore Your Majesty's confidence somewhat. We shall have this proof in a few days without the publicity and scandal that would destroy a poor girl."

"I will have this proof at once; and I summon you to furnish me with it, under pain of having your accusations disbelieved."

"Sire, I obey," said Doña Maria, painfully moved.

"I am waiting, and very impatient, madame."

"Sire, you shall be obeyed."

"If you have told the truth, Doña Maria, there shall not be to-morrow in Spain a single Moor who is not an outlaw or a fugitive."

"Then, to-morrow, seigneur, you will be a great king; and I, poor abandoned fugitive though I be, shall give thanks to God for the greatest happiness that has ever been granted to me in this world, — the certainty of your prosperity."

"Señora, you turn pale, you stagger; do you wish me to call for some one?"

"Do not call, sire. No; I shall return to my apartments. I have ordered wine and refreshments; they are on my table. I am burning, but, once I have quenched my thirst, I shall be quite well again; think not any longer of me, sire, I entreat you —

"But I swear to you," said Maria, suddenly, running to the neighboring chamber, "I swear to you that there has been some one there; this time I have heard, beyond any doubt, the step of a man —"

Don Pedro seized a flambeau, Maria another, and both

rushed into this chamber. It was deserted; nothing indicated that any one had been there.

But one of the hangings was trembling still at the outer door of which Hafiz had spoken.

"Nobody!" said Maria, surprised; "yet I am sure I heard something."

"I told you it was impossible. Oh, Mothril! Mothril! the vengeance I shall inflict upon thee for thy treason! You are going to return, then, madame?"

"Yes, by the secret passage, as soon as I have warned Aïssa."

Having thus spoken, Doña Maria took leave of the king, who, in his feverish impatience, almost confounded his gratitude for the service rendered with his memory of the love that was past.

And the reason was that Doña Maria was a beautiful and impassioned woman, a woman whom no one who had once seen her could ever forget.

Proud and daring, she imposed respect and compelled love. More than once had this royal despot trembled at her anger; oftener still had his listless heart throbbed in expectation of her coming.

And therefore, when she passed out after this explanation, Don Pedro wished to run after her and cry out, —

"What to me is Aïssa? What to me are the petty villanies that are hatched in darkness? You are she whom I love; you are the fruit that can alone slake my burning thirst!"

But Doña Maria had already shut the iron door, and the king heard naught save the rustling of her robe against the walls, and the crackling of the withered branches as they broke under her footsteps.

XXIX.

THE RING OF DOÑA MARIA AND THE PONIARD OF AÏSSA.

MOTHRIL'S foot had barely touched the ground when Doña Maria believed she had heard a noise in the chamber. Mothril had taken off his sandals, and then approached the tapestry to listen to the plot contrived for his ruin.

The revelation of Aïssa's secret had penetrated him with dread and horror. That Doña Maria hated him he did not doubt; that she should seek to destroy him by belittling his policy and unveiling his ambition was what the Moor expected. But what he could not endure was the idea of Don Pedro becoming indifferent to Aïssa.

Aïssa, betrothed to Mauléon, Aïssa, fallen from her priceless purity, was become for Don Pedro an object without charm or value; and not to hold Don Pedro through Aïssa was to lose the curb that held the indomitable courser in check.

A few moments more and all this scaffolding, so laboriously constructed, would be shattered to pieces. Aïssa, sure of protection, was coming with her companion to reveal to Don Pedro the entire secret. Then Doña Maria was restored to all her rights; then Aïssa lost all hers; then Mothril, shamed and dishonored, banned and stigmatized as a wretched forger, took the dolorous road of exile with his fellows, supposing that he was not swept into the tomb by the first hurricane of the royal anger. Such, then, was the future that unrolled before the eyes of the Moor while Maria was speaking to Don Pedro, and her words were falling one by one, like drops of melted lead, upon the smarting wound of this ambitious man.

Gasping, bewildered, now cold as marble, now hot as seething sulphur, Mothril was asking himself, with his hand on his poniard, why he did not slay, at one stroke, the master who listened, and the informer who spoke; that is to say, why he did not save his life and his cause.

If Don Pedro had had near him another guardian angel beside Maria, that angel would not have failed to warn him of the terrible danger he was at that moment running.

Suddenly, the brow of Mothril cleared, the sweat fell down his face in less copious and icy streams. Two words, uttered by Maria, had opened the path to safety, as well as the path to crime.

He let her finish her story tranquilly, then; she might unbosom herself fully to Don Pedro. And it was only at the last words of the conversation, when he had no longer anything to learn, that he left his hiding-place; it was then the tapestry trembled behind him, as noticed by Don Pedro and Doña Maria.

Once outside, Mothril paused for about two seconds, and said,—

"It will take her three times as long to return to her chamber by the secret lobby as it will take me to go there by the patio.

"Hafiz," he continued, tapping on the shoulder of the young tiger, who was watching eagerly for any order he might give, "run to the gallery passage, stop Doña Maria as soon as you meet her, beg her pardon, as if you were fully repentant, accuse me if you wish, confess, reveal, — do whatever you like, but detain her for five minutes from entering the gallery."

"Very well, master," said Hafiz; and, climbing like a lizard up the wooden column of the patio, he entered the lobby, where he could already hear the footsteps of Doña Maria approaching.

Mothril, during this time, made the tour of the garden, ascended the staircase of the gallery, and entered the apartment of Doña Maria.

In one hand he held his poniard; in the other, a little gold flask, which he had just taken from one of the folds of his broad girdle.

When he entered, the wax, half consumed, was running down in large flakes from the flambeau. Aïssa, with closed eyelids, was gently sleeping upon the cushions. Her parted lips breathed forth a beloved name with her perfumed breath.

"She first," said the Moor, with a gloomy look. "Dead, she will not confess what Doña Maria would have her avow."

"Oh, to strike my child!" he murmured, — "my child asleep! she for whom, if my fears do not urge me on, the Most High reserves a crown. I must pause. Let her be the last to die, so that I may nurse my hopes as long as possible."

He advanced quickly towards the table, took the silver cup, still half filled with the drink prepared by Maria herself, and poured into it the entire contents of the gold flagon.

"Maria," said he, in an undertone and with a hideous smile, "what I pour out for you is, perhaps, not as effective as that hidden in your ring, but, excuse me, we poor Moors are barbarians. If my draught does not please you, I will make you a present of my poniard."

He had scarcely finished when the suppliant voice of Hafiz reached him, intermingled with the more animated voice of Doña Maria, detained in the secret lobby.

"For pity's sake," said the young monster, "pardon my youth! I knew not what my master was about to do."

"I will see later; leave me!" was Doña Maria's answer. "I shall make inquiries, and the testimony brought to me concerning you will enable me to find out the truth you are now concealing."

Mothril at once crouched behind the tapestry that veiled the window. Placed there, he could see, could hear everything, and could rush out upon Maria, should she attempt to leave the room.

After dismissing Hafiz, she disappeared slowly under the sombre gallery.

Then Doña Maria again entered her apartment and gazed upon Aïssa, now sunk in slumber, with a strange emotion.

"I have profaned," she said, "in the eyes of men your sweet secret of love; I have blackened the beauty of the dove; but the wrong I have done you, poor child, shall be well repaired! You are sleeping under my protection. Sleep! for the moment, I leave you to your sweet dreams."

She took a step towards Aïssa. Mothril clutched his poniard in his fingers.

But the movement just made by Doña Maria drew her near the table, upon which she saw the silver cup and the ruddy liquid that seemed to invite her thirsty lips.

She took the cup and drank greedily.

Before the last mouthful had touched her palate, the fatal chill of death was at her heart.

She staggered, her eyes became fixed, she pressed her two hands against her breast, and, divining a new calamity in her inexplicable suffering, she looked around her with anxiety and terror, as if to question solitude and sleep, twin witnesses of her agony.

The pangs that shot through her had sprung to life with the rapidity of a conflagration. Her cheeks flushed, her hands moved convulsively; it seemed as if her heart mounted to her throat, and she opened her mouth to utter a cry.

Quick as lightning, Mothril stifled that cry in a deadly embrace.

Vainly did Maria struggle in his arms, vainly did she bite the fingers pressed against her lips.

Mothril, while he was thus fettering the arms and voice of the unfortunate woman, at the same time extinguished the taper, and Maria sank down at once into darkness and death.

Her feet beat the floor for a few seconds, and the sound awoke her young companion.

Aïssa arose, and, groping in the darkness, stumbled over the dead body.

She fell into the arms of Mothril, who seized her hands and threw her down near Maria, also ripping up her shoulder with a thrust of his poniard.

Bathed in blood, Aïssa fainted. Then Mothril plucked from Maria's finger the ring which contained the poison.

He emptied this ring into the silver cup and again placed it on the finger of his victim.

Next, staining the poniard worn by the young Morisca in her girdle, he laid it beside Maria, so that her fingers touched it.

This mystery of horror was accomplished in less time

than it takes a serpent of the Indies to strangle two gazelles which it has watched playing in the grass of some savanna. Mothril, to bring his task to a successful termination, had now only to shelter himself from all suspicion.

Nothing was easier. He went back to the neighboring patio, just as if he were returning from a tour of inspection.

He asked the king's servants whether His Majesty had retired. They answered that they had seen him walking up and down his gallery in a kind of agitation.

Mothril ordered his cushions to be brought to him; then he bade a servant read aloud some verses of the Koran, and appeared to sink into a profound slumber.

Hafiz, although he had been unable to consult his master, had understood what he wanted, thanks to his instinct. He had strolled round among the guards of the king with his customary gravity. In this way half an hour passed. The greatest silence reigned in the palace.

Suddenly, a heart-rending cry resounded from the depths of the royal gallery, and the voice of the king shrieked out these frightful words: —

"Help! help!"

Every one rushed to the gallery, the guards with their naked swords, the servants with the first weapons that came to their hands.

Mothril, rubbing his eyes and sitting up as if he were still heavy with sleep, asked, —

"What is the matter?"

"The king! the king!" answered the excited crowd.

Mothril rose and walked behind the others. He saw Hafiz advancing in the same direction; he, too, was rubbing his eyes and seemed amazed and bewildered.

Then Don Pedro was seen, with a torch in his hand, on the threshold of the apartment of Doña Maria. He was uttering awful cries, was pale, and, every time he turned round towards the chamber, his groans and imprecations became more vehement.

Mothril forced his way through the crowd that in trembling silence surrounded the half-maddened prince.

Ten torches threw over the gallery their ruddy glare.

"Look! look!" cried Don Pedro. "Dead! both dead!"

"Dead!" repeated the crowd, hoarsely.

"Dead!" said Mothril; "who are dead, seigneur?"

"Look, shameless Saracen!" said the king, whose hair stood on end.

The Moor took a torch from the hands of a soldier, slowly entered the apartment, and recoiled, or feigned to recoil, at sight of the two dead bodies and the blood that stained the floor.

"Doña Maria!" he cried, "Doña Aïssa! dead! Allah!"

The crowd repeated, with a shudder, "Doña Maria! Doña Aïssa! dead!"

Mothril knelt down and gazed upon the two victims, sadly and attentively.

"Seigneur," said he to Don Pedro, who was reeling, and whose two hands, upon which he rested his head, were bathed in sweat, "a crime has been committed here; have the goodness to order every one to retire."

The king did not answer. Mothril made a sign, and all slowly retired. "Seigneur," repeated Mothril, in the same tone of affectionate persistence, "a crime has been committed."

"Wretch!" cried Don Pedro, "do I see you again in my presence, you who have betrayed me?"

"My king must indeed suffer since he thus ill-treats his best friends," said Mothril, with unchangeable meekness.

"Maria!—Aïssa!" repeated Don Pedro, frantically, "dead!"

"And yet, sire, you hear no complaint from me."

"Complaint from you, miscreant! And why should you complain?"

"Because I see in the hand of Doña Maria the weapon that has shed the illustrious blood of my kings and slain the daughter of my venerated master, the great caliph."

"It is true," murmured Don Pedro, "the poniard is in the hand of Doña Maria; but Doña Maria herself, whose features present an aspect so frightful, whose eye threatens, whose lips are covered with foam,—who has killed her?"

"How can I tell, seigneur? I was asleep and only entered after you."

And the Saracen, after another lingering look at the livid face of Maria, silently shook his head; but he began to examine curiously the cup, which was still half full.

"Poison!" he murmured.

The king bent over the corpse and seized the hand in a fit of gloomy terror.

"Ah," cried Don Pedro, "the ring is empty!"

"The ring!" repeated Mothril, with well-acted surprise; "what ring?"

"Yes," continued the king, "the ring with the deadly poison. Ah! look there! Maria has killed herself!" he cried; "Maria whom I was waiting for. Maria who might again have won my love."

"No, seigneur, I think you are mistaken. Doña Maria was jealous, and has long known that your heart was filled by another woman. Consider well, seigneur, that

Doña Maria must have been stricken with fear, as well as mortally wounded in her pride, on seeing Aïssa come where you had summoned her. Once her anger was past, she preferred death to desertion. Moreover, she did not die unavenged, and for a Spanish woman revenge is a pleasure sweeter than life."

This discourse was masterly in its perfidy; the tone of artless confidence with which it was uttered imposed for a moment on Don Pedro. But he was suddenly carried away by grief and resentment, and, seizing the Moor by the throat, he cried, —

"Mothril, you lie! Mothril, you are playing with me! You attribute the death of Doña Maria to regret at my desertion; you know not, then, or you pretend not to know, that I preferred that noble friend to all the world."

"Seigneur, you did not say so the other day, when you accused Doña Maria of wearying you."

"Repeat not that, accursed wretch, in presence of yonder corpse!"

"Seigneur, I will fetter my tongue, I will fling away my life rather than offend my sovereign; but I would wish to moderate his sorrow, and, as a loyal friend, I am trying to do so now."

"Maria! Aïssa!" cried Don Pedro, wildly. "My kingdom as ransom for one hour of your life!"

"What God does He does well," chanted the Moor, lugubriously. "He has bereft me of the joy of my old age, the flower of my life, the pearl of innocence that enriched my house."

"Infidel!" cried Don Pedro, whose egotism and, consequently, whose fury these words had designedly aroused; "you speak still of the candor and innocence of Aïssa, though knowing full well of her love for the French knight, though knowing full well she is dishonored!"

"I," replied the Moor, in a choking voice, —"I know of the dishonor of Doña Aïssa! Aïssa dishonored! Ah!" he roared, with a wrathful bellow that was not the less terrible for being affected, "who has said so?"

"She whom your hatred will no longer injure, she who never lied, she whom death has just ravished from my side."

"Doña Maria!" rejoined the Saracen, contemptuously; "it was her interest to say it. She might well have said that because of her love, for she has died because of her love; she might well have calumniated because of revenge, for she has killed because of revenge."

Don Pedro remained silent and thoughtful in presence of an accusation so logical and bold.

"If Doña Aïssa had not been stabbed with a poniard," added Mothril, "it would, perhaps, have been said that she tried to assassinate Doña Maria."

This last argument outstripped all the limits of audacity. Don Pedro turned it to account.

"Why not?" said he. "Doña Maria revealed to me the secret of your Morisca; might not the latter have revenged herself on the informer?"

"Observe," answered Mothril, "that Doña Maria's ring is empty. Now, who emptied it if not herself? King, you are blind if you do not see, by the death of these two women, that Doña Maria deceived you."

"Why so? She was to have brought me the proof, she was to have led Aïssa before me, who would have repeated the words of Maria."

"Did she come?"

"She is dead."

"Because she could not return without her proof, and proof she had not."

Don Pedro was again terribly bewildered.

"The truth!" he murmured, "who will tell me the truth?"

"I am telling it to you."

"You!" cried the king, with a renewal of his hatred; "you are the monster who persecuted Doña Maria, and tried to make me abandon her; you are the cause of her death! Well! you shall disappear from my dominions, you shall take the road of exile; 'tis the only grace I shall accord you."

"Hush, seigneur! a miracle!" answered Mothril, who paid not the slightest attention to this violent outburst of Don Pedro; "the heart of Doña Aïssa beats under my hand; she lives, she lives!"

"She lives!" cried Don Pedro; "are you sure?"

"I feel the beating of her heart."

"The wound is not mortal, perhaps — a doctor —"

"No Christian," said Mothril, with sombre authority, "shall lay his hand upon a noble damsel of my nation. Aïssa will not, perhaps, be saved; but, if she be, it shall be by me alone."

"Save her, Mothril! save her! — that she may speak —"

Mothril looked intently at the king.

"That she may speak, seigneur!" said he; "she shall speak."

"Well, Mothril, we shall see afterwards."

"Yes, seigneur, we shall see whether I am a calumniator, and whether Aïssa is dishonored."

Don Pedro, who was on his knees before the two bodies, then gazed upon the ghastly features of Maria, contracted by a hideous death; afterwards, upon the calm, sweet face of Aïssa, sleeping in her deathlike swoon.

"Undoubtedly," he said to himself, "Doña Maria was very jealous; and I still remember she did not defend

Blanche de Bourbon formerly, whom I had killed for her sake."

He rose, his thoughts now diverted to the young girl.

"Save her, Mothril!" he said to the Saracen.

"Fear nothing, seigneur; I wish her to live, and she shall live."

Don Pedro retired, struck with a sort of superstitious terror; it seemed to him as if the spectre of Doña Maria had risen from the ground, and was following him in the gallery.

"When the young girl is in a condition to speak," said he, "bring her to me, or rather give me notice; I wish to question her."

It was his last word. He returned to his apartments, without regrets, without love, and without hope.

Mothril ordered the doors to be closed; he directed Hafiz to gather certain balms, the juices of which he squeezed out upon the wound of Aïssa, a wound his ready poniard had made with the dexterity of a surgeon's knife.

Aïssa recovered consciousness as soon as Mothril had made her inhale divers powerful perfumes. She was very weak; but no sooner did her memory and strength return than the first use she made of life was to utter a cry of terror.

She had just perceived the inanimate body of Maria Padilla lying at her feet, the eyes still laden with menace and despair.

XXX.

THE PRISON OF THE GOOD CONSTABLE.

MEANWHILE, Du Guesclin had been conducted to Bordeaux, the residence of the Prince of Wales, and he saw that, although he was treated with the utmost respect, he was very narrowly watched as a prisoner.

The castle in which he was incarcerated had a governor and a jailer. The guard consisted of a hundred men-at-arms, who took good care that no one should approach the constable without permission.

Nevertheless, the most distinguished officers in the English army felt bound in honor to visit the prisoner. John Chandos, the Sire d'Albret, and the principal lords of Guyenne often obtained leave to dine and sup with Du Guesclin, who, being a good comrade and a merry boon companion, received them with open arms. To enable him to treat his guests well, he borrowed money from the Lombards of Bordeaux on his properties in Bretagne.

Gradually, the constable lulled the suspicions of the garrison. He appeared to take pleasure in his prison, and nothing in his demeanor showed that he was anxious for his liberty.

When the Prince of Wales called upon him and spoke of his ransom, laughingly, —

"Patience, Your Highness!" he said; "they are getting it ready."

The Prince of Wales then confided his troubles to him. Du Guesclin, with his customary frankness, re-

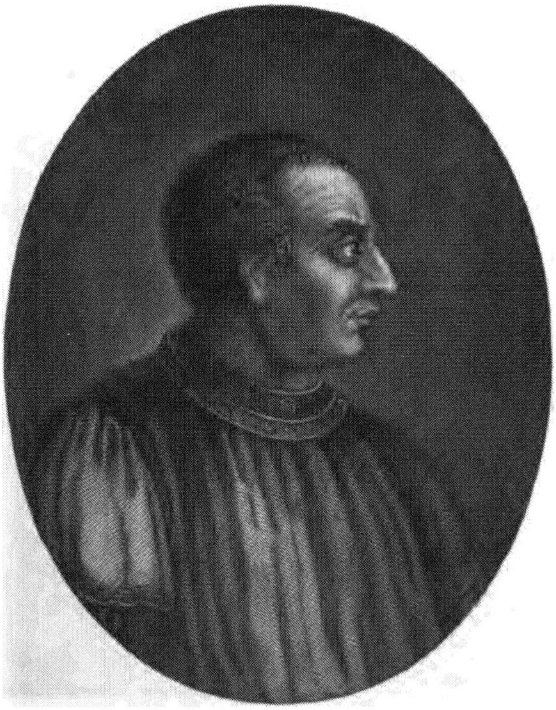

proached him with placing his genius and his power at
the service of such a bad cause as that of Don Pedro.

"How," said he, "came a knight of your rank and
merit to stoop so low as to defend that robber and assassin, that crowned renegade?"

"State reasons," answered the prince.

"And a desire to trouble France, was it not?" replied the constable.

"Ah! Messire Bertrand, do not make me talk politics," said the prince.

And they laughed.

Sometimes the duchess, the prince's wife, sent Bertrand refreshments, presents that were the work of her own hands, and these gentle attentions rendered the prisoner's sojourn in the fortress more endurable.

But he had no one near him to whom he might confide his vexations, and his vexations were profound. He saw that time was slipping by, he felt that the soldiers of the army he had levied with such pains were scattering more and more every day, and that it would be all the more difficult to gather them together again when it was necessary.

He had, almost under his eyes, the spectacle of the captivity of twelve hundred officers and men-at-arms, his comrades taken at Navaretta, the nucleus of an invincible army, and who, were they once free, would collect with ardor the fragments of that great force that had been crushed by a defeat no one had expected.

He often thought of the King of France, who must doubtless be very much embarrassed at the present moment.

He beheld, from the depths of his gloomy prison, that dear and venerated monarch walking, with drooping head, under the arbors of the garden of Saint-Paul, now lamenting, now hoping, and murmuring like Augustus, "Bertrand! give me back my legions!"

"And at this very time," added Du Guesclin, in his internal soliloquies, "France is devoured by the returning tidal wave of the companies; the Caverleys and the Green Knights, like the locusts, will eat up the remainder of the poor harvest."

Then Du Guesclin thought of Spain, of the insolent tyranny of Don Pedro, the abject condition of Henry, hurled forever from a throne upon which he had barely laid his hands.

And the constable could not refrain from censuring the cowardly indolence of this prince, who, instead of devoting himself earnestly to his work, consecrating his life and fortune to it, stirring up one half the Christian world against the faithless Spaniards attached to Don Pedro, was now doubtless basely begging his bread at the hands of some unknown castellan.

When this flood of thoughts inundated the soul of the good constable, the prison seemed odious to him. He looked at the iron bars as Samson must have looked at the hinges of the gates of Gaza, and he felt within him the strength to bear off the wall upon his shoulders.

But prudence prompted him to receive his guests heartily, and, as his Breton loyalty was combined with a good deal of the astuteness of the native of Lower Normandy, as he was at once virile and shrewd, the constable was never so joyously uproarious, never so noisy in his cups as during his hours of depression and weariness.

Consequently, he threw some of the craftiest Englishmen off the scent.

A superior authority, however, maintained the most rigorous surveillance around the prisoner. Too proud to complain, Bertrand knew not to whom or to what he was to attribute a display of severity that went so far as even to prevent the letters he sent to France reaching their address.

The court of England had regarded the capture of Du Guesclin as one of the happiest results of the victory at Navaretta.

And naturally, for the constable was the only serious obstacle the English, under the command of a hero like the Prince of Wales, could encounter in Spain.

King Edward, who had able advisers, wished to extend his power gradually in a country ravaged by civil war. He saw clearly that Don Pedro, the ally of the Moors, would be dethroned sooner or later, and that, with Don Henry vanquished and slain, there would no longer remain any pretender to the throne of Castile, which, from that moment, would fall an easy prey to the victorious army of the Prince of Wales.

But, if Bertrand were free, matters would assume a different complexion; he could return to Spain, recover the advantage lost at Navaretta, seat Don Henry again upon his throne, and that forever, and it would be all over with the scheme of conquest which had been monopolizing the attention of the royal council of England for the last five years.

Edward's judgment of men was less chivalrous than that of his son. He supposed the constable could escape; that, if he did not escape, he might be carried off; and that, even as a shackled prisoner, powerless within the four walls of his dungeon, he could still give good counsel, suggest a good plan of invasion, a hope to the conquered party.

So Edward had placed two incorruptible spies near Du Guesclin, the governor and the jailer, both of whom were amenable only to the direct authority of the grand council of England.

Edward did not communicate the secret intentions of his advisers to the Prince of Wales, a man surpassingly noble and loyal. He feared this prince might oppose a magnanimous resistance to his plans.

The fact is, the English monarch did not wish the prisoner released, no matter how high the ransom; and he hoped, by gaining time, to take him out of the hands of the Prince of Wales, and have him brought to London, where the Tower would be a safer storehouse for such a treasure than the castle of Bordeaux.

Now, it was quite certain that, should the Prince of Wales get any intimation of this resolution, he would at once set Du Guesclin at liberty before receiving any official order in connection with him. For this reason, they were waiting in London until the affairs of Spain were settled. Once Don Pedro was seated firmly on his throne, and France held rigorously in check, they would, with one bold stroke, by an order of the grand council, suddenly summon the prince to come to London with his prisoner.

So the English monarch was waiting for the favorable moment.

Du Guesclin had no warning of the approaching storm. He was living in full reliance upon the all-powerful authority of the conqueror of Navaretta.

At length the day so ardently longed for by the illustrious prisoner shone upon the bars of his chamber.

The Sire de Laval had just arrived at Bordeaux with the ransom.

This noble Breton informed the Prince of Wales of his mission and its object.

It was noon. The sun descended obliquely on the

THE PRISON OF THE GOOD CONSTABLE.

apartment of the constable, who was alone at the moment, and sadly regarding its rays as they flickered upon the bare wall.

The trumpets sounded, the drums beat; Bertrand was aware that he was to receive some illustrious visitor.

The Prince of Wales entered, bareheaded, with a smiling countenance.

"Well, sir constable," said he, while Du Guesclin bent a knee in homage, "were you not longing for the sun? It is bright this morning."

"The fact is, monseigneur," answered Du Guesclin, "that I would much prefer the singing of the nightingales of my country to the little squeak of the mice of Bordeaux; but what God does man must accept in silence."

"Quite the contrary, sir constable, sometimes God proposes and man disposes. Have you heard any news from your country?"

"No, monseigneur," said Bertrand, in a voice that trembled with emotion, so much anguish and pleasure stirred his heart at that sweet name.

"Well, sir constable, you are going to be free; the money has arrived."

After saying these words, the prince offered his hand to the amazed Bertrand, and passed out, smiling.

At the door, —

"Messire governor," said he to the officer whose duty it was to guard the prisoner, "you will allow the constable to receive the friend and the money that are coming to him from France."

Having thus spoken, the prince left the castle.

The governor, gloomy and anxious, remained alone with the constable.

This unexpected arrival of Laval destroyed all the

schemes of the English council, and Du Guesclin would be free in spite of everything.

Without an express order from King Edward, the governor could not oppose the will of the Prince of Wales, and that order had not arrived.

However, the governor knew the innermost ideas of the English council; he knew that the release of the constable would be a source of misfortune for his country and a vexation for King Edward. He resolved, then, to make an effort to do of himself what the government had not yet been able to do, because of the rapid success of the expedition of Mauléon, and the eager enthusiasm of the Bretons to liberate their hero.

The governor, therefore, instead of giving orders to the jailer, according to the direction of the Prince of Wales, made a friendly call upon the prisoner.

"So you are free, then, sir constable," said he; "it will be a real misfortune for us to lose you."

Du Guesclin smiled.

"In what particular?" he asked jestingly.

"It is so great an honor, Messire Bertrand, for a mere knight like me to guard so mighty a warrior as you!"

"Good!" said the constable, with his customary playfulness. "But I am one of those who always manage to get themselves taken in battle. The prince is sure to make me a prisoner again; that is an absolute certainty; and when he does, you will have the keeping of me a second time, for, by my soul, you are a good keeper!"

The governor sighed.

"At least, one consolation is left me," he said.

"What is it?"

"I have the keeping of all your companions; twelve

hundred Bretons, prisoners like yourself. I can talk to them about you."

Du Guesclin's joy abandoned him at the thought of the friends he should leave prisoners, while he, rescued from slavery, would again behold the sun of his country.

"These worthy companions," added the governor, "will be deeply grieved at your departure; but I will do my best to lessen the irksomeness of their captivity."

A fresh sigh from Bertrand, who this time began to stalk silently up and down the flagstone pavement of his chamber.

"Ah," went on the governor, "what splendid advantages genius and valor have! The merit of one man makes him of as much value as twelve hundred men."

"How is that?" asked Bertrand.

"I mean, messire, that the sum brought by the Sire de Laval for your ransom would suffice for the ransom of your twelve hundred companions."

"It is true!" murmured the constable, more pensive and gloomy than ever.

"It is the first time," continued the Englishman, "I have had ocular demonstration of the fact that a man may be worth an army. In fact, sir constable, your twelve hundred Bretons are really an army, and could make a campaign by themselves alone. By Saint George, messire, if I were in your place, and as rich as you are, I should never leave this spot except as an illustrious captain at the head of my twelve hundred soldiers!"

"Spoken like a brave man," said Du Guesclin to himself, thoughtfully; "he shows me my duty. It really is not right that a man, made of flesh and bone like any one else, should cost his country as much as twelve hundred valiant and honest Christians."

The governor followed with attentive eye the progress of his suggestion.

"Come now!" said Bertrand, suddenly; "do you believe the ransom of the Bretons would cost only seventy thousand florins?"

"I am certain of it, sir constable."

"And that the prince would release them on receipt of this sum?"

"Yes, and without any chaffering either."

"Do you pledge yourself to that?"

"On my honor and life!" said the governor, with a thrill of joy.

"It is well; have the goodness to bring hither the Sire de Laval, my countryman and friend; tell my scribe also to come and have with him everything required to draw up a memorandum in due form."

The governor lost no time; he was in such good spirits that he forgot he had orders not to let any persons approach the prisoner except the English and Navarrese, his natural enemies.

He acquainted the astonished jailer with the wishes of Bertrand, and ran himself to inform the Prince of Wales.

XXXI.

THE RANSOM.

BORDEAUX was full of tumult and agitation caused by the arrival of the Sire de Laval with his four mules laden with gold and the fifty men-at-arms bearing the banners of France and Bretagne.

A considerable crowd had followed the imposing escort, and on all faces were read either anxiety or vexation, if the face was that of an Englishman, or joy and triumph, if it belonged to a Frenchman or Gascon.

The Sire de Laval marched along amid the congratulations of some, the hearty imprecations of others. But his countenance was calm and impassive; he followed the trumpeters at the head of the procession, one hand on his poniard, the other on the reins of his powerful black steed, and, with visor raised, he pushed on through the swarming multitude, neither hastening nor slackening his pace before any obstacle.

When he reached the castle where Du Guesclin was a prisoner, he dismounted, gave his horse to the squires, and ordered the four muleteers to take down the chests containing the money.

His people obeyed him.

While they were lifting, one after the other, the four heavy burdens, and while the curious crowd was pressing eagerly around the escort, a knight, with lowered visor, and without colors or device, approached the Sire de Laval and said in pure French, —

"Messire, you are about to enjoy the happiness of seeing the illustrious prisoner and the still greater happiness of setting him at liberty, when you will lead him away with the brave men-at-arms who follow you. I am one of the loyal friends of the constable, but cannot, perhaps, find an opportunity of speaking with him, except you are kind enough to allow me to go with you to his donjon; might I ask you to do so?"

"Sir knight," said Messire de Laval, "your voice sounds pleasantly in my ear, you speak the language of my country, but I do not know you, and, if I were asked your name, I should have to lie —"

"You would answer," said the unknown, "that I am the Bastard of Mauléon."

"But you are not he," said Laval, quickly, "since the Sire de Mauléon has left us in order to pass more rapidly into Spain."

"I come on his part, messire; do not refuse me. I have just one word to say to the constable, a single —"

"Say this word to me, then; I will transmit it to him."

"I can tell it to none but him, and even he would not understand it except I showed my face. I entreat you, Sire de Laval, do not refuse me, in the name of the honor of the French arms of which, I swear to you before God, I am one of the most zealous defenders."

"I believe you, messire, but you are showing very little confidence in me, — knowing who I am," he added, with an expression of wounded pride.

"When you know who I am, sir count, you will not use such language. I have spent three days in Bordeaux trying to reach the constable; but neither gold nor artifice has succeeded with me."

"I distrust you thoroughly," replied the Comte de Laval, "and I have no notion of charging my conscience with a lie for your sake. Besides, what interest have you in going near the constable now, who is to leave in ten minutes? In ten minutes, in fact, he will be here where you are standing, and then you can say to him this important word."

The stranger shook his head, impatiently.

"In the first place," said he, "I am not of your opinion, and I do not regard the constable as free. Something tells me that his departure from prison will involve more difficulties than you imagine. Moreover, admitting that he may leave in ten minutes, those ten minutes would be so much time gained for the journey I am about to make, for I should thus avoid all the delay incidental to the ceremonies connected with his release: his visit to the prince, for instance, his thanks to the governor, the farewell banquet. I entreat you to take me with you. I can be useful to you."

At this moment, the stranger was interrupted by the jailer, who came to invite the Sire de Laval to enter the donjon.

The count took leave of his petitioner, bluntly and imperiously.

The unknown knight, who, he thought, was trembling under his armor, retired behind the men-at-arms, and waited, as he was still hopeful, until the last chest had disappeared on the way to the donjon.

While the Sire de Laval was going up the staircase, the Prince of Wales was seen passing through an open gallery connecting the two wings of the castle, preceded by the governor and followed by Chandos and a few officers.

The conqueror of Navaretta was about to pay his last visit to Du Guesclin.

All the populace cried: "Noël! and Saint George for the Prince of Wales!"

The French trumpets sounded in honor of the hero; the Prince of Wales bowed courteously.

Then the doors were shut, and the crowd, approaching the steps, awaited with noisy murmurs the coming forth of the constable.

The hearts of the Breton men-at-arms beat violently; they were on the point of seeing their great captain once more, that captain for whose liberty every one of them would have freely given his life.

Half an hour passed; the by-standers were becoming impatient and the Bretons anxious.

The unknown knight tore at his right gauntlet with his left gauntlet.

Chandos was seen a second time in the open gallery, talking eagerly with some officers who seemed not only amazed but astounded.

Then, when the door of the castle was again thrown open, instead of giving passage to the liberated hero, it exposed to view the Sire de Laval, pale and disconcerted, trembling with emotion, and with eyes that wandered over the crowd in search of some one.

Several Breton officers hurried up to him.

"What is the matter?" they asked nervously.

"Oh! a great disaster! a strange event!" replied the count. "But where, then, is that unknown knight, that prophet of woe?"

"Here I am," said the mysterious knight; "here I am. I was waiting for you."

"Do you still wish to see the constable?"

"More than ever."

"Then make haste, for in ten minutes it will be too late. Come on! come on! He is now more of a prisoner than ever."

"We shall see," replied the unknown, lightly springing

up the steps behind the count, and following in his train.

The jailer opened the door for them with a smile, and all the assembled gathering began to comment in a thousand different fashions upon the event that was delaying the departure of the constable.

"Hark ye!" said the chief of the Bretons, in an undertone to his men-at-arms, "keep a good grip of your swords, and look out!"

XXXII.

HOW THE GOVERNOR, INSTEAD OF SURRENDERING A PRISONER, LIBERATED AN ENTIRE ARMY.

THE Englishman was not mistaken: he knew his prisoner.

Hardly had the Sire de Laval received the order to enter the castle, hardly had he had time to fling himself into the arms of the constable, — hardly, in a word, had this first moment of mutual joy passed, when Du Guesclin, fixing his eyes upon the chests that were being carried up to the landing by the muleteers, exclaimed,—

"My dear friend, what a lot of money!"

"And yet never was tax raised with less trouble," answered the Sire de Laval, whose pride in his fellow-countryman was so great that he found it impossible to give sufficient expression to his respect and friendship.

"And this is the way my brave Bretons have been robbing themselves," said the constable; "and you, of course, the first amongst them."

"You ought to have seen the coins raining into the purses of the collectors," cried the Sire de Laval, delighted at the chance of nettling the English governor, who had returned from visiting the prince, and was listening unmoved.

"Seventy thousand florins of gold; what a sum!" repeated the constable.

"Yes, a large sum when it has to be collected; a small one when it is collected, and about to be handed over."

"My friend, sit down, I pray you," interrupted Du Guesclin. "You know that there are twelve hundred of my countrymen here, prisoners like myself?"

"Alas! yes, I know it."

"Well, I have discovered a way to set them free. They were taken through my fault. I shall repair that fault to-day."

"How?" said the Sire de Laval, astonished.

"Have you had the kindness, messire governor, to send for the scribe?"

"He is at the door, sir constable, and awaiting your orders," said the Englishman.

"Let him enter."

The governor tapped the floor three times with his foot. The jailer ushered in the scribe, who, having doubtless been forewarned, had pen and ink and parchment ready in his five lean fingers.

"Write, my friend, what I am going to dictate to you," said the constable.

"We, Bertrand du Guesclin, Constable of France and of Castile, Count of Soria, make known by these presents that our repentance is great for having, on one day of insensate pride, estimated our personal worth at the value of twelve hundred good Christians and brave knights, who, certainly, are worth more than we."

Here the good constable paused, but not to study on the faces of the by-standers the effect of this preamble.

The scribe continued writing faithfully.

"We humbly ask pardon of God and of our brothers," went on Du Guesclin; "and to repair our folly we devote the sum of seventy thousand florins to the ransom of the twelve hundred prisoners made by His Highness the Prince of Wales at Navaretta of fatal memory."

"And you are pledging your property!" cried the Sire

de Laval. "It is abusing your generosity in a signal fashion, sir constable."

"No, my friends, my property is squandered, and I cannot reduce Madame Tiphaine to misery. She has already suffered only too much through me."

"Then what are you going to do?"

"The money you bring me is mine beyond any doubt, is it not?"

"Certainly; but—"

"That is enough. If it is mine, I can dispose of it as I like. Write, messire le scribe: 'I devote this sum of seventy thousand florins, which the Sire de Laval has brought me, to this ransom.'"

"But, seigneur constable," cried Laval, in dismay, "you remain a prisoner."

"And covered with immortal glory," interrupted the governor.

"This is impossible," continued Laval; "reflect."

"You have written?" said the constable to the scribe.

"Yes, monseigneur."

"Give me the parchment, so that I may sign it."

The constable took the pen and signed rapidly.

At this moment the trumpets announced the arrival of the Prince of Wales.

The governor had already laid hold of the parchment.

As soon as the Sire de Laval perceived the English prince, he ran up to him, and, bending the knee, said,—

"Monseigneur, here is the money required for the ransom of M. le Connétable; do you accept it?"

"According to my word, and with the greatest pleasure," answered the prince.

"This money is certainly yours, monseigneur; take it," continued the count.

"A moment," said the governor. "Your Highness is

not aware of the incident that has just taken place; be pleased to read this parchment."

"To annul it," cried Laval.

"To have it executed," said the constable.

The prince cast his eyes over the document, and, deeply moved,—

"It is a noble deed," said he, "and one I should like to have done myself."

"But it would have been useless in your case, monseigneur," replied Du Guesclin, "for you are the victor."

"Your Highness will not detain the constable?" cried Laval.

"Certainly not, if he wishes to leave," said the prince.

"But I wish to stay, Laval, it is my duty; ask those lords what they think of it."

Chandos, Albret, and the others loudly expressed their admiration.

"Well," said the prince, "let the money be counted, and do you, gentlemen, set the Breton prisoners at liberty."

It was not until the English captains had passed out that Laval, half mad with grief, recalled the sinister prophecy of the unknown knight, and ran from the castle to summon him to his aid.

An officer was calling the roll of the prisoners; the chests of gold were empty and the money heaped up in piles, when Laval returned to the castle with the unknown knight.

"Tell the constable now what you have to tell him," murmured Laval in his ears, while the prince was conversing familiarly with Du Guesclin. "And, since you have so much power, whether magical or natural, persuade him to take the money for his own ransom instead of giving it to others."

The unknown started. He advanced two steps, and his golden spur resounded on the pavement.

The prince turned round at the noise.

"Who is this knight?" asked the governor.

"One of my companions," said Laval.

"Then let him raise his visor, and he is welcome," interrupted the prince.

"Monseigneur," said the unknown, in a voice that made Du Guesclin start also, "I have made a vow to keep my face covered; permit me to fulfil it."

"Be it as you will, sir knight; but it is not your purpose to remain unknown to the constable?"

"To him as well as to all, seigneur."

"In that case," cried the governor, "you must leave the castle, for I have orders not to let any enter save those who are known to me."

The knight inclined, as if to show he was willing to obey.

"The prisoners are free," said Chandos, returning to the hall.

"Adieu, Laval, adieu!" cried the constable, with a heartfelt reluctance that did not escape the count, for he seized Bertrand's hands, saying, —

"For God's sake relinquish your purpose! it is still time."

"No," answered the constable, "on my life, no!"

"Would you wrong his honor to such a degree as that?" said the governor. "If he is not free to-day, he may be in a month. Money is found easily, but such chances of glory as this are not met with twice."

The prince seemed to applaud; his captains imitated him.

The unknown knight at once advanced gravely towards the governor, and, in a majestic voice, —

"It is you," he said, "who would wrong the glory of your master, sir governor, by allowing him to do what he has done."

"What say you, messire?" cried the governor, turning pale. "You insult me; I wrong the glory of my prince? By God's death, you have lied!"

"Do not fling down your gauntlet unless you know that it is fitting in me to pick it up. Messire, I speak with truth and openness. His Highness the Prince of Wales is acting against his glory in holding Du Guesclin a prisoner in this castle."

"You lie, you lie!" cried angry voices, while at the same time many a sword stirred in its scabbard.

The prince had turned pale like the others, so rude and uncalled-for did this attack appear.

"Who, then, would have me do his will here?" said he. "Is he, perchance, a king that he dare speak thus to a king's son? The constable can pay his ransom and depart. If he does not pay, he remains, that is the whole matter; why these hostile complaints?"

The unknown knight was not disturbed.

"Monseigneur," he added, "this is what I have heard on my journey hither: 'They are bringing the ransom for the constable; but the English are too much afraid of him to let him go.'"

"*Vrai Dieu!* they are saying that?" murmured the prince.

"Everywhere, monseigneur."

"You see they are mistaken, since the constable is free to go. Is it not so, constable?"

"It is, monseigneur," replied Bertrand, strangely and inexplicably moved ever since he had heard the voice of the unknown knight.

"Now," said the governor, "since the constable has

disposed of the sum intended for his ransom, it will be necessary to wait until a sum equal to it arrive."

The prince remained thoughtful for an instant.

"No," said he, at length, "the constable shall not wait. I fix his ransom at a hundred livres."

A murmur of admiration ran through the assembly.

Bertrand wished to protest; but the unknown knight placed himself between him and the prince.

"Thank God," said he, arresting him with his hand, "France can pay twice for her constable! Du Guesclin must not be the debtor of any one. There are in this roll drafts upon the Lombard Agosti of Bordeaux; they are for eighty thousand florins, payable at sight. I shall see to the counting of the sum myself, which will be here in two hours — "

"And I," interrupted the prince, angrily, "I tell you the constable leaves this castle upon payment of a hundred livres, or he does not leave at all! If Messire Bertrand is offended at being called my friend, let him say so. Yet I remember him declaring one day that I was as good a knight as he."

"Oh, monseigneur!" cried the constable, kneeling before the Prince of Wales, "I accept with so much gratitude that to pay the hundred livres I will ask a loan from your captains."

Chandos and the other officers hurried up to him with their purses; he dipped into them, and then brought the hundred livres to the prince, who embraced him, saying, —

"You are free, Messire Bertrand; let the doors be flung open, and let none ever again say that the Prince of Wales fears any one in this world."

The governor, in a state of absolute dismay, begged to have the order repeated; the unfortunate man had played so badly that, instead of a single prisoner, he was losing a whole army along with its captain.

While the prince was questioning his officers, and even Laval himself, on the subject of the mysterious author of this political counterstroke, the unknown approached Du Guesclin and said, in a low voice, —

"A false generosity was keeping you in prison, a false generosity releases you; you are free. Good-bye till we meet again in a fortnight under the walls of Toledo!"

And, bowing profoundly to the Prince of Wales, he disappeared, leaving Bertrand astounded.

An hour after, the most active search would not have discovered a trace of him in that city which the constable, free and joyous, rode through in triumph at the head of his Bretons, whose acclamations reached the skies.

There was one person, however, who did not join the jubilant procession that followed Du Guesclin.

He was an officer of the Prince of Wales, one of those leaders of the Free Companies called captains, who had votes in the council, although their opinions were never attended to.

He was, in a word, a personage with whom we are acquainted. He had entered the chamber of Bertrand in the train of Chandos, had kept his visor always closed, and, having been struck by the voice of the unknown knight, had never lost sight of him for a moment afterwards.

So, no sooner did the knight disappear than this captain collected some of his men, ordered them to take horse and follow the traces of the fugitive, and he himself, having gathered what information he could, pushed forward on the road to Spain.

XXXIII.

THE POLICY OF MUSARON.

MEANWHILE, Agénor, spurred on by the endless anxiety of the lover who has no news, was advancing at a rapid pace towards the dominions of Don Pedro.

On the way, he had, thanks to a certain reputation won for him by his journey to France, recruited his party from among the Bretons who, after the collection of the ransom, had come in search of Du Guesclin with the aim of fighting by his side.

He also met a goodly number of Spanish knights going to the meeting-place appointed by Henry of Trastamare, who, it was said, was about to return to Spain, and was beginning to come to terms with the Prince of Wales, as the latter was dissatisfied with Don Pedro.

Every time that Agénor slept at a town or village of any importance, he made inquiries about Hafiz, Gildaz, and Maria Padilla, asking if any one had seen a courier who was looking for a Frenchman, or a beautiful young Morisca followed by two servants and travelling to France.

Every time also that an answer in the negative struck his ear, the young man plunged deeper the rowels into the flanks of his horse.

Then Musaron would say, in his cross-grained philosophical fashion, —

"Monsieur, this young woman is a young woman you ought to love well, for she is costing us a great deal of trouble."

Agénor rode so hard that he cleared much ground, and he made so many inquiries that he grew resigned.

Twenty leagues still separated him from the court of Burgos.

He knew that an army, which was very devoted, very warlike, very fresh, and, consequently, very dangerous to Don Pedro, was awaiting only the signal to come together and confront the conqueror of Navaretta with a new hydra's head more destructive and venomous than the old one.

Agénor asked himself and asked Musaron if it would not be proper, before proceeding further with any political negotiation, to enter upon an amorous one with Maria Padilla.

Musaron acknowledged that diplomacy is good, but he claimed that, by taking Don Pedro, Maria, Mothril, and Spain, they would take Burgos, in which Burgos they would not fail to take Aïssa, if she was still there.

Which consoled Agénor exceedingly, and he advanced some leagues further.

And this was how the circle gradually contracted that was fated to stifle Don Pedro, blinded as he was by prosperity, and stimulated to the pursuit of trifles by the intrigues of his favorites at the very time his crown was in jeopardy.

Musaron, the most obstinate of men, especially since he felt he was rich, would not allow his master for a moment to run the risk of pushing on towards Burgos, shutting himself up in that city, and holding a conference with Doña Maria.

He made use, on the contrary, of his dejection and his amorous forgetfulness to retain him in the midst of the Bretons and the partisans of Henry of Trastamare, so that the young knight soon became the leader of a considerable party, a distinction he owed as much to his mission in France as to his assiduity in upholding the warlike spirit of his companions.

He kept open table for the new arrivals and corresponded with the constable, as well as with his brother Olivier, who was preparing to pass the frontier at the head of five thousand Bretons, being determined to succor his brother and help him to win his first battle.

Musaron became a tactician. He passed entire days in writing out plans of battles and computing the number of crowns Caverley must have piled up since the last affair, in order to have the satisfaction of not falling into any mistake the first time they should fight.

It was in the midst of these warlike arrangements that important tidings reached Agénor: in spite of the vigilance of Musaron, an adroit emissary had succeeded in announcing to him the departure of Don Pedro for the royal pleasure-house, and the disappearance of Aïssa and Maria exactly at the time the king went on this excursion.

The same courier informed Mauléon that Gildaz had died on his way home, and that Hafiz alone had returned to Doña Maria.

To learn all this good news, Agénor had only to give thirty crowns to a man of the country, who had conversed with Maria's nurse, the mother of poor Gildaz.

And so, now that Agénor at last knew what was in store for him, in spite of Musaron, in spite of his companions in arms, in spite of everything, he flung himself on the best of his horses, and turned the rein in the direction of the road that led to the castle Don Pedro had selected for his residence.

Musaron fretted and fumed and cursed and swore; but he, too, set out for this castle.

XXXIV.

HOW MOTHRIL'S CRIME HAD A HAPPY SUCCESS.

AT Don Pedro's castle, the lamentations became more noisy and terrible when daylight shone on the apartments of Doña Maria.

Don Pedro had not been able to rest; his servants claimed they had heard him weeping.

Mothril had spent the night in a fashion more serviceable to his interests. He had been making arrangements to destroy the last vestige of his crime.

Being alone with Aïssa, and lavishing on her the tenderest care with all the skill of the most expert physician, he had, from the beginning of his conversation with her, moulded the still unsettled mind of the young girl as if it were soft wax.

So, when Aïssa cried out on seeing the body of Doña Maria, he pretended to be shaken with involuntary horror, and threw a cloak over the lifeless remains of the king's mistress.

Then, when Aïssa regarded him with terror, —

"Poor child!" he said, "give thanks to God who has saved you."

"Saved! saved me?" she asked.

"From a frightful death, yes, my dear child."

"Who has struck me, then?"

"She whose hand still holds your poniard."

"Doña Maria! she, so kind, so generous! impossible."

Mothril smiled, with that disdainful compassion which always imposes on minds overpowered by some engrossing self-interest.

"The mistress of the king, generous and kind to Aïssa whom the king adores! You do not believe it, my daughter."

"But," said Aïssa, "since she purposed sending me away —"

"To unite you to this French knight, she said, did she not?" continued the Moor, in a tone of calm, unvarying kindness.

Aïssa started up and turned pale on seeing that the secret of her love was in the hands of the man who was specially interested in combating it.

"Fear nothing," went on the Moor; "what Maria could not do, because of the love and jealousy of the king, I shall do. Aïssa, you say you love. Well! I give my consent, and I will aid you; provided the daughter of my king lives and lives happy, I care for nothing further on earth."

Aïssa was so astounded at hearing such sentiments from Mothril that she could not turn away her eyes from his face, those eyes still weary with the sleep of death.

"He is deceiving me," she said to herself; then, her mind recurring to the body of Doña Maria, "Doña Maria is dead," she repeated wildly.

"And now for the cause of it, my dear child: the king loves you passionately, and declared his love yesterday to Doña Maria, who returned to her apartments, drunk with rage and jealousy. It was Don Pedro's intention to unite himself to you in the bonds of marriage, and this had always been the ambition of Doña Maria. Thereupon, she relinquished life, emptied her ring into the silver cup, and, that she might not leave you behind her a triumphant queen, that she might at the same time be avenged on Don Pedro and on me, both of whom love you in a different fashion, she seized your poniard and smote you."

"During my sleep, then, for I remember nothing," said Aïssa. "A cloud veiled my eyes, I heard something like hushed heart-throbs and stifled death-rattles. I think I rose and felt some hands upon mine and, immediately afterwards, the cold steel tearing my flesh — "

"It was the last effort of your enemy; she fell beside you, for the poison had more effect on her than the poniard had on you. I found you had still a spark of life, I quickened it, and so I have had the happiness to save you."

"Oh, Maria! Maria!" murmured the young girl, — "and yet you were kind."

"You say so, daughter, because she favored your love for Agénor de Mauléon," said Mothril, in an undertone, and with an amiability that had too much affectation in it not to hide a secret fury, — "because she introduced him into your apartments at Soria."

"You know?"

"I know everything; so does the king. Maria revealed your dishonor to Don Pedro before assassinating you. But she feared the calumny would slip away from the soul of the king, and that he would pardon you for having belonged to another, — those who love are so indulgent, — and so, to cut you off from the world of the living, she employed the dagger."

"The king knows that Agénor — "

"The king is mad with anger and love, — the king, who had already bribed Hafiz, leaving me in ignorance of everything, to draw you to the castle; the king,

I say, expects to bring you to his side again when you are restored to health. He is excusable; he loves you."

"This time I shall die," said Aïssa; "for my hand will not tremble, will not glide over my bosom as has done the hand of Maria Padilla."

"Die! you die! my idol! my adored child!" cried the Moor, kneeling. "No, you shall live; live happy, and blessing my name forever!"

"Without Agénor I cannot live."

"He is of a different religion from yours, my daughter."

"I will adopt his religion."

"He hates me."

"He will pardon you when he sees that you no longer stand between us. Besides, what is that to me? I love, and see nothing in the world except the object of my love."

"Not even him who has just saved you for your lover?" said Mothril, humbly and with an affected sorrow that touched the heart of the young girl deeply. "You sacrifice me even at the very time I am exposing myself to death for your sake!"

"How?"

"Assuredly I am, Aïssa. You wish to live with Don Agénor; I will aid you."

"You?"

"I, Mothril, yes, Aïssa."

"You are deceiving me—"

"Why?"

"Prove your sincerity."

"It is easy. You fear the king; well! I promise to prevent you from seeing the king. Does that satisfy you?"

"Not entirely."

"I understand: you wish to see the Frenchman again."

"Beyond aught else."

"Then wait until you are able to endure the journey. I will lead you to him, will confide to him my life."

"But Maria, too, was leading me to him —"

"Undoubtedly, she had an interest in getting rid of you, and she would have preferred to spare herself an assassination. An assassination is a heavy burden to bear on that day when we must all appear before God."

In uttering these words, Mothril's countenance betrayed for a moment that agony the damned suffer, the damned who have neither respite nor hope in their tortures.

"Well! what do you intend to do, then?" asked Aïssa.

"I intend to conceal you until you are cured; then, as I have just told you, I will unite you to the Seigneur de Mauléon."

"That is all I demand; by acting as you say, you will become for me a divine being. But the king —"

"Oh! if he guessed our design, he would oppose it with all his might. My death would be his best resource. If I were dead, you would surely belong to him, Aïssa."

"Or rather to death."

"Would you rather die than live for the Frenchman?"

"No, oh, no! — speak, speak!"

"Should Don Pedro, perchance, my dear child, come to see you, should he talk and question you about Agénor de Mauléon, you must declare boldly that Doña Maria lied when she asserted you loved this Frenchman, especially when she asserted you had given him possession of your love. The result will be that the king will no longer distrust the Frenchman, will no longer watch your conduct, and will make both of you free and happy. You must also, and this is the most important point of all, my dear child, you must try and recall your recollections and remember this: Doña Maria spoke to you before she struck you; she told you, doubtless, to confess your dishonor to the king, and, upon your refusal, she stabbed you."

"I remember nothing," cried Aïssa, terrified, as every simple, upright soul would have been, at the Moor's disclosure of his infernal theory. "I do not wish to remember anything. I do not wish to deny, either, my love for Mauléon; that love is my light and my religion, his name is the star that guides my life. I am so proud of belonging to him that I would proclaim it before all the kings of the earth. Do not depend on me for these falsehoods. If Don Pedro speaks to me I will answer."

Mothril turned pale. This last feeble obstacle destroyed all the results of a murder; the simple stubbornness of a child bound, hand and foot, the vigorous man who would have dragged a world in his train.

He understood that further persistence was useless. Yet he had performed the feat of Sisyphus. He had rolled the rock up to the summit of the mountain, and then the rock had rolled down again.

Mothril had neither the time nor the chance to begin anew.

"My daughter," said he, "you will act as you please. Your interest, as your heart or your fancy understands it, is my only law. Whatever you wish I wish. Tell the king, therefore, only what you like. I know well that your confession will cost me my head, for I have always felt it my duty to proclaim your innocence and your purity; I have never consented to allow a suspicion to hover over you. Let my head pay for your fault, that is to say, for your happiness. Allah wills it; may his will be done!"

"Still, I cannot lie," said Aïssa. "Besides, why should you permit the king to come and speak to me? Keep him away; it is easy. Can you not transport me to some isolated dwelling; in a word, can you not conceal me? Are not my wounds and health sufficient pretexts? In this respect, my present position helps you, — but to lie, never! to deny Agénor, never!"

Mothril vainly tried to hide the joy the words of Aïssa had just created in his soul. To depart with Aïssa, to remove her for a time from the questions of Don Pedro, to give him time for his anger, hatred, regrets, his recollection of Maria, to grow fainter, to gain a month, — why, it was to gain everything! And this chance of salvation was offered by Aïssa herself. Mothril seized it eagerly.

"Since you wish it, my daughter," said he, "we shall start. Have you any objection to the castle of Montiel of which the king has named me governor?"

"I have no objection to anything save the presence of Don Pedro. I will go wherever you wish."

Mothril kissed the hand and robe of Aïssa, and carried her gently in his arms into the next chamber. He then ordered the body of Doña Maria to be taken away, and, calling two women of his nation upon whose fidelity he could rely, he placed them near the wounded girl, cautioning them on their lives not to speak to Aïssa or to suffer any one else to address her.

Everything being thus arranged, he went to see Don Pedro, having first composed his mind and the expression of his face.

Don Pedro had just received various letters from the city. It was announced to him that envoys from Bretagne and England had appeared in the neighborhood, that rumors of war were in circulation, and that the Prince of Wales was drawing his ring of steel tighter around the new capital, with the object of forcing his protégé of Navaretta, by the pressure of an invincible army, to pay the expenses of the war and coin his gratitude into ready money.

These tidings saddened Don Pedro, but did not dishearten him. He sent for Mothril, who entered the royal chamber at the very moment the king was making known his desire for his presence.

"Aïssa?" said Don Pedro, anxiously.

"Seigneur, her wound is deep and dangerous; we shall not save this victim."

"A fresh misfortune!" cried Don Pedro. "Oh! another one would be too much. To lose Doña Maria who loved me so much, and Aïssa whom I love to distraction, and, at the same time, to begin anew a fierce, implacable war, — it is too much, Mothril, too much for the heart of a single man."

And Don Pedro showed his minister the warnings he had received from the governor of Burgos and from the neighboring cities.

"My king," said Mothril, "you must for the moment forget love and prepare for war."

"The treasury is empty."

"A tax will fill it. Sign the tax I have asked you to sign."

"I suppose I must. Can I see Aïssa?"

"Aïssa hangs like a flower above the abyss. A breath may hurl her into death."

"Has she spoken?"

"Yes, seigneur."

"What did she say?"

"A few words that explain everything. It seems Doña Maria tried to force her to dishonor herself by an avowal that would have ruined her in your regard. The courageous child refused, and the jealous Doña Maria struck her."

"And Aïssa has said that?"

"She will repeat it as soon as her strength returns. But I fear that never again in this world shall her voice be heard."

"Great God!" cried the king.

"One remedy alone can save her. A tradition of my country promises life to the wounded who, at night, during the mists of the new moon, touch their wound with a certain magical herb."

"That herb must be found," said the king, with the fury of superstition and of love.

"It is not found in this country, seigneur. I have seen it only at Montiel."

"At Montiel! Send to Montiel, Mothril."

"I have said, seigneur, that the wound must touch this herb while it is still on the stem. Oh, it is a sovereign remedy! I can easily bring Aïssa to Montiel, but will she endure the journey?"

"She must be borne as gently as the bird is borne when it soars through the air on its two wings. Let her depart, Mothril, let her depart! but you will stay with me."

"I am the only person, seigneur, who can recite the magic formula during the operation."

"Then I am to remain alone."

"No, seigneur; for, when Aïssa is cured, you can come to Montiel and you need never more leave her."

"Yes, Mothril, yes, you are right; I shall never leave her more, and so I may be happy at last. But what about the body of Doña Maria? I wish the highest honors to be paid to her remains."

"I have heard, seigneur," said Mothril, "that, in your religion, the body of a suicide is deprived of burial. The church, therefore, must not know that Doña Maria committed suicide."

"No one must know it, Mothril."

"But your servants —"

"I shall say in full court that Doña Maria died of fever, and, when I have so spoken, no one will dare to raise his voice."

"Blind! blind and mad!" thought Mothril.

"Then, Mothril, you will set out with Aïssa?"

"This very day, seigneur."

"And I shall attend to the obsequies of Doña Maria, sign the edict, and make an appeal to my army and my nobility. I shall charm away this storm."

"And I," thought Mothril, "shall shelter myself from it!"

XXXV.

HOW AGÉNOR LEARNED THAT HE ARRIVED TOO LATE.

LEAVING officers and soldiers and lovers of war generally to waste their time in plans and devices and strategies, Agénor pursued his own aim, which was to find Aïssa, the dearest possession he had in the world.

Love had begun in his case to have the whip-hand over ambition, and even over duty; for, as we have seen, the young man, in his impatience to enter Spain and get tidings of Aïssa, had suffered the envoys of the King of France and of the Comte de Laval to go to Bordeaux and pay the ransom the constable had fixed himself in a moment of heroic pride.

So, as this page would be lacking in our story, since it is lacking in that of Agénor, if we did not replace it by the facts of history, we must say, in a few words, that Guyenne shuddered with grief on the day when the Prince of Wales, with his usual generosity, allowed the prisoner, who had been ransomed by the gold of all France, to slip through the gates of Bordeaux.

We will add that the first care of Bertrand was to run to Paris and thank the king. Those who do not already know the rest will have their curiosity satisfied. From this out, we are, as far as the constable is concerned, sincere and impartial historians.

Don Agénor and his faithful Musaron travelled by long stages towards the castle in which Don Pedro had hoped to possess Aïssa.

Agénor guessed there was no time to lose. He knew Don Pedro and Mothril too well to indulge in false illusions.

"Who knows," said he to himself, "but Maria Padilla, through weakness or fear, may have compounded with her dignity, and that an alliance with the Moor Mothril may not have appeared to her preferable to the chances of a rupture with Don Pedro? What if the favorite were to have played the part of the indulgent spouse and shut her eyes on the caprice of her royal lover?"

These ideas made the impetuous blood of Agénor boil. For the time, he reasoned only like a lover, that is to say, his reason was unreason with a varnish of common sense.

He struck, as he rode along, mighty blows with his lance, which fell partly on Musaron's mule and partly on Musaron's spine. But the result was the same in either case: when the good squire was thus belabored, he belabored his steed. They also relieved the tedium of the road by discourses, the substance of which we shall extract for the delectation and instruction of the reader.

"You see, Musaron," said Agénor, "when I have talked a single hour with Doña Maria I shall know how things are at present and also what I am to expect in future."

"But, monsieur, you will learn nothing at all, and, in the end, you will fall into the clutches of that rascally Moor, who watches you as a spider does a fly."

"Ah, you are always repeating the same thing, Musaron! do you think a Saracen is as good as a Christian?"

"When a Saracen has things in his head, he's as good as three Christians. It's just as if you said, Is a woman as good as a man? Yet we see men subjugated and beaten by women every day. Now, do you know why, monsieur? because women always think about what they want to do, while men almost never do what they ought to think about."

"And your conclusion?"

"Is that Doña Maria has been prevented by some intrigue of the Saracen from sending Doña Aïssa to you."

"What next?"

"What next? The next thing is that Mothril, who has succeeded in preventing Doña Maria from sending your mistress to you, is waiting, well armed with courage and strength, until he catches you in the toils, just as larks are caught in the green wheat; and then he will kill you and you will not have Aïssa."

The answer of Agénor was a cry of rage, and he clapped spurs to his horse.

In this way, he arrived at the castle, the aspect of which smote him as with a pang. Places are eloquent; they speak a language intelligible to chosen souls.

Agénor examined, by the first rays of moonlight, the building that inclosed all his love and all his life. And, while he was looking, the awful assassination, the crowning triumph of Mothril, was attaining its fulfilment within these mysterious and impenetrable walls.

Worn out with having ridden so much and learned so little, sure of henceforth meeting face to face that which he sought, Agénor, after spending many a long hour in gazing upon the walls, pushed forward, followed by Musaron, towards a little village situated on the other side of the mountain.

In that spot dwelt, as we know, some goatherds: Agénor asked them for lodging, for which he paid generously. He was successful in obtaining parchment and ink, and he directed Musaron to write a letter to

Doña Maria, a letter full of affectionate regrets and expressions of gratitude, but also full of anxiety and distrust, though couched in all the delicate forms known to the French mind.

Agénor would have wished to confide the missive to Musaron, so as to be surer of it reaching its address; but the squire proved to his master that, as he was known to Mothril, there would be less danger in selecting their ambassador from amongst the simple shepherds of the mountain.

Agénor saw the wisdom of the advice, and despatched a shepherd with the letter.

He then stretched himself alongside Musaron on a couple of sheepskins, and waited.

But the sleep of lovers is like that of madmen, robbers, and ambitious statesmen, — it is easily interrupted.

Two hours after lying down, Agénor was standing upon the declivity of a hill, from which he could see distinctly the gate of the castle, although it was at a great distance, and watching for the return of his messenger.

This was the letter he sent to Doña Maria: —

"Noble lady, you who are so generous and so devoted to the interests of two poor lovers, I have returned to Spain, like the dog that draws his chain after him. No news of you, none of Aïssa. For Heaven's sake, give me some information! I am at the village of Quebra, where your answer will bring me death or life. What has happened? What am I to hope or to fear?"

The shepherd did not return. Suddenly the gates of the castle were flung open. Agénor felt his heart beat; but it was not the goatherd who came forth.

A long file of soldiers, women, and courtiers, issuing no one knew from where, — for the king had come to this residence but scantily attended, — a long procession, in a word, followed a litter that bore a dead body.

This could be seen from the mourning tapestries with which the litter was hung.

Agénor said to himself that the omen was sinister.

He had hardly given expression to this thought when the gates were again shut.

"The delay of the messenger is strange, and what we see is stranger still," said he to Musaron, who shook his head in sign of dissatisfaction.

"Go, then, and try to get some information," added Mauléon.

And he sat down at the back of the hillock, in the dusty furze.

Before a quarter of an hour had slipped by Musaron returned, bringing with him a soldier who seemed to require a good deal of persuasion to be induced to come.

"I tell you," Musaron was shouting, "my master will pay you, and pay you well."

"Who will pay, and for what?" said Agénor.

"For the news, seigneur."

"What news?"

"Seigneur, this soldier is one of the escort that is conducting the body to Burgos."

"For God's sake! what body?"

"Ah, seigneur! ah, my dear master! even from me you might not have believed it, but from him, perhaps, you will believe it: the body they are conducting to Burgos is that of Doña Maria Padilla."

Agénor uttered a cry of doubt and despair.

"It is true," said the soldier; "and I am in a hurry to resume my place in the escort."

"Misfortune on top of misfortune!" cried Mauléon; "but is Mothril in the castle?"

"No, seigneur," answered the soldier; "Mothril has just started for Montiel."

"Started! he started!—with his litter?"

"In which the dying young girl is resting, yes, seigneur."

"The young girl, Aïssa, dying! Ah, Musaron, this kills me!" sighed the unhappy knight, falling back on the ground as if he were really dead; and this frightened the good squire, who was little accustomed to see his master in a swoon.

"Sir knight, that is all I know," said the soldier; "and even that I only know by chance. It was I who aided in lifting to-night the young girl, who was stabbed, and Doña Maria, who was poisoned."

"Oh, cursed night! oh, misfortune, misfortune!" repeated the young man, who was almost frantic. "Stay, my friend; take these ten florins, although you have announced to me a life-long sorrow."

"Thanks, sir knight, and adieu!" said the soldier, starting away briskly across the furze.

Musaron, with his hand over his eyes, examined the horizon.

"Hold, hold, my dear master!" he cried; "look yonder, and you will see, at a great distance, a litter and some men with it who have crossed the mountain, and are now travelling over the plain. And yonder, too, in his white mantle, is the Saracen, our enemy, on horseback."

"Musaron, Musaron," said the knight, restored to life by rage and grief, "to horse, and let us crush the wretch! and if Aïssa must die, let me at least receive her last sigh!"

Musaron took the liberty of placing his hand on the shoulder of his master.

"Seigneur," said he, "we never reason correctly on an

event that has but recently occurred. We are two and they are twelve. We are tired and they are fresh. Moreover, we know they are going to Montiel; we shall meet them at Montiel. Look you, my dear monseigneur, we must, above all, know thoroughly the story the soldier has related to us only partially; we must know why Doña Maria has died of poison, and why Doña Aïssa has been wounded by a poniard."

"You are right, my faithful friend," said Agénor. "Do with me what you like."

"I will make you a happy and triumphant man, my master."

Agénor shook his head, despairingly. Musaron knew that the sole remedy for this disease was agitation of mind and body.

He led his master back to the camp, where the Bretons and the Spaniards, loyal to Henry of Trastamare, lay less in ambush and proclaimed their plans more loudly, ever since vague tidings had reached them of the liberation of Du Guesclin, and, especially, since they saw their strength and numbers increasing from day to day.

XXXVI.

THE PILGRIMS.

At some leagues from Toledo, on a sandy road lined with stunted pines, Agénor and his faithful Musaron were riding sadly, seeking, for the evening was declining, some venta or other in which they might rest their weary limbs, and get a hare cooked that an arrow of the squire had struck in its form.

Suddenly, they heard in the sand behind them a hurried movement: it was the gallop of a swift mule, bearing on its stout flanks a pilgrim whose face was concealed by a broad-brimmed hat, and, still better, by a veil that fell from the brim of the hat.

This pilgrim spurred his mule and controlled it with all the skill that befits the perfect cavalier.

The animal, evidently of a goodly race, flew rather than ran over the sand, and was lost so quickly to sight, that all our travellers could distinguish was the sound of the rider's voice as he passed, saying to them, " *Vayan ustedes con Dios!* " (Go with God.)

Ten minutes had scarcely elapsed when Musaron heard another noise like to the first. He turned round, and had barely time to draw aside his master's horse and his own, when four horsemen dashed up to them with lightning speed.

The leader, who was in advance of the others, was habited in a pilgrim's dress, like that of the cavalier first seen by the travellers.

But, under this dress, the prudent pilgrim wore a coat of mail; even his face was hidden by a visor, and, although it was night, the face of this knight afforded a singular spectacle under his broad-brimmed hat.

The unknown had evidently come up, like a bloodhound, so to speak, to scent our travellers; but Agénor wisely lowered his visor and laid his hand upon his sword.

Musaron kept on the defensive.

"Seigneur," said a hollow voice in bad Spanish that seemed to issue from the depths of a gulf, "you have seen, have you not, one of my companions, a pilgrim like myself, ride by you on a black mule as swift as the wind?"

The sound of this voice made a disagreeable impression on Agénor: he had an indistinct recollection of having heard it before. But his duty was to answer; he did so, courteously.

"Seigneur pilgrim, or seigneur knight," he replied, also in Spanish, "the person you speak of passed about ten minutes ago; and, as you have remarked, he rode a mule so fleet that there are few horses in the world could follow it."

Musaron thought he noticed that the voice of Agénor struck the pilgrim with a kind of surprise; for he advanced and said boldly, —

"This information is more precious than you think, knight; moreover, it has been given with such good grace that I should be charmed to make the acquaintance of the giver. I see by your foreign accent that we both come from the north; it is a reason that invites us to become more intimate. Raise your visor, then, that I may have the opportunity of thanking you after seeing your face."

"First raise your own, sir knight," answered Mauléon,

whom the voice and the question were affecting more and more disagreeably.

The pilgrim hesitated. Finally, he refused in a way that proved how perfidious and interested was his demand.

And, without another word, he beckoned to his companions, and was off again on the road followed by the first pilgrim.

"What an impudent rascal!" said Musaron, when he had lost sight of him.

"And what a villanous voice, Musaron! I am pretty sure I have heard that same voice, and at times, too, when the sound of it was far from pleasant."

"I am of your opinion, seigneur, and, if our horses were not too tired, it would not be a bad thing to run after these caitiffs. I am quite certain they are up to something that is well worth looking into."

"What concern is that of ours, Musaron?" replied Mauléon, in the tone of a man whom nothing could ever concern again. "We are going to Toledo where our friends are likely to be assembled. Toledo is near Montiel: that is all I know and all I care to know."

"At Toledo we shall have tidings of the constable," said Musaron.

"And also of Henry of Trastamare, probably," rejoined Agénor. "We shall receive orders, become machines, mere automatons, and, after all, that is the only resource, the only consolation for those who have lost their soul and, consequently, no longer know what they ought to say or what they ought to do in life."

"There! there!" said Musaron, "you'll always have time enough for despair. 'The last day brings victory,' says one of the proverbs of our country."

"'Or death,' — does it not run so? That is what you are afraid to add."

"Supposing so, seigneur; you can die only once."

"Do you think I am afraid of death?"

"Oh, monseigneur, you're not afraid of it enough; that's the very thing that annoys me."

And, discoursing thus, they reached the longed-for venta at last.

It was an isolated house, as are in Spain those shelters, those providential asylums that protect the traveller against the sun at noon and the cold at night, — bourns ardently desired and often as impossible to reach as oases in the desert, for the traveller who does not meet one of them on his way may die of cold and thirst and hunger before he meet another.

When Agénor and Musaron had stabled their horses, or rather, when the worthy squire had taken this entire task on his own shoulders, Agénor perceived the two pilgrims in the low hall of the venta, seated before a bright fire among a group of muleteers who were sunk in the deepest slumber; but these two pilgrims, instead of conversing, had their backs turned to each other.

"And I believed they were companions!" said Agénor to himself, in surprise.

The pilgrim of the veil buried himself deeper in his shadow when the two new travellers entered.

As to the pilgrim of the visor, he seemed to be watching with unutterable curiosity for the moment when a corner of his assumed companion's veil should open.

This moment did not arrive. Mute and impassive, but evidently annoyed, the mysterious personage at last feigned a profound sleep, to avoid answering his troublesome neighbor.

One by one, the muleteers went out to the yard and lay down under their mules, wrapped up in their mantles; all who remained now before the fire were Mauléon, who had just supped with his squire, and the two pilgrims, the one still occupied in watching, the other in sleeping.

The man of the visor began a conversation with Agénor by offering some commonplace excuses for the fashion in which he had left him on the road.

Then he asked him whether he was not going to retire to his room, where he surely could rest much better than on a stool like that.

Agénor, with his visor still lowered, had determined on keeping his place, were it only to thwart the unknown, when the idea came into his head that, if he stayed where he was, he should learn nothing. It was clear to him the other pilgrim was not sleeping. Something or other was going to happen, then, between these two men, each of whom wished to remain alone.

Agénor lived in an age and in a country in which curiosity often saved the lives of the curious.

He pretended, therefore, to withdraw to the room assigned him by his host, but he stopped behind the door which, although massive and solid, was, nevertheless, so badly joined that his eyes could see what was going on at the fireplace.

He had shown his wisdom, for a spectacle well worthy of his attention was reserved for him.

When the pilgrim of the visor saw that he was alone with his neighbor, whom he believed asleep, he rose up and took some steps in the hall to test the intensity of this sleep.

The sleeping pilgrim did not budge.

The man of the visor approached on tiptoe, and stretched out his hand to raise the veil that hid the features of the pilgrim.

But before his hand touched it, the pilgrim was on his legs, and, in a wrathful voice, —

"What do you want," said he, "and why do you disturb my sleep?"

"Which was not very profound, sir pilgrim of the veil," said the other, jeeringly.

"But which ought to be respected, messire inquisitive of the iron face."

"You have good reasons, no doubt, for preventing it being known whether yours is iron or flesh, sir pilgrim."

"My reasons concern nobody, and, if I wear a veil, it is because I do not wish to be seen; that is plain."

"Señor, I am very inquisitive, and I will see you," said the man of the visor, in a bantering tone.

The pilgrim at once raised his robe, and drawing a long poniard, —

"You shall first see this," he answered.

Then the man of the visor, after reflecting for a moment, drove in the heavy bolts of the door behind which Agénor was listening and looking.

At the same time, a window looking on the road opened and let in four men all armed and clad in coats of mail.

"You see," said he to the pilgrim, "defence would be useless and even impossible, seigneur. Be pleased, then, to answer simply — and so save a life I believe very precious — the following question."

The pilgrim, his hand on his poniard, was trembling with rage and anxiety.

"Are you, or are you not," continued the aggressor, "Don Henry of Trastamare?"

The pilgrim started.

"To such a question, put in such a form and with such preliminaries," he replied, "a person ought not to answer, if that person be the one you mention, without looking forward to death. I shall defend my life, then, for I am really the prince whose name you have uttered."

And, with a majestic gesture, he bared his noble face.

"The prince!" cried Mauléon, from behind the door which he now tried to break through.

"He!" cried the man of the visor, with savage joy, "I was quite sure of it; comrades, we have been following him long enough. It is a far road to Bordeaux! Oh, sheathe your poniard, my prince! no one wants to kill you, but we all want to put you to ransom. By the bodies of all the saints, you will find us easy to deal with! Sheathe your poniard, prince, sheathe it!"

Agénor struck blow after blow, and with all his might, on the door, but his efforts to splinter it were vain; the oak resisted.

"Stand at that door and keep the man who is striking it inside; leave me to deal with the prince."

"Brigand!" retorted Henry, contemptuously, "you would deliver me to my brother!"

"If he pays better than you, yes."

"I spoke truly, when I said it was better to die here," cried the prince. "Help! help!"

"Ah, seigneur!" said the bandit, "we shall be forced to kill you; your head, perhaps, will not be paid for so liberally as your whole living body would, but we shall have to be contented with carrying your head to Don Pedro."

"We'll see about that," cried Agénor, who, by one supreme effort, had broken in the door, and now rained blow after blow on the brigand's four followers.

"Yes, this makes it necessary for us to kill him," said the leader, drawing his sword to attack Henry.

"You have a very indiscreet friend there, seigneur; bid him keep quiet."

But, before the bandit had finished, a third pilgrim entered from the outside, and one that was certainly unexpected.

The new arrival wore neither mask nor veil, evidently believing that his pilgrim garb covered and clothed him sufficiently. His broad shoulders, enormous arms, and square, intelligent head announced a vigorous and intrepid champion.

He appeared on the threshold of the door, and gazed with astonishment, but without anger or fear, on the tumult in the hall of the hostel.

"So there's fighting going on here!" said he. "Ho there! Christians, which of you are right and which wrong?"

And his manly and imperious voice rose above the disorder as that of the lion rises above the tempest in the gorges of the Atlas.

The attitude of the combatants at the mere sound of that voice was singular enough.

The prince uttered a cry of joy and surprise; the man of the visor recoiled in dismay, and Musaron shouted, —

"Upon my life, it is M. le Connétable!"

"Help, constable, help!" said the prince, "they are trying to assassinate me!"

"You, my prince?" roared Du Guesclin, tearing asunder his robe to be more at his ease; "and who are they, pray?"

"Friends," said the brigand to his followers, "we must kill these men or die here. We are armed, they are not; the devil has given them into our hands. Instead of a hundred thousand florins, it is two hundred thousand that are within our reach! Forward!"

The constable, with incomparable coolness, stretched out his arm, before the brigand had finished his phrase, seized him by the throat as easily as if he had been a sheep, and laying him at his feet, pounded him on the flagstone. Then, snatching away his sword, —

"Now I am armed," said he; "three against three. Come on, my night-birds."

"We are lost," murmured the companions of the brigand, flying through the still open window.

Meanwhile, Agénor hurried forward, untied the visor of the prostrate brigand, and cried, —

"Caverley! I had guessed as much!"

"He is a venomous beast and ought to be crushed here and now," said the constable.

"I'll take charge of that," answered Musaron, about to cut Caverley's throat with his hunting-knife.

"Mercy!" murmured the robber, "mercy! do not abuse your victory."

"Yes," said the prince, embracing Du Guesclin, in a transport of joy, "yes, mercy! We have too many reasons for thanking God who has brought us together to trouble ourselves about this wretch. Let him live, and go and get hanged elsewhere."

Caverley, in an outburst of gratitude, kissed the feet of the generous prince.

"Let him be off, then," said Du Guesclin.

"Begone, bandit!" growled Musaron, opening the door.

Caverley did not wait for a second order; he ran so swiftly that horses would not have come up with him, if the prince had changed his mind.

After mutual congratulations, the prince, the constable, and Agénor discussed the coming war.

"You see," said the constable, "that I keep my appointments punctually. I was going to Toledo in obedience to your orders at Bordeaux. Have you hopes of Toledo, then?"

"I am very hopeful," answered the prince, "if Toledo opens her gates to me."

"But that is not certain," rejoined the constable. "Since I have been travelling in this habit, that is, since four days, I have learned more than I did in the previous two years. These Toledans are for Don Pedro. We shall have to besiege them."

"Dear constable, to expose yourself to so many dangers for my sake!"

"Dear sire, I have only one word. I have promised that you should reign in Castile, and in Castile you shall reign or I shall die there. And so I had no sooner gained my liberty at Bordeaux, through your presence of mind, than in ten days I saw King Charles and gained the frontier. I have been running through Spain during eight days in search of you; for Olivier, my brother, and Le Bègue de Vilaine had been warned that you had just passed through Burgos on your way to Toledo."

"It is true I passed through it; I expect to meet the great officers of my army before Toledo. I did not disguise myself until I came to Burgos."

"And they did the same, monseigneur, and it was from them I took the hint of doing so also. In this disguise, the leaders pass unnoticed, and are able to prepare lodgings for the army. The pilgrim garb is in fashion, and to-day every one wishes to make a pilgrimage in Spain, so that even that rascal Caverley assumed the habit as well as we. Well, now we are all together. You will select a residence and summon all Spaniards of your party to rally round you, and I shall do the same for the knights and soldiers of other countries; let us lose no time. Don Pedro is still wavering; he has just lost his best adviser, Doña Maria, the only creature in the world that loved him. Let us profit by his lethargy, and force a battle before he has had time to recover his senses."

"Doña Maria is dead!" said Henry; "is it certain?"

"I am certain of it," said Agénor, sadly; "I saw her body pass by."

"And Don Pedro, what is he doing?"

"Nobody can tell. He has had his unhappy victim interred at Burgos; then he disappeared."

"Disappeared! is it possible? But you say Doña Maria is his victim. Tell me all about it, constable. I have not dared to speak to a living soul for the last week."

"This is what happened," said the constable, "as I have learned from my spies: Don Pedro loved a Morisca, the daughter of that accursed Mothril. Doña Maria suspected as much; she even discovered there was an understanding between this Morisca and the king; stung to madness, she took poison, after stabbing her rival to the heart."

"Oh," cried Agénor, "oh, that is not possible, messeigneurs! It would have been a crime so odious, a treason so black that the sun would have recoiled in horror."

The king and the constable looked with astonishment upon the young man who expressed himself in this fashion. But they could not draw from him any explanation.

"Pardon me, messeigneurs," said Agénor, humbly. "I have a young man's secret, a secret at once sweet and bitter, half of which Doña Maria carries with her into the tomb, the other half I wish to guard as a religious possession."

"In love, poor boy!" said the constable.

Agénor's only answer was, —

"I am at your orders, messeigneurs, and ready to die in your service."

"I know," said Henry, "that you are a man of unselfish devotion, a loyal, gifted, and indefatigable servant, and so you may count on my gratitude; but, tell us, do you know anything about the loves of Don Pedro?"

"I know everything, sire, and if you command me to speak — "

"Where is Don Pedro at present? that is all we wish to know."

"Messeigneurs," said Agénor, "be pleased to grant me a week, and I will answer with certainty."

"A week?" said the king. "What do you think of it, constable?"

"I think, sire," replied Bertrand, "that a week is absolutely required to organize our army and wait for money and re-enforcements from France. We, therefore, really risk nothing — "

"So much the better, seigneur," added Mauléon, "since, if my plan succeed, you will have in your power the true cause, the actual firebrand of the war, Don Pedro, whom I will deliver up to you with much joy."

"He is right," said the king; "with the capture of either of us the Spanish war is ended."

"Oh, no, sire!" cried the constable. "I swear solemnly that were you made prisoner, which, with God's help, is not likely to happen, I should, though you were cut in pieces, continue to track and punish that miscreant Don Pedro, who would kill his prisoners in cold blood, and who is the ally of infidels."

"And that feeling is mine also, Bertrand," rejoined the prince; "do not trouble yourself about me. But, if I am taken and slain, recover my body by a victory, and place my lifeless remains upon the throne of Castile; provided that bastard, assassin, and traitor lie dead at the foot of that throne, I proclaim myself fortunate and triumphant."

"Sire, no more need be said," added the constable; "and now let us give this young man his liberty."

"And an order to meet you at Toledo," said Mauléon, "which we shall invest, shall we not?"

"In a week."

"In a week."

Henry tenderly embraced the young man, who was quite confused by the honor.

"Be of good cheer," said the king. "I wish to show you that as you have shared in my adversity you shall also have a right to share in my prosperity."

"And I," added the constable, "I who partly owe you my liberty, promise to aid you with all my power, on whatever day you demand my help, no matter where, or for what, or against whom that help may be needed."

"Oh, messeigneurs, messeigneurs!" cried Mauléon, "you overwhelm me with joy and pride. Two such puissant princes to treat me thus! But for me you represent God himself upon this earth, you open to me heaven."

"You are worthy of it, Mauléon," said the constable; "do you require money?"

"No, seigneur, no."

"The plan you are meditating, however, will cost a good deal; you may, who knows, have to bestow gifts."

"Seigneurs," answered Mauléon, "you remember that I captured one day the money-box of that brigand Caverley; it contained a king's fortune. It was too much; I lost it without regret. Afterwards, I received a hundred livres from the king in France; it is a treasure quite as large, since it is all that I need."

"How well he speaks!" murmured Musaron from his corner, with tears in his eyes.

The king heard him.

"Is that your squire?" said he.

"A faithful and brave servant," replied Mauléon, "who has saved my life more than once and now renders it endurable."

"He shall also be rewarded. Come here, squire," said the king, unfastening one of the shells on his robe; "take this, and, on whatever day you or your descendants, no matter to what generation they belong, are in want of anything, place this shell in my hand or in that of any of my successors and it will be worth a fortune. Go, good squire, go."

Musaron knelt, his heart swelling as if it would burst through his bosom.

"Now, sire," said the constable, "let us profit by the night to reach the place where your officers await you. We have done wrong in letting this Caverley escape; he is capable of returning with triple numbers and taking us once for all, if it were only to prove to us that he is anything but a fool."

"To horse, then," said the king.

They armed, and, trusting to their courage and their fortunes, they gained a wood where it would be hard to attack them and impossible to pursue them.

Then Agénor dismounted and took leave of his two

powerful protectors, who wished him good luck and a pleasant journey.

Musaron waited for orders, so that he might know to which one of the cardinal points he was to direct the horses.

"Where are we going?" said he.

"To Montiel. My hatred tells me that, sooner or later, we shall find Don Pedro there."

"Yes," said Musaron, "there is some good in jealousy; it shows us more things than really exist. Let us go to Montiel."

XXXVII.

THE CAVERN OF MONTIEL.

AND they pushed on rapidly. In two days Agénor reached the goal of his ambition and of his love.

Aided by Musaron, he had taken so many precautions during the journey to Montiel that no one in the country could boast of having seen them.

Only, on the other hand, their precautions were of such a very strict character that they lost the chance of gaining any information. Whoso speaketh not cannot learn.

When Musaron beheld Montiel, seated like a giant of granite on its rocky base and lifting its head even to the heavens, while its feet seemed plunged into the waters of the Tagus; when he contemplated by the light of the moon the winding spirals of a road thickset with brushwood, and the flights of steps cut at such an acute angle that the traveller going up them could not see more than twenty paces before him, while, from above, the most diminutive sentinel could see everything that mounted, Musaron said to his master, —

"It is a regular vulture's nest, my dear master, and, if your dove is shut up therein, we can never get at her."

In fact, Montiel was impregnable, except by famine and two men are hardly capable of investing a fortress.

"The important things to learn," said Agénor, "are whether Mothril is living in this den with Aïssa, the condition of Aïssa in the midst of our enemies, and, in a word, the conduct of Don Pedro throughout the whole business."

"We shall learn all this, if we have patience," rejoined Musaron; "only we have but four days to have patience; reflect on that, seigneur."

"I shall stay here until I see Aïssa or meet some one who can speak of her."

"So it is a hunt we have to engage in; but turn this over in your mind, my master: while we are hunting about this castle, a Mothril or a Hafiz can let fly an arrow at us that will nail us like toads on a stone. Oh, yes, an admirable position! I congratulate you on your wisdom."

"You are right."

"Then we must use means more ingenious than ordinary means are. As to believing that Doña Aïssa is in that den, I do believe it; knowing Mothril, I would even have my doubts, if he had not shut her up there. As to knowing whether Don Pedro is there also, I think, if we wait two days, we shall know."

"Why?"

"Because the castle is small, cannot hold much provisions, cannot have a garrison, and, to renew the larder of so great a king, his people must go out often."

"But where are we to lodge?"

"We need not go far. I can see the very thing we want from here."

"Yon cavern?"

"Is a cleft in the rock; a spring gushes forth from it; it is damp, but it is retired. No one comes there except to drink or draw water. We shall be safely hidden inside, and we can snap up the first one who comes, and either force or bribe him to speak. Meanwhile, we shall be living in the open air."

"You are a brave and judicious companion, my Musaron."

"Oh! you may be quite sure Don Pedro has not many counsellors of quite my size. Do you accept the cavern?"

"You forget two things: our food, which we are not likely to find in that opening, and our horses, which cannot enter."

"It is true, — one man can't think of everything. I have found the beginning, do you find the end."

"We shall kill our horses and fling them into the Tagus, which runs below."

"Yes, but what shall we eat?"

"We can watch whoever comes out for provisions, and, when he is returning, we can fall upon him, and so have something to eat."

"Admirable," retorted Musaron; "only you forget that when the people in the castle do not see their caterer return, they will become suspicious."

"What matter, if we get the information we need."

It was decided that both plans should be followed. Nevertheless, at the very moment Agénor was about to knock his horse down with his battle-mace, his heart failed him.

"Poor beast," said he, "you have served me well!"

"And he would serve you still better," added Musaron, "in case you had to carry Doña Aïssa off from here."

"You speak like fate. I shall not slay my poor horse, you may stake your life on it, Musaron. Unbridle him, hide the harness and the other trappings in the grotto. The animal can wander around without being recognized and can feed himself well, being in this respect more industrious than a man. If he is seen, the worst that can happen to him, and to us. also, is to be taken to the castle, and we can always be near enough to defend him, can we not ? "

" Yes, monsieur."

Musaron untied the horse, took off the harness and hid it at the back of the cavern, the soil of which was of solid loam. Musaron, to secure a more healthful condition of things, heaped sand on the floor, which he had collected in his mantle on the banks of the Tagus, and strewed this with heather.

The close of the night was spent in these labors. Daylight surprised our two adventurers at the back of their solitary asylum.

A singular phenomenon struck their ears.

The voices of people walking upon the terrace came down to them along the sort of spiral staircase that led from the foot of the hill to the castle.

The sound of these voices, instead of simply ascending, as usually happens, reverberated in turning along the sides of this funnel; then it sprang up anew, like a stick from the heart of a whirlpool.

The result was that Agénor, in the depths of the cavern, could distinguish voices three hundred feet over his head.

The first fortification was situated above the cistern; every one could approach it easily, but the country was so deserted and wasted that, except the people of the castle, none ventured into this labyrinth.

Agénor and Musaron spent the first half of the day very sadly. They drank water, for they were very thirsty, but they could not eat, although they were very hungry.

Towards the end of the day, two Moors came down from the castle. They were leading an ass which was to carry the provisions they intended purchasing in the next market-town, about a league distant.

At the same time, four slaves arrived from the market-town with jars they were going to fill at the fountain.

The two Moors of the castle entered into conversation with the slaves. But the dialect was so barbarous that our adventurers could not make out a single word.

The Moors left for the market-town with the slaves, and returned two hours after.

Hunger is a bad adviser. Musaron wished to slay these poor devils mercilessly, throw them into the river, and seize the provisions.

"It would be a foul assassination and would injure with God the success of our plan," said Agénor. "What if we were to try a stratagem, Musaron? You see the road is narrow and the night is dark. The ass with its baskets will have much difficulty in making its way through the path along the rock. We have only to give it a push when passing; it will roll down to the bottom of the hill. Then, during the night, we can pick up whatever provisions we find on the ground."

"What you say is right, and worthy of a charitable Christian, monsieur," answered Musaron; "but I was so hungry that I no longer felt any pity."

No sooner said than done. The four hands of the two adventurers gave a rough push to the little ass when it passed, grazing the rock; it lost its footing and fell upon the steep declivity.

The Moors uttered cries of rage and beat the poor animal; but all their efforts could not fill the empty baskets again. One of them returned to the market-town with the bruised ass, and the other went back to the castle, and both were loud in their lamentations.

However, our two hungry travellers ran bravely

among the rocks and briers, picking up here and there the bread, the raisins, and the skins of wine.

At one stroke they had got enough provisions to last them a week.

After a bountiful repast, they were all afire with hope and courage.

And, not to mince matters, they had need of both.

In fact, for the next two mortal days, they perceived nothing, heard nothing save the voice of Hafiz, who wandered on the terrace and deplored his servitude, the voice of Mothril who gave orders, and the exercises of the soldiers. No evidence that the king was at Montiel.

Musaron had the courage to sally out at night to the neighboring market-town in quest of news; nothing to be learned there.

Agénor also made inquiries; he had his labor for his pains.

When a man begins to despair, time creeps along with ever increasing slowness.

The position of our two spies was critical: in daytime they dared not show themselves; at night they feared to go out, for somebody might enter during their absence, and that somebody might be the king.

But when two days and a half were gone, Agénor was the first to lose courage.

On the night of this second day, Mauléon had gone to the village and returned with an empty purse, but with no news.

He found Musaron in the cavern, in a state of utter despair and tearing out his hair by fistfuls, and his supply of hair was limited.

On questioning the honest servitor, he learned from him that, tired out with his lonely watch in the grotto, he had fallen asleep; that, during his sleep, something like a horseman had ridden up to the castle and Musaron had not seen him. He had only heard the steps of a horse or mule.

"We are fated to be unfortunate!" cried the squire.

"Don't take it to heart; it cannot have been the king. The people of the market-town know that he is at Toledo; besides, he would not ride alone, and the noise made by his suite would have awakened you. No, it was not the king; he will not come to Monteil. Instead of losing our time here, let us start for Toledo."

"You are right, my master; all we can hope for in these quarters is to hear the voice of Doña Aïssa. A sweet voice it is, but the song of the bird is not the bird, as we say in Béarn."

"To work at once, then, Musaron! Pick up the harness, and let us be off immediately."

"The job won't take me long, sir knight; you could never believe how I have been bored in this cavern."

"Up!" said Agénor.

At the same moment, just as he was rising, —

"Hush!" whispered Musaron.

"What is the matter?"

"Silence, I tell you! I hear footsteps."

Agénor entered the grotto again, and Musaron was so disturbed that he ventured to pull his master in by the wrist.

It was no false alarm; hurried steps could be distinguished on the road leading to the castle.

The night was dark; the two Frenchmen hid themselves at the back of the cavern.

Soon three men came into view: they were walking cautiously, and each had his head covered with branches of the madroño,[1] so as not to be seen from the citadel.

[1] The wild strawberry plant.

When they reached the fountain, they stopped.

They were garbed like peasants, but each had a battle-axe and a knife.

"Certainly," said one of them, "this is the road he followed; here are the shoe-prints of his horse on the sand."

"Then we have missed him," said another. "By the devil! we have been having a nice run of ill-luck for some time."

"The game you hunt is too big," added the first.

"Lesby, you reason like a clown; the captain will say the same."

"But —"

"Hold your tongue! Kill big game and it will feed the hunter for a fortnight. Ten larks or a hare make but one meal, and that a poor one."

"Yes, but you catch your hare or lark; you don't catch your boar or stag often."

"That was a pretty miss of ours, the other day, was it not, captain?"

He who was thus designated heaved a big sigh. It was his only answer.

"And then," continued the stubborn Lesby, "why change the scent and the prey every moment? Stick to one and you take it."

"Did you take the one we followed the other night from Bordeaux at the venta?"

"Whew!" whispered Musaron, in his master's ear.

"'Sh!" answered Mauléon, with his ear to the ground.

The man called captain by his companions then drew himself up, and, in an imperious voice, —

"Both of you hold your tongues," said he; "do not criticise my orders. What have I promised you? Ten thousand florins to each. If you get them, what do you ask more?"

"Nothing, captain, nothing."

"Henry of Trastamare is worth a hundred thousand florins to Don Pedro; Don Pedro is worth a hundred thousand florins to Henry of Trastamare. I thought I could take the one; I have been mistaken. I have very nearly left my skin in the lion's den, as you saw. Well, as the lion saved my life, in common gratitude I ought to take his enemy, — and I shall. It is true I do not intend giving him up to Henry of Trastamare for nothing, I 'll sell him; it is all the same to him, provided he has him. In this fashion, we shall all be content."

A growl of satisfaction was the answer of the rascal's two followers.

"Why, God pardon me, if it is not Caverley I have there at the end of my hand!" said Musaron, in the ear of his master.

"'Sh!" repeated Mauléon.

Caverley, for it was really he, ended his profession of faith as follows: —

"Don Pedro has left Toledo, he is in this castle. He is very brave and has taken the journey alone, as a measure of precaution. In fact, a single man is never noticed."

"No," said Lesby, "but he is taken."

"Ah! one cannot foresee everything," answered Caverley. "And now to come to the end of our plan: you, Philips, will hold the horses; you, Becker, will stay here with me. The king will not leave the castle later than to-morrow, because he is, as we know, expected at Toledo."

"And then?" said Becker.

"We'll keep a watch on him as he passes. But we must be on our guard against one thing."

"Against what?"

"He may have given orders for horsemen from Toledo to come and meet him; we ought, therefore, to arrange matters where we stand. To work, then: Lesby, you are a keen fox hunter; find us a good hole among these rocks where we may burrow."

"Captain, I hear the sound of water close by; it is some spring or other. Generally, springs hollow out for themselves a bed in the rock; there must be a grotto near."

"Goodness gracious, we are lost! they are coming here," said Musaron, while Agénor applied his hand as a gag to his lips.

"Stay," cried Lesby, "yonder is the grotto."

"All right," said Caverley. "Leave us, Lesby; go and join Philips, and let the horses be near here at daybreak."

Lesby withdrew; Caverley and Becker remained alone.

"See what it is to have brains," said the bandit to his companion. "I look like a land-pirate, and I am the only statesman who comprehends the situation. Two men quarrel about a throne; suppress one, and the war is over. Moreover, in doing what I am doing, I am acting like a Christian, like a philosopher; I am sparing the blood of men. I am virtuous, Becker, I am virtuous!"

And the bandit began laughing, at the same time trying to moderate his voice.

"And now," said he, at last, "let us enter this hole; but be on the watch, Becker, be on the watch!"

XXXVIII.

HOW CAVERLEY LOST HIS PURSE AND AGÉNOR HIS SWORD.

THIS was the nature of the grotto: —

First, the spring, a crystal stream falling from a stony vault upon pebbles among which it had hollowed out a bed.

Then, in the depression behind it, a winding grotto, reached by two natural steps.

This cavern was dark during the day, and the man who could have guessed its existence at night must indeed have had something of the fox in him.

Caverley avoided the perpendicular fall of the spring by groping along the natural steps.

Becker, more ingenious, or fonder of comfort, advanced towards the back in pursuit of more shelter and warmth.

Agénor and Musaron heard them, could almost see and touch them.

Becker settled down at last, and invited Caverley to imitate him, saying, —

"Come, captain, there's room for two."

Caverley allowed himself to be persuaded, and entered.

But, as he found his progress rather difficult, he repeated, in a tone of ill-humor, —

"Room for two, indeed! it's easy talking!"

And he stretched out his hands to avoid knocking against the stone vault or the sides of the rock.

But, unfortunately, he encountered the leg of Musaron, and seized it, shouting to Becker, —

"Becker, a corpse!"

"No, *pardieu!*" cried the valiant Musaron, taking him by the throat, "it is a very live man, and he's going to strangle you, my hero."

Caverley was too upset and nonplussed to add another word. Musaron held his wrists and tied them with the girth of one of his horses.

Agénor had only to reach out his hand and do the same for Becker, who was half dead from superstitious terror.

"Now, my dear captain," said Musaron, "we shall talk of ransom. Give your closest attention to the fact that we are a numerous body, and that the least gesture or cry on your part would be echoed by a multitude of dagger-thrusts in your ribs."

"I won't budge, I'll say nothing," murmured Caverley; "but spare me."

"It behooves us first to take our precautions," said Musaron, stripping Caverley of his arms, offensive and defensive, piece by piece, with the dexterity of a monkey peeling a nut.

Then, this work finished, he did the same for Becker.

The arms removed, Musaron passed to the purses. His fingers alone imparted some delicacy to this operation. His conscience did not impart the least scruple to it. Plethoric purses and well-lined girdles passed into the power of Musaron.

"What! you a plunderer, you also?" said Agénor to him.

"Messire, I am simply taking away from them the means of doing harm."

The first moment of terror over, Caverley demanded permission to make a few observations.

"You may do so," said Agénor, "if you speak in a low voice."

"Who are you?" said Caverley.

"Ah! that is a question, my dear," replied Musaron, "we do not intend answering."

"You heard all my conversation with my men?"

"We did not lose a single word."

"The devil! You know my plan, then?'

"As well as you do yourself."

"Hum! What are you going to do with me and my companion Becker?"

"The answer is easy. We are in the service of Don Pedro; we shall deliver you to Don Pedro, and, at the same time, inform him of your kind intentions in his regard."

"That's not charity," answered Caverley, who must have turned pale in the darkness. "Don Pedro is cruel: he will make me suffer a thousand tortures. Kill me at once with a good stab in the heart."

"We do not assassinate," answered Mauléon.

"Yes, but Don Pedro will assassinate me."

And the long silence of his conquerors taught Caverley that he had persuaded them, since they found nothing to reply.

Agénor was reflecting.

The unexpected presence of Caverley had also revealed to him the presence of Don Pedro at Montiel. This man had been the hound of unerring scent that tracks the prey of its master. The service done to Mauléon appeared to him great enough to urge him to clemency. Moreover, his enemy was disarmed, stripped, and powerless to do him harm.

On the other hand, the very same thoughts occurred to Musaron. He was so accustomed to the ideas of his master that their conceptions had got to run simultaneously in the same groove.

But Caverley had turned this silence to account, like the clever and artful fellow that he was. He had reflected that, ever since the beginning of the conversation he had with his unknown conquerors, only two voices had spoken; while groping and turning round he had become convinced that the grotto was too small and narrow to hold more than four men.

Except in arms, then, the balance was even.

To get back his arms he must use his hands, and his hands were tied.

That darksome providence which protects scoundrels, and which is nothing else but the weakness of honest folk, came to the aid of Caverley.

"This Caverley," Agénor had said to himself, "is going to be a terrible embarrassment. In my place, he would get rid of it with a stroke of his dagger, and would fling my body into the Tagus. But these are methods I do not wish to employ. He will be an embarrassment, I say, when I want to leave here; and I want to leave here as soon as I have reliable tidings of Aïssa and Don Pedro."

No sooner was this observation made than Mauléon, who was prompt to act, seized Caverley by the arm and began untying him, saying, —

"Master Caverley, you have, without knowing it, rendered me a service. Yes, Don Pedro would kill you, and I would not have you die thus, when there are so many good gibbets in England and France."

And, at each word, the imprudent boy loosened a knot.

"So," continued Mauléon, "I give you your liberty; profit by it to make your escape, and try to amend your life."

And he made an end of his work by untying the strap.

Scarcely had Caverley his arms free, when, leaping upon Agénor, he tried to wrest his sword from him, saying, —

"Along with my liberty, give me back my purse!"

Already he held the blade and was inserting a hand in the hilt to strike, when Mauléon dealt him a blow with his fist that sent him rolling in the pool of water beyond the steps of the grotto.

Caverley, like the fish that, escaping from the basket of the fisherman, feels anew the ambient element wherein for it is life, sucked in the air voluptuously, bounded outside the cavern, and took to his heels along the road leading to the market-town.

"By Saint James! my master," said Musaron, furiously, "you have just done something to be proud of, you have. Let me run after him and catch him."

"Eh, why should you," said Agénor, "since I have given him leave to beat a retreat?"

"Madness! the very height of madness! the knave is sure to play us some trick or other; he will return, he will speak — "

"Hold your tongue, you donkey!" said Agénor, shoving Musaron with his elbow, so that his squire might not, in his frenzy, let out anything before Becker; "if he returns, we shall hand him over to Don Pedro, whom we must inform of the affair this very night."

"That's different," grumbled Musaron, who understood his master's artfulness.

"Come, my friend, untie the arms of honest Master Becker, and be sure you tell him that if Caverley, Philips, Lesby, and Becker, those four illustrious knights, are in this neighborhood to-morrow, they will be hanged from the battlements of Montiel; for they maintain order in stricter fashion on this side the border than in France."

"Oh! I will not forget it, señor," said Becker, intoxicated with joy and gratitude.

He never dreamt of taking up arms against his benefactors. He kissed their hands and disappeared, light as a bird.

"Ah! my master," sighed Musaron, "what a lot of adventures!"

"Why, sir squire," said Agénor, "what a number of lessons you'll have to take before you are fully proficient! What! don't you see that this Caverley has unearthed Don Pedro for us; that, as he does not know who we are, he believes us to be the protectors of Don Pedro, and that, consequently, he will leave the country the quicker? And then, what more do you want? you have money and arms!"

"Messire, I am wrong."

"Not much doubt about that."

"But let us watch, messire, let us watch! The devil and Caverley are very sly!"

"A hundred men would be no match for us in this grotto!" answered Mauléon; "we can sleep alternately, and so wait for tidings of my dear mistress, since Heaven has already given us tidings of Don Pedro."

"Messire, I despair of nothing now, and, if some one said to me, 'The Señora Aïssa is about to come down and visit you in this lair of serpents,' I would believe it and say, 'Thank you for your news, my good man.'"

At this moment a faint sound, distant but timed and measured, smote the trained ear of Musaron.

"By my faith," said he, "you were right! that is Caverley galloping. Stay, I swear I hear four horses. He has come up with his Englishmen, and all are flying from the gibbet you threatened him with, unless they are coming back here. But no, the noise grows weaker, it dies away. Good luck to you on your journey till we meet again, you devil's own captain!"

"Musaron! Musaron!" suddenly cried Agénor, "I haven't my sword."

"The rascal stole it from you," said Musaron; "it was a pity, it was so fine a blade!"

"And my name engraved on the hilt! Ah, Musaron, the brigand is sure to learn all about me!"

"Not before night, seigneur, and then, you may trust me, he will be very far. That damned Caverley! he must always steal something."

The next morning, at daybreak, they heard two men descending from the castle and talking eagerly. They were Mothril and Don Pedro. The latter was leading his horse by the bridle.

At this sight, every drop of blood in Agénor's veins boiled.

He was about to rush upon his two enemies, poniard them and end the struggle, but Musaron stopped him.

"Are you mad, seigneur?" said he. "What! you would kill Mothril without having Aïssa? And how do you know but that, just as at Navaretta, those who guard Aïssa have received orders to slay her, if Mothril died or you made him prisoner?"

Agénor shuddered.

"Oh, you love me truly!" he said; "yes, you love me!"

"I should say so, *pardieu!* Do you fancy I should take no pleasure in killing that ruffianly Moor who has done so much evil? Yes, I will kill him, but in due time; and may the opportunity be a good one!"

They saw these two objects of their legitimate hatred pass within reach of their hands; they were almost brushed by them, and yet they did not dare to rid the world of the wretches.

"Fortune is making sport of us!" cried Agénor.

"You do well to complain," retorted Musaron; "you who, but for Caverley, would have set out yesterday without knowing where Don Pedro was, and without any news of Aïssa. But hush! listen."

"Thanks," said Don Pedro to his minister. "I believe she will get better and that she will love me."

"Have no doubt of it, seigneur. She will get better because Hafiz and I are going to gather, according to the prescribed rite, the herbs you know of. Then she will love you, because there is no longer anything in your court to offend her. But let us speak of serious matters. Find out if these tidings are certain. Ten thousand of my countrymen should by this time have debarked at Lisbon and sailed up the Tagus as far as Toledo. Go to Toledo where you are loved. Encourage those faithful defenders. On the day that Henry is in Spain, you will take him and his army at one stroke between the city he will besiege and the army of your Saracen allies, at whose head I shall place myself as soon as they come in sight of Toledo. There, your success will be sure and safe and thorough."

"Mothril, you are an able minister; whatever happen, you have been devoted to me."

"What ugly faces the Moor must make to seem gracious!" said Musaron in the ear of Agénor.

"Before I leave you to return to the castle," said Mothril, "this last counsel. Refuse to settle the money question with the Prince of Wales until he has taken your side. The English are noted for their treachery."

"Yes, and, besides, I have no money."

"An additional reason. Adieu, seigneur, you are henceforth victorious and happy."

"Adieu, Mothril."

"Adieu, seigneur."

The two adventurers had again to undergo the torture of witnessing the slow ascent of Mothril who, with an infernal smile on his lips, was returning to the castle, admission to which was so ardently longed for by Agénor.

"Let us seize him," said the young man, "and go up along with him; then we can tell him that if he does not give up Aïssa we shall kill him; he will give her up."

"Yes; and on the road down he will crush us under masses of rock. Much better off we shall be then! Patience, I tell you, God is good!"

"Well, though you refuse to have anything to do with Mothril, you will not, at least, refuse the opportunity that offers in the case of Don Pedro. He is alone, we are two. Let us take him, and, if he resist, kill him; if he does not resist, let us bring him to Henry of Trastamare, to prove that we have found him."

"An excellent idea! I adopt it," cried Musaron. "I follow you."

They waited till Mothril had reached the terrace of the castle; then they ventured to leave their hole.

But, when they turned their eyes on the plain, they saw Don Pedro at the head of a band of at least forty men-at-arms. He continued peaceably his journey to Toledo.

"Ah, *pardieu!* we were very stupid, — pardon me, seigneur, very credulous, I mean," said Musaron. "Mothril was not likely to let the king start alone: guards have come from the market-town to meet him."

"Told to do so by whom?"

"Oh, by the Moors yesterday evening, or by a signal from the castle."

"You are right; let us think of nothing now but either of seeing Aïssa or returning to Don Henry!"

XXXIX.

HAFIZ.

THE hoped-for opportunity did not come for an entire day.

No one left the castle save the caterers.

A messenger arrived, but the horn of the castellan had signalled his approach. Our adventurers did not deem it prudent to stop him.

Towards evening,—when all nature grows still, when the sounds that ascend from the river to the mountain are themselves hushed and muffled, when the sky turns pale at the horizon, and even the rocks appear less cool,— our two friends heard an animated conversation between two old acquaintances of theirs.

Mothril and Hafiz were quarrelling, as they descended from the terrace of the castle to the path that ended at the gates.

"Master," said Hafiz, "you had me confined when the king was here, yet you promised to present me to him; you promised me much money also. It is tiresome being with this young girl you force me to watch. I wish to make war along with our countrymen who are returning from the country, and, at this moment, sailing up the Tagus on vessels with white sails. Therefore, you must pay me at once, so that I may go away to the king."

"You would leave me, my son; have I been a bad master?"

"No; but I no longer care to have any master."

"I wish to keep you," said Mothril, "for I love you."

"But I do not love you. You have made me do evil deeds that haunt my sleep with frightful dreams. I am too young to go on living thus. Pay me and give me my freedom, or I shall find some one to whom I will tell everything."

"Then you are right," answered Mothril. "Come up to the castle, and I will pay you immediately."

When they were descending, Hafiz was in the rear and Mothril in front. The road was so narrow that, in returning, Hafiz had to be in front and Mothril in the rear.

The screech-owl began to hoot in the hollow of the rocks. The violet-hued tints on the walls of stone had shaded into purple.

Suddenly, an awful cry, a hideous blasphemy, rent the air, and a something heavy, flabby, bloody, fell flattened in front of the cavern where our two friends were listening attentively.

They answered that dismal shriek with a cry of dismay.

The birds of night flew away in alarm from the bosom of their rocky nests, and the very insects fled, scared from their holes.

Soon a pool of blood reached the waters of the cistern, which it reddened.

Agénor, pale and trembling, projected his face outside of his hiding-place, and Musaron came and placed his livid face beside his.

"Hafiz!" cried they both, on seeing the motionless and mangled body of the companion of Gildaz at three paces from where they stood.

"Poor child!" murmured Musaron, running out to afford him succor, if there was still time for it.

But the shadow of death was already moving across that bronzed face; the dilated eyes were growing dim, and a heavy breathing, accompanied by a stream of blood, escaped with difficulty from the crushed breast of the Moor.

He recognized Musaron; he recognized Agénor, and his features expressed a superstitious terror.

The wretch believed that in them he saw their avenging shades.

Musaron raised his head; Agénor brought fresh water and bathed his forehead and his wounds.

"The Frenchman! the Frenchman!" said Hafiz, drinking greedily. "Allah! pardon me!"

"Come with us, my poor boy," said Agénor; "we will cure you."

"No, I am dead; dead like Gildaz," murmured the Saracen. "I meet the death I have merited,— assassination. Mothril hurled me down from the top of the steps at the castle."

A gesture expressive of horror that escaped Mauléon was noticed by the dying Moor.

"Frenchman," said he, "I have hated you; but I do not hate you to-day, for you can avenge me. Doña Aïssa still loves you. Doña Maria also protected you. It was Mothril who poisoned Maria; it was he who took advantage of Aïssa when she swooned, and struck her with his poniard. Tell this to Don Pedro, tell it to him very quick, but save Aïssa if you love her; for, in a fortnight, when Don Pedro returns to the castle, Mothril is to deliver Aïssa, sent to sleep by a magic potion, to Don Pedro. I have done you evil, but I am doing you good now. Pardon and avenge me. Allah!"

He fell back exhausted, turned his eyes with a painful effort towards the castle to curse it, and expired.

For more than a quarter of an hour, the two friends could not collect their ideas and recover their coolness.

This hideous death, this revelation, the menacing aspect of the future,—all had stricken them with unutterable dismay.

Agénor was the first to rise. "From now until a fortnight," he said, "we are safe. In a fortnight, Don Pedro, Mothril, or I shall be dead. Come, Musaron; now for the camp of Don Henry to render him an account of the mission I undertook. But we must make haste; go search for our horses in the plain."

And, in fact, Musaron, though he was hardly able to stand, did find the horses, which, moreover, came at his call.

He harnessed and equipped them; then, jumping lightly into the saddle, he took the road to Toledo, whither his master had already preceded him.

When they were in the plain, and that baleful castle projected its black profile upon the bluish-gray of the heavens,—

"Mothril!" cried Agénor, in a loud, resonant voice, shaking his fist at the windows of the castle, "Mothril, till our next meeting! Aïssa, my love, I'll see you soon!"

XL.

THE PREPARATIONS.

POWDER does not flame up with more rapidity than did the revolt in the states of Don Pedro.

Having no fear of an invasion by the neighboring kingdoms, the inhabitants of Castile, for the most part, declared themselves in favor of Henry, as soon as a manifesto from him informed Spain that he had returned with an army, and that this army was commanded by the constable Bertrand Du Guesclin.

In a few days, the roads were covered with soldiers of fortune, monks of every order, and Bretons, all on the way to Toledo.

But Toledo, faithful to Don Pedro, as Bertrand had predicted, closed its gates, armed its walls, and awaited the issue.

Henry lost no time. He invested the city and began a siege in due form. These hostilities served him marvellously, for it gave his allies time to range themselves under his banners.

On the other hand, Don Pedro was unflagging in his efforts. He sent courier after courier to his old friends, the kings of Granada, Portugal, Aragon, and Navarre.

He negotiated with the Prince of Wales, who lay sick at Bordeaux, and seemed to have lost a little of his warlike energy. He was calmly awaiting that cruel death which was to bear him away from a glorious future, while still young.

The Saracens, announced by Mothril, had landed at Lisbon. After resting for some days, they sailed up the Tagus, in vessels furnished by the King of Portugal, preceded by three thousand horse sent to Don Pedro by the same monarch.

Henry had for him the cities of Galicia and Leon and a homogeneous army, of which five thousand Bretons, commanded by Olivier Du Guesclin, formed the mighty nucleus.

The prince was now only waiting for trustworthy news from Mauléon, when the latter entered the camp with his squire, and recounted all he had done and seen.

The king and Bertrand listened in profound silence.

"What!" said the constable, "Mothril did not leave with Don Pedro?"

"He will remain until the Saracens arrive, then he will put himself at their head."

"The first thing we must do is to send a hundred men and capture him in Montiel," said Bertrand. "Agénor will command the expedition, and, as I do not suppose he has any very strong reasons for loving Mothril, he will order a lofty gibbet to be erected on the banks of the Tagus and hang up the Saracen, the assassin, the traitor —"

"Seigneur, seigneur," pleaded Agénor, "you have been good enough to promise me your friendship, to promise me your support. Do not refuse me to-day. Grant me the favor of permitting the Saracen Mothril to live calm and undisturbed in his castle of Montiel."

"Why? it is a nest that ought to be destroyed."

"Seigneur constable, it is a lair with which I am well acquainted and which can be useful to you, as the future will prove. You know that those who want to drive out a fox pretend not to notice its hole and pass by without looking at it; otherwise the animal departs and never returns."

"What follows, knight?"

"Seigneurs, let Mothril and Don Pedro believe they are unspied and inviolable in the castle of Montiel; who knows but we shall take them there later on, with a single casting of the net?"

"Agénor," said the king, "is that your only reason?"

"No, sire, — and I have never lied, — no, that is not my sole reason. My real reason is that this castle holds within it a friend, and that friend Mothril will slay, if he is too closely pressed."

"You have your wish," cried Bertrand, "and never believe that we are likely to refuse anything you may desire."

After this conversation, which reassured Mauléon as to the fate of Aïssa, the leaders of the army pressed on the siege of Toledo vigorously. The inhabitants defended themselves so bravely that the city became the centre of many feats of arms, and several renowned and experienced besiegers were killed or wounded in skirmishes and sorties.

But these inconclusive combats were but the preludes to a general action, as the lightning flash and the clashing clouds are the preludes of the storm.

XLI.

STARVING TOLEDO.

Don Pedro had just regulated all his affairs with his subjects and allies in Toledo, a well-defended city with numerous resources.

The Toledans had wavered between party and party during this interminable series of civil wars; now was the time to strike a blow that would bind them forever to the cause of the conqueror of Navaretta.

In doing so, Don Pedro displayed his shrewdest ingenuity. He convinced the Toledans that, if they did not support their prince this time, and, if he conquered in the next battle, as he had done in the last, it was all over with Toledo forever; Don Pedro would never pardon.

This crafty man knew well that the only real stimulants of the population of a great city are hunger and greed.

Mothril repeated this to him every day. The important point, therefore, was to feed the Toledans and inspire them with the hope of rich spoils.

Don Pedro did not succeed in achieving both results.

He promised much in the future, but everything was lacking in the present.

When the Toledans perceived that there were no provisions in the markets and that the granaries were empty, they began to murmur.

A society, formed of twenty wealthy citizens who were devoted to Henry of Trastamare or simply animated by a spirit of opposition, fomented the murmurs and mischievous disposition of the people.

Don Pedro consulted Mothril.

"These persons will play you a bad turn," answered the Moor, "and open the city to your rival, while you are sleeping. Ten thousand will enter, seize you, and then the war will be over."

"What am I to do, then?"

"A very simple thing. In Spain you are called Pedro the Cruel."

"I know it, and I merit this title solely by acts of justice that were a little energetic."

"I am not arguing the matter; but, if you have merited this name in the past, you must not be afraid of meriting it in the present; if you have not merited it, hasten to justify the title by some excellent executions that will teach the Toledans the strength of your arm."

"I agree with you," answered the king. "I will act this very night."

He did so. He had the malcontents of whom we have spoken pointed out to him, and took note of their dwellings and habits; then, on that very night, with a hundred soldiers whom he commanded in person, he forced open the house of each rebel and butchered him.

The bodies were flung into the Tagus. A little nocturnal noise, much blood carefully washed away, and that was all there was left to instruct the Toledans as to the king's notions of how justice ought to be administered and the city ruled.

They stopped murmuring, and set to eating their horses with much enthusiasm.

The king congratulated them.

"You have no need of horses in the city," said he.

"The distances are not long; and, when we make a sortie on the besiegers, we can make it on foot."

After their horses, the Toledans were constrained to eat their mules. For a Spaniard that is a hard necessity. The mule is a national animal, regarded almost as a fellow-countryman. It is the horses that are sacrificed in the bull-fights, while the mules have the office of picking up on the arena horses and bulls killed on top of one another.

The Toledans then ate their mules, sighing.

Don Pedro let them sigh.

This execution of the mules raised the energy of the besieged; they made a sortie in quest of provisions, but Le Bègue de Vilaine and Olivier de Mauny, who had not eaten their Breton horses, beat them cruelly, and forced them to remain within their ramparts.

Don Pedro suggested to them a new idea.

It was to eat the provender the horses and mules were no longer eating, because they were — dead!

This lasted a week, and then something else had to be thought of.

In fact, matters were by no means pleasant.

The Prince of Wales, annoyed at not receiving the sums of money owed him by Don Pedro, had just sent three envoys to Toledo to present the bill for the expenses of the war.

Don Pedro consulted Mothril on this new difficulty.

"The Christians are very fond," replied Mothril, "of the pomp of ceremonies and public festivals; if we had bulls, I should counsel you to give a splendid bull-fight, but we have none, we must think of something else."

"What do you advise?"

"These deputies come to ask you for money; all Toledo awaits your answer. If you refuse, it is because your coffers are empty; in that case, count no longer on the Toledans."

"But I cannot pay, there is no money."

"I am well aware of that, seigneur, for I administer your finances; so as we have not money, we must make up for it by shrewdness.

"Invite the envoys to come to the cathedral in grand parade. There, in presence of the whole people, who will be enchanted to see your royal robes, the gold and precious stones of the sacerdotal ornaments, the splendid armor of your knights, and the fifty horses still left in the city as samples of the curious species now extinct, — there you will say to the envoys, —

"'Seigneurs, have you full powers to treat with me?'

"'Yes,' they will answer, 'we represent His Highness the Prince of Wales, our gracious lord.'

"'So then,' you will say, 'His Highness demands the sum of money I have agreed to pay?'

"'Yes,' they will answer.

"'I do not deny the debt,' you will say, my prince. 'But it was agreed between His Highness and me that I should have the protection, alliance, and co-operation of the English in return for the sum due.'"

"But I have had all you mention," cried Don Pedro.

"Yes, but you have it no longer, and you risk having the opposite. Above all, you must insist on their neutrality; for, if you have to fight the Prince of Wales and his twenty thousand Englishmen, along with the army of Henry of Trastamare and the Bretons commanded by the constable, you are lost, my prince, and the English will pay themselves out of your spoils."

"They will refuse me, Mothril, since I cannot pay them."

"If they had intended to refuse, they would have done so already. But the Christians have too much self-love to confess to one another that they have been deceived. The Prince of Wales would rather lose all you owe him, and pass for being paid, than be paid without any one knowing it. Let me finish: these envoys will summon you to pay them; you will answer:—

"'I am threatened on all sides with the hostility of the Prince of Wales. If it were so, I would rather lose all my realm than allow the shadow of an alliance to exist between me and so disloyal a prince. Swear, then, that for the ensuing two months the Prince of Wales will keep, I do not say the promise he made me of coming to my help, but the promise he made me of remaining neutral, and I swear on the Holy Gospels here present that in two months you shall be paid. I have the money ready.'

"The envoys will swear, because they will want to return home as speedily as possible; then your people will feel elated and relieved, being now sure they shall not have to encounter fresh enemies, and, after eating all their horses and mules, they will eat the rats and lizards of Toledo,—a rather numerous tribe on account of the neighborhood of the rocks on the river-side."

"But in two months, Mothril?"

"You will not pay either, it is true; but the battle we wish to force will be won or lost; in two months you will not need to pay your debts, whether you conquer or are conquered. If you conquer, you will have more credit than you require; if you are conquered, you are worse than bankrupt."

"But my oath on the Gospels?"

"You have often spoken of turning Mahometan; this will be your opportunity, my prince. Become a devotee of Mahomet, and then Jesus Christ, the other prophet, will have no claim on you."

"Execrable pagan!" murmured Don Pedro; "what hateful counsels!"

"I do not say you are wrong," replied Mothril; "but your faithful Christians give you none at all; mine, therefore, are better than none."

But, after reflection, Don Pedro put in action every point of the plan of Mothril.

The ceremony was imposing; the Toledans forgot their hunger at the sight of the magnificence of the court and the pageantry of warlike state.

Don Pedro displayed so much magnanimity, made such fine discourses, and swore so solemnly, that the envoys, after pledging their prince to neutrality, seemed more happy than if they had been paid in ready money.

"What is the difference, after all?" said Don Pedro; "this will last as long as I."

He had more luck than he hoped, for, as Mothril had foreseen, a large body of Africans arrived by the Tagus, broke through the enemies' lines, and revictualled Toledo, so that Don Pedro, on reckoning up his resources, found himself at the head of an army of eighty thousand men,— Jews, Saracens, Portuguese, and Castilians.

He kept in the shade during all these preparations, taking extreme care of his person, and leaving nothing to chance, which might, by some isolated accident, destroy the result of the great stroke he was meditating.

On the other hand, Don Henry was already organizing a government. He acted, in fact, as any sovereign might have been expected to act, who was the elect of the people and firmly seated on his throne.

He was determined that, on the morrow of an action which would deliver to him the crown, his royalty should be as sound and solid as if it had been consecrated by a long peace.

In the midst of the measures taken by the two sovereigns, Agénor had his eye on Montiel, and knew, through well-paid spies, that Mothril, having established a cordon of troops between the castle and Toledo, rode almost every day, on a barb fleet as the wind, to visit Aïssa, now entirely recovered from her wound.

The young knight had tried all means to get an entrance into the castle, or to communicate with Aïssa, but none succeeded.

Musaron had so many schemes in his head that it threw him into a fever.

But, after all their planning, the only hope of safety Agénor saw was in an early general engagement that would permit him to kill Don Pedro with his own hand, take Mothril alive, and make the freedom and safety of Aïssa the price of that rascal's ransom.

This sweet thought, this haunting dream wearied the brain of the young man with its ardent companionship.

He fell into a profound disgust with everything that was not active and decisive war; and, as a member of the council of the leaders, he always voted in favor of abandoning the siege and forcing Don Pedro to a pitched battle.

But he met earnest opponents in the council, for Henry's army barely consisted of twenty thousand men, and many officers thought it would be madness to risk such a venture with the chances all against them.

Agénor, on the other hand, represented that, though Don Henry had but twenty thousand men since his manifesto, still, if he did not distinguish himself by some brilliant exploit, his army, instead of increasing, would melt away, while the Tagus was bringing re-enforcements of Saracens and Portuguese every day to Don Pedro.

"The cities are restless," said he; "they waver between two banners. See the skill with which Don Pedro reduces you to inaction; and, in the eyes of everybody, your inaction is a proof of your impotence.

"Abandon Toledo, which you cannot take. Remember that, if you conquer, the city will be compelled to surrender, while, at the present moment, nothing presses it to do so; on the contrary, Mothril's plan is in process of execution. You will be shut in between the walls of stone and the walls of steel. Behind you is the Tagus, lined with eighty thousand combatants. If you delay, you will fight only to die bravely. To-day you can attack and conquer."

True, at bottom this discourse was selfish; but what good advice was ever given that had not a touch of selfishness?

The constable was too shrewd and too experienced in war not to support Mauléon. Still, the indecision of the king had to be conquered, for he risked much in taking chances without seeing which way the wind blew.

But what men do not, God does, according to his will.

XLII.

THE BATTLE OF MONTIEL.

Don Pedro was in as great a hurry as Agénor to possess the chattel which, next to his crown, he desired more than anything else in the world.

Whenever he was able, after the day's work was done, to gallop at nightfall to Montiel between two lines of trusty soldiers, and gaze upon the fair but pale and sad features of Aïssa, he felt happy.

But it was a happiness that Mothril seldom granted him. The plan of the Saracen was ripe. He had cast his net successfully and landed his prey. The trouble was now to keep it, for a king in ambush is like a lion in the toils: you have him just as long as he is there.

Don Pedro had begged Mothril to deliver Aïssa to him; he promised to marry her and seat her beside him on the throne.

"No," replied Mothril, "it is not in time of war a king celebrates his espousals, it is not when so many brave men die for him that he takes thought of love. No; wait for victory; then you may do what pleases you."

In this fashion, he held back the fiery king. And yet his policy was clear as day. Don Pedro would have seen through it, had he not been blind.

Mothril wished to make Aïssa queen of Castile, because he knew that an alliance between a Christian and a Mahometan would incense Christendom; because then the whole world would forsake Don Pedro, and because then, the Saracens, so often vanquished, would conquer Spain once more, and forever.

Then would Mothril become King of Spain, — Mothril who exercised such commanding influence among his compatriots, Mothril who for ten years had been guiding them to this promised land, advancing step by step, but at a rate that was evident to all except to the drunken or frenzied king.

But, while surrendering Aïssa and while planning a return of adversity for Don Pedro, it was necessary to act slowly and surely. Mothril, therefore, was waiting until a decisive victory should destroy the most furious enemies the Moors could ever encounter in Spain. The Moors must first win a great battle under the leadership of Don Pedro, must kill Henry of Trastamare, Bertrand Du Guesclin, and all the Bretons, and make Christendom at length understand that, when Spain had determined to dig tombs for her invaders within her borders, she rendered the crossing of her frontiers easy.

It was necessary also that Agénor de Mauléon, the greatest obstacle to the plans of Mothril, should be killed, in order that the young Morisca, having been first subdued by her father's promises and the assurance of a speedy union with her lover, and then utterly disheartened by the knowledge of that lover's undoubted death on the field of battle, might yield to despair, and second the schemes of Mothril, whose honesty she would no longer suspect.

The Moor became more tender and sympathizing than ever; he even accused Hafiz of having had an understanding with Doña Maria to deceive Agénor or kill him. Hafiz was dead and could no longer defend himself.

He procured for her tidings of Agénor, some true, some invented.

"He thinks of you," he would say, "he loves you, he lives with his lord the constable, and never misses an opportunity of corresponding with the messengers I send to him for news."

Aïssa, reassured by such words as these, waited patiently. She even found a certain charm in this separation, confident as she was that it was a proof of Mauléon's desire to be as near her as possible.

Her days were passed in the most remote apartments of the castle. There, indolent and dreamy, alone with her women, she often gazed out upon the country through a window that hung perpendicularly above the gulf of rocks below Montiel.

When Don Pedro visited her she met him with that formal, icy politeness which, in women incapable of dissimulation, is the supreme effort of hypocrisy. A coldness so incomprehensible that the presumptuous sometimes take it for the timidity love feels at the beginning of love.

The king had never experienced any resistance. Maria Padilla, the haughtiest of women, had loved him, had preferred him to the whole world. Why should he not believe in the love of Aïssa, especially as the death of Maria and the calumnies of Mothril had persuaded him that the young girl's heart was pure from every thought of love?

Mothril kept an active watch on the king at each one of his visits. Not a word of this prince but had its value for the Moor, while he did not allow Aïssa to utter a single reply. Her state of health, he said, required absolute silence.

Still, Mothril was constantly in dread of an understanding between Don Pedro and the servants in the castle; such an understanding might result in the surrender of Aïssa to the king, as so many women had been surrendered to him before.

Mothril, who was supreme master in Montiel, had, therefore, taken his precautions. The best of all was to convince Aïssa that he approved of her love for Agénor. And the young girl had been convinced.

As a result of all this, when Mothril left Montiel to take the command of the African troops who had come for battle, he had only two recommendations to make, the one to his lieutenant, the other to Aïssa herself.

This lieutenant was the same that had so badly defended the litter of Aïssa after the battle of Navaretta, but he burned to take his revenge.

He was a soldier rather than a servant. Incapable of stooping to the grovelling submission of Hafiz, he understood only the obedience due to his leader and the respect due to the prescriptions of his religion.

Aïssa understood only one thing also, — an eternal union with Mauléon.

"I leave for battle," said Mothril to her. "The Sire de Mauléon and I have made a compact to spare each other during the fray. If he conquer, he must come and take you out of this castle, the doors of which I will open for him, and then you will fly with him, — and with me, if you love me as a father. If he be conquered, he is to come to me and I am to lead him to you; he will thus owe me his own life and the possession of you. Such devotion ought to make you love me well, Aïssa; will it? You know that if Don Pedro had the slightest idea, the slightest suspicion of this plan, my head would roll at his feet before an hour, and you would be forever lost to the man you love."

Aïssa was profuse in her protestations of gratitude, and hailed this day of sorrow and of blood as the dawn of her liberty and love.

When he had thus prepared the young girl, he gave his instructions to his lieutenant.

"Hassan," said he, "the Prophet is about to decide the fate of Don Pedro. We are on the point of engaging in battle. If we are conquered, or even if we are conquerors, and I do not return to the castle on the evening of the combat, it will be because I am killed, wounded, or a prisoner; then, you will open the door of Doña Aïssa's room, — here is the key, — you will poniard her and her two women and fling them into the ravine from the top of the rocks, because it is not fitting that good Mussulman women be exposed to the insults of a Christian, whether that Christian be Don Pedro or Trastamare. Keep a better guard than you did at Navaretta. There your vigilance was found wanting. I pardoned you and allowed you to live; this time the Prophet would punish you. Swear, then, to execute my orders."

"I swear it," said Hassan, coldly; "and when the three women are dead, I will poniard myself also, so that my spirit may watch over theirs."

"Thanks," answered Mothril, throwing his golden collar around the neck of the lieutenant; "you are a good servant, and, if we are victorious, you shall have the command of this castle. Let Doña Aïssa be ignorant of the lot that awaits her until the last moment; she is a woman, she is weak, she must not suffer death more than once. And, speaking of victory," he hastened to add, "I do not believe it can escape us. So, my order is a precaution to which we shall not be obliged to have recourse."

After these words, Mothril took his arms, his best horse, ordered ten of his most devoted men to follow him, and, leaving the command of Montiel to Hassan, started during the night to find Don Pedro, who was impatiently awaiting him.

Mothril was sure of victory, and had good grounds for his confidence.

These were the chances in his favor.

Four against one. Fresh auxiliaries arriving every moment, all the gold of Africa hurried into Spain by a secret and immutable determination, the determination to conquer the country once more, a determination never abandoned, though often rendered fruitless; while, on the other hand, the knights of Europe were fighting, some in the hope of gain, others from religious devotion, all coldly enough and very likely to be discouraged by a reverse.

If ever an event burst forth from the midst of well concerted plans, it was that of the battle to which history has given the poetic and chivalrous name of Montiel.

Don Pedro, who was in a fever of impatience, massed all his troops between Montiel and Toledo.

They covered two leagues of country, and were echeloned up to the mountains, cavalry as well as infantry.

Hesitation was now out of the question for Don Henry. To enter the field as an involuntary agent would be shameful for a pretender who had borne this device when in Castile before: —

"To stay here a king or dead."

He went in search of the constable and said, —

"Once more, Sire Bertrand, do I commit my realm to your care. It is you who will command. You may be more fortunate than at Navaretta, you cannot be more brave and skilful. But you know that what God does not permit a first time, he graciously deigns to permit a second."

"Then, sire, I command!" cried the constable, eagerly.

"As a king, I am your first or your last lieutenant, sir constable," replied the king.

"And you say to me what King Charles V., my wise and glorious master, said at Paris when he gave me the constable's sword."

"What did he say, brave Bertrand?"

"He said, sire: 'Discipline is badly kept in my armies, which are lost for want of submission and justice. There are princes who blush at the thought of obeying a mere knight. But never yet has battle been won without the concord of all and the supremacy of one. Therefore, Bertrand, you will command, and every disobedient head, though it were my brother's, shall bend or fall if it will not submit.'"

These words, pronounced in full council, were a brief but inoffensive summary of the misfortune of Navaretta, where the imprudence of the king's brothers, Don Tello and Don Sancho, had caused the ruin of the greater part of the army.

The princes, who were present, reddened as they heard them.

"Sir constable," returned the king, "I have said you commanded; therefore, you are master. Whoever complies not with your orders or your humors, I will strike with this axe, though he were my ally, my relative, or even my brother. In fact, he who loves me should wish me victory, and I can only conquer by the obedience of all to the wisest captain in Christendom."

"So be it," answered Du Guesclin; "I accept the command; to-morrow, we shall deliver battle."

The constable spent the whole night in listening to the reports of his spies and couriers.

Some of them announced that fresh bands of Saracens were landing at Cadiz.

Others gave extended accounts of the disasters of the country districts, which these eighty thousand men had been desolating for a month like a cloud of locusts.

"It is time for this to end," said the constable to the king, "else these people will have so ravaged your realm that even after a victory you will hardly have anything worth having left."

Agénor was joyous, and yet his joyousness was accompanied by that shrinking of the heart felt on the eve of an event by those who desire it but know that it will decide an important question. He tried to banish his pain and anxiety by an incredible display of activity.

Always on horseback, he carried orders, collected and ranked the companies, reconnoitred the ground, and assigned to each troop its place for the morrow.

Du Guesclin divided his army into five corps.

Four thousand five hundred horse, commanded by Olivier Du Guesclin and Le Bègue de Vilaine, formed the vanguard.

The Frenchmen and a chosen body of Spaniards, numbering six thousand, formed the division commanded by Don Henry of Trastamare.

The Aragonese and the other allies made up the rear.

A reserve of four hundred horse, commanded by Olivier de Mauny, was to protect the retreat.

As to the constable, he took charge of the three thousand Bretons commanded by the younger De Mauny, Carlonnet, La Houssaie, and Agénor.

This division, composed of men well mounted and

invincible, was, like a mighty arm, to strike in whatever direction the eye of the leader deemed its presence necessary to the success of the day.

Bertrand had his soldiers roused before daylight, and each of them marched slowly to his post, so that at dawn the army was ranged in battle array without fatigue and without noise.

It was not his custom to make long speeches.

"Let this be your thought," said he: "you have each four enemies to kill, but you are worth ten of them. Yon heap of Moors, Jews, and Portuguese cannot stand against the soldiers of France and Spain. Strike without pity, kill all who are not Christians. I have never shed blood wantonly, but to-day necessity enjoins us to do so.

"There is no bond between the Moors and Spaniards. They detest each other mutually. Interest alone unites them; but, as soon as the Moors shall see themselves sacrificed to the Spaniards, as soon as they shall see us spare the Christian and kill the infidel, distrust will run through the ranks of the Moors, and, once their despair past, they will quickly seek the path of safety. Kill the Moors, then, and kill without mercy."

This harangue produced the usual effect. The soldiers were roused to extraordinary enthusiasm.

However, Don Pedro was also at work. He could be seen laboriously manœuvring the undisciplined but immense African battalions, whose splendid arms and garb shone in the rising sun.

When Du Guesclin reconnoitred this innumerable multitude from the top of a hill he had selected as his observatory, he feared the small number of his soldiers might give too much confidence to the enemy. He therefore detached men from the rear ranks, and closed up those in front in such a way that both seemed equal.

Moreover, he had bundles of standards planted behind the back of the hills, in order that the Saracens might believe soldiers were beneath these standards.

Don Pedro saw all this; his genius grew with the danger. He addressed an eloquent discourse to his faithful Spaniards, and brilliant promises to the Saracens. But, however brilliant they might be, they could not equal the hopes his allies founded on the ultimate despoiling of himself.

The trumpets sounded from Don Pedro's side, those of Du Guesclin at once replied, and a great trembling, like as if two worlds were rushing upon each other, shook the ground, and even the trees on the hills.

The effect of Du Guesclin's advice could be discerned from the very first assault. The Bretons, by refusing to make any prisoners among the Mahometans and killing every one who was not a Spaniard or a Christian, created the deepest suspicion in the minds of the Saracens, and this suspicion spread among the infidels like a cold chill, damping all their ardor.

They fancied the Christians of the two parties had an understanding, and that, whether Henry conquered or was conquered, the Saracens would be the only victims.

Their battalions had been attacked by Du Guesclin's brother and Le Bègue de Vilaine; these intrepid Bretons made such a massacre around them that, the Moorish chiefs being slain, among them even the Prince of Bennemarine, the Saracens took fright and fled after their first corps was cut in pieces.

The second wavered, but still advanced bravely. Du Guesclin ordered his three thousand Bretons to charge in double quick time, and the shock was so rude that half of the enemy's column turned rein.

It was a second massacre: generals, nobles, soldiers, all were slain. Not a single one escaped.

Du Guesclin returned to his post, and, while he was wiping his flushed face, he saw Don Henry also returning from the pursuit, who, in obedience to orders, took his station beside the constable.

"You ought to be pleased, messeigneurs," said Bertrand. "All goes well. We have lost only about a thousand men, and twenty-five thousand Saracens have fallen; see what fine heaps are before you. All goes well."

"If this last!" murmured Henry.

"At least we shall do our best to make it last," replied the constable. "Look at Mauléon yonder, who is dashing on the third corps of Saracens commanded by Mothril. The Moor sees him and is ordering him to be surrounded; horsemen are already riding from the ranks to do so. He will get killed; sound the retreat, trumpets."

Ten trumpets sounded. Agénor pricked up his ears, and, as submissively as if he had been going through an exercise in a riding-school, he returned to his post under a hail of arrows hammering at his well-tempered armor.

"Now," said the constable, "my vanguard is about to attack the Spaniards; these are good troops, messeigneurs, and we shall not get the upper hand easily. We must divide into three bodies and attack on three sides. The king," he continued, "will take the left, Olivier the right, and I shall wait."

The Spaniards received the shock like people who want to conquer or die.

' Henry, in attacking the division of Don Pedro, encountered the resistance of hatred and intelligent valor.

The two kings perceived each other from afar and exchanged threats, but could not come to close quarters. Around them rose mountains of men and of opposing arms, then these mountains sank down engulfed, and the earth drank rivers of blood.

King Henry's division suddenly grew weak. Don Pedro had the upper hand; he was fighting, not as a soldier, but as a lion. Already one of his squires had been slain; he changed for the second time his horse; he had not a wound, and he brandished his battle-axe with so much dexterity and so good an aim that every stroke brought down a man.

Henry saw himself encompassed by the Moors of Mothril, among them Mothril himself, who was the tiger, just as Don Pedro was the lion. The French lords were mowed down in numbers by the yataghans and scimitars of these Moors; their ranks were beginning to thin, and the arrows reached even the breast of the king; nay, a daring soldier had succeeded in touching him with his lance.

"It is time," cried the constable. "Forward, my friends! Notre Dame, Du Guesclin, and victory!"

The three thousand Bretons moved forward with a terrible noise, and, forming into an angle, penetrated, like a wedge of steel, the division of Don Pedro, consisting of twenty thousand men.

At last, Agénor had the long coveted permission to fight and take Mothril.

In a quarter of an hour the Spaniards were broken, crushed. The Morisco cavalry could not hold out against the weight of the men-at-arms and the blows of that terrible angle.

Mothril tried to fly, but he met the Aragonese and the men of Bègue de Vilaine, commanded by Mauléon. He must pass at any price, if he was not to be shut in by this terrible wall. Agénor was already looking on himself as the master of Mothril's life and liberty, when the Moor, with three hundred men at most, broke through the Bretons, lost two hundred and fifty horsemen, and passed; in passing, he struck the head of Agénor's horse, which was within two paces of him, with a blow of his scimitar.

Agénor rolled in the dust. Musaron let fly a shaft, but missed, and Mothril, like a fleeing wolf, disappeared behind heaps of dead bodies in the direction of Montiel.

At this moment, Don Pedro saw that his men were giving way. He felt, so to speak, the breath of his most implacable enemies on his face. One of them broke the golden crest of his helmet and killed his standard-bearer. What was the shame of the prince was the safety of the man.

Don Pedro was no longer recognizable; the carnage made around him was without direct object. It was at this moment that an English knight in black armor, with visor carefully lowered, took his horse by the bridle and forced him from the field of battle.

Four hundred horsemen, concealed behind a hillock by this prudent friend, formed the only escort of the fugitive king. It was all that remained to him of the eighty thousand men that were ready to die for him at daybreak.

As the plain in all directions was covered with fugitives, Bertrand could not discover the company of the king from the other scattered bands; it was, indeed, no longer known whether Don Pedro was living or dead. The constable, therefore, launched at haphazard his reserve and the fifteen hundred horse of Olivier de Mauny on all the fugitives; but Don Pedro, thanks to the excellence of his horse, was far in advance of every one.

No one thought of following him, for, in fact, no one recognized him. In the eyes of all he was an ordinary fugitive.

But Agénor, who knew the road to Montiel and the interest Don Pedro had in taking refuge there, — Agénor was on the lookout.

He had seen Mothril galloping in that direction.

He guessed who the Englishman was that was showing such kindness to Don Pedro.

He saw a body of four hundred horsemen escorting a man who was well in their front, thanks to the fleetness of his magnificent steed.

He recognized the king by his broken helm, his gold spurs reddened with blood, and the ardor with which he gazed upon the towers of Montiel in the distance. Agénor cast his eyes around to see if there was any corps near that could aid him in following this precious fugitive and cutting off the retreat of his four hundred horse.

He saw only Le Bègue de Vilaine, who with eleven hundred horsemen, all out of breath, were taking a rest before joining with the others in the general pursuit.

Bertrand was too far away to reach the fugitives and so make his victory complete in all respects.

"Messire," said Agénor to Le Bègue, "come to my aid quick, if you wish to take the King Don Pedro, for it is he who is galloping yonder to the castle."

"Are you sure?" cried Le Bègue.

"As of my life, messire!" answered Mauléon. "I recognize the man in command of these horsemen, it is

Caverley; no doubt his object in escorting the king so faithfully is to take and sell him, it is his trade."

"Yes," cried Le Bègue; "but an Englishman must not have such a fine piece of luck, when we have so many valiant French lances here." And turning to his soldiers, "To horse all of you!" he said, "and let ten men go and warn M. le Connétable that we are going towards Montiel in search of the conquered king."

The Bretons charged with such fury that they reached the escort.

Immediately the English leader drew up his men in two companies: one followed him who was supposed to be the king, the other confronted the Bretons firmly.

"Charge! charge!" cried Agénor; "they only want to gain time for the king to enter Montiel."

Unfortunately for the Bretons, a defile opened in front of them; they could enter it only by sixes to come up with the fugitive English.

"We shall lose them! they are escaping us!" cried Mauléon; "courage, Bretons, courage!"

"Yes, we shall escape you, Béarnese of hell!" howled the English knight at the head of the escort; "however, if you want to take us, come on!"

He spoke with confidence, because Agénor, carried away by his energy and jealousy, had distanced all his companions, and appeared almost alone before these two hundred English lances.

The fearless young man did not pause in presence of this terrible danger. He plunged the rowels deeper in the sides of his foam-flecked steed.

Caverley was daring, and, moreover, his natural ferocity was intensified by the prospect of a victory that seemed assured.

Placed as he was in the midst of his men, he awaited Mauléon, steadying himself in his stirrups.

Then was seen a curious spectacle: a knight rushing headlong upon two hundred cavaliers, each with lance in rest.

"Oh, the coward Englishman!" cried Le Bègue from afar. "Ah, coward! coward! — Halt, Mauléon, you are over-chivalrous! — Coward! coward Englishman!"

Caverley was moved to shame; after all, he was a knight and owed a lance-thrust to the honor of his golden spurs and his nation.

He left the ranks and prepared for the combat.

"I have your sword already," he cried to Mauléon, who was advancing like a thunderbolt. "It is not here as it was in the cavern of Montiel, and, before long, I shall have your armor."

"Take the lance first, then," replied the young man, rushing at him so furiously with his lance that Caverley was unhorsed and flung on the ground, where he lay beside his horse.

"Hurrah!" shouted the Bretons, coming ever nearer and nearer.

Which seeing, the English turned rein and sought to join their companions, now flying across the plain, abandoning the king, who was carried in the direction of Montiel by his horse.

Caverley tried to rise; his back was broken. His horse, in freeing itself, kicked him in the breast and nailed him again on the ground, which was covered with a stream of dark blood.

"By the devil!" he murmured, "it is over. I shall never stop any one again; this is death."

And he fell back.

At the same moment, all the Breton cavalry arrived,

and the eleven hundred mail-clad horses swept like a hurricane over the mangled corpse of this famous capturer of kings.

But the delay had saved Don Pedro. In vain did Le Bègue, by heroic efforts, give a threefold energy to men and beasts.

The Bretons dashed on, mad with rage, at the risk of killing their horses, but they only arrived on the track of Don Pedro just at the moment he was entering the first barrier of the castle, and that safely, for the gate closed on him; he praised God for having thus escaped a second time. Mothril had been there since a quarter of an hour before.

Le Bègue tore his hair in despair.

"Patience, messire!" said Agénor; "let us lose no time, but do you invest the fortress; what we have not done to-day, we shall do to-morrow."

Le Bègue followed this advice: he scattered all his horsemen around the castle, and, when night fell, every issue leading from Montiel had been shut up securely.

Soon afterwards, Du Guesclin arrived with three thousand men, and learned the important news from Agénor.

"It is unfortunate," he said, "for the place is impregnable."

"We shall see, seigneur," replied Mauléon; "at least, if no one can enter, it is safe to say that no one can get out either."

XLIII.

A TRUCE.

THE constable was not a credulous man. His opinion of the talents of Don Pedro was as favorable as that of his character was the reverse.

When he had made the tour of Montiel, reconnoitred the fortress, and convinced himself that, with a good and trusty guard, even a mouse could be prevented from leaving the place, he said, —

"No, Messire de Mauléon, we have not the good fortune you led us to hope. No, Don Pedro has not shut himself up in Montiel, because he is very well aware that he would be blockaded, and that he would have to surrender to famine."

"I assure you, monseigneur, that Mothril is in Montiel, and the King Don Pedro is there with him," replied Mauléon.

"I will believe that when I see it," said the constable.

"How many are in the garrison?" asked Bertrand.

"About three hundred men, seigneur."

"These three hundred men, by simply hurling down stones on the heads of our men, can kill five thousand of them without giving us a chance of firing an arrow at them. Don Henry will be here to-morrow. When he comes, we shall deliberate whether it is better to leave, or waste a month here for nothing."

Agénor wished to answer; but the constable had all a Breton's obstinacy, and would not suffer a reply, or, rather, would not submit to be persuaded.

The next day, in fact, Don Henry arrived, radiant after his victory.

He led with him his army, intoxicated with joy; and when his council had deliberated on the question as to whether Don Pedro was or was not in Montiel,—

"I think as the constable does," said the king. "Don Pedro is too crafty to have openly shut himself up in a fortress from which there is no issue. We ought, then, to leave a small force here to alarm Montiel, and compel the castle to capitulate, for it would not be well to leave behind us a place proud of having never been taken; but we shall go elsewhere. We have, thank God, something more important to attend to, and Don Pedro is not there."

Agénor was present at the discussion.

"Sire," said he, "I am very young and very inexperienced to raise my voice among so many valiant captains; but my conviction is such that nothing can shake it. I recognized Caverley following the king, and Caverley has been killed. I saw Don Pedro enter Montiel, and I recognized his broken helm, his broken shield, and his blood-stained spurs of gold."

"But might not Caverley himself have been mistaken? I exchanged armor at Navaretta with a faithful knight," replied Don Henry; "might not Don Pedro have done the same?"

This last remark obtained general assent. Agénor saw himself again defeated.

"I hope you are persuaded?" said the king.

"No, sire," he answered humbly; "but I cannot oppose the wise ideas of Your Majesty."

"You must try to be convinced, Sire de Mauléon, you must try to be convinced."

"I will try," said the young man, with a grief he could not dissemble.

In fact, for a tender lover, what position could be more cruel? Don Pedro was shut up with Aïssa,— Don Pedro, exasperated by defeat, and without any motive for forbearance now. With the prospect of a coming death, would not this faithless prince seek to make a last paroxysm of voluptuousness the harbinger of his doom? Would he leave inviolate, and in the power of another, the young girl whom he loved, and whom violence could place in his arms?

Moreover, was not Mothril there, that artisan of odious stratagems, capable of all that could advance him a step in his greedy and sanguinary policy.?

All this drove Agénor wild with anger and vexation.

He understood that, by hiding his secret longer, he would let Don Henry, the army, and the constable depart, and that then Don Pedro, far superior in spirit and talent to the disgusted lieutenants compelled to remain behind in front of Montiel, would succeed in escaping after sacrificing Aïssa to the caprice of a moment's idleness.

He took his resolution, and demanded a private interview with the king.

"Sire," said he, "this is why Don Pedro, in spite of all appearances, has taken refuge in Montiel. It is a secret I have kept, for it is mine. But I must reveal it in the interest of your glory. Don Pedro loves passionately Aïssa, the daughter of Mothril. He wishes to marry her. This is why he allowed Mothril to assassinate Doña Maria Padilla; just as, for the sake of Maria, he had ordered the assassination of Madame Blanche de Bourbon."

"Oh!" said the king, "then Aïssa is in Montiel?"

"Yes," replied Agénor.

"But that is a thing of which you are not surer than you were of the other, my friend."

"I am sure of it, seigneur, because a lover always knows where his beloved mistress is."

"You love Aïssa,— a Morisca?"

"I love her passionately, seigneur, with this reservation: that for me Aïssa will become a Christian, while she will kill herself if Don Pedro tries to possess her."

Agénor turned pale in pronouncing these words, for he did not believe them, the poor knight; and even though Aïssa killed herself to escape dishonor, she was not the less lost to him forever.

This confession threw Don Henry into deep perplexity.

"It is a reason," he murmured; "but tell me why you think Aïssa is in Montiel."

Agénor related, in all their details, the death of Hafiz and the wounding of Aïssa.

"Have you a plan, however?" said the king.

"I have one, seigneur; and, if Your Majesty will lend me your aid, I promise to place Don Pedro in your power before a week, as surely as that, on the last occasion, I gave you trustworthy news of him."

The king summoned the constable, to whom Agénor repeated his story. "For all that, I do not believe that a prince so crafty and relentless would ever let himself be ensnared by love of a woman," replied the constable; "but the Sire de Mauléon has my promise to help him in whatever may give him pleasure, and I will help him."

"Let the fortress continue to be invested, then," said Agénor; "cause a trench to be dug around it, and, with the earth of this trench, raise a rampart, behind which skilful and vigilant officers, not soldiers, will lie concealed.

"My squire and I will lodge in a spot with which we are acquainted, and where we can hear whatever goes on in the castle. Don Pedro, if he sees a strong besieging army, will believe that his arrival at Montiel is known and will become distrustful. Now, distrust is the salvation of a man so able and dangerous. Order all your troops to depart for Toledo, leaving only two thousand men behind the earthen rampart; they will be quite sufficient to invest the castle and resist a sortie.

"When Don Pedro believes that the guard is kept negligently, he will try to escape, and I shall warn you."

Hardly had Agénor developed his plan and succeeded in attracting the attention of the king, when the bearer of a flag of truce, sent by the governor to the constable, was announced.

"Let him enter," said Bertrand, "and explain what he wants."

The bearer was a Spanish officer, named Rodrigo de Sanatrias. He informed the constable that the garrison of Montiel saw with anxiety such a considerable display of force, and that the three hundred men, shut up in the castle with a single officer, did not care to continue the struggle for very long, as they had no longer any hope since the departure and defeat of Don Pedro.

At these words, the constable and the king looked at Agénor, as much as to say, "You see he is not there?"

"You would surrender, then?" asked the constable.

"Yes, messire, but, like brave soldiers, after a certain time, because we do not wish that Don Pedro, on his return, should accuse us of betraying his cause without striking a blow."

"It is said the king is with you," answered Don Henry.

The Spaniard burst out laughing.

"The king is very far away," said he. "Why should he have come here, where people besieged as you are besieging us can only die of hunger or surrender?"

A new look of the king and the constable addressed to Agénor.

"What do you want actually, then?" asked Du Guesclin; "lay down your conditions."

"A truce of ten days," said the officer, "so that Don Pedro may have time to relieve us. After that time, we shall surrender."

"Listen," said the king; "you are positive Don Pedro is not in the castle?"

"Positive, seigneur. If he were, we would not ask to leave the castle; for, when we left, you would all see us, and, consequently, recognize the king. Now, if we lied, you would punish us; and, if you took the king, you would, doubtless, not spare him?"

This last phrase was a question; the constable did not answer. Henry of Trastamare had sufficient self-control to extinguish the deadly flash that shone in his eyes at the supposition of the capture of Don Pedro.

"We grant you the truce," said the constable, "but no one must leave the castle."

"But our provisions, seigneur?" said the officer.

"They shall be furnished to you. We shall go to you, but you cannot leave."

"It is not an ordinary truce, then," murmured the officer.

"Why should you wish to go forth? to escape? But, as we promise that after ten days your lives shall be safe—"

"I have no more to say," answered the officer. "I accept; have I your word, messire?"

"May I give it, seigneur?" asked Bertrand of King Henry.

"Yes, constable."

"I give it," replied Du Guesclin; "ten days' truce and life to the entire garrison."

"The entire?"

"Of course," cried Mauléon, "there can be no restrictions, since you declare Don Pedro is not in the fortress."

These words escaped the young man, in spite of the respect he owed his two chiefs, and he congratulated himself on having uttered them, for a visible pallor passed like a cloud over the features of Don Rodrigo de Sanatrias.

He saluted and withdrew.

When he had passed out, —

"Well!" asked the king, "are you convinced, my obstinate young friend and unhappy lover?"

"Convinced that Don Pedro is in Montiel? yes, sire, and that you will have him in your power in a week."

"Ah!" cried the king, "there is stubborness for you!"

"And yet he is not a Breton," said Bertrand, laughing.

"Messeigneurs, Don Pedro is playing the same game we were trying to play. Sure of not being able to escape us by force, he is trying stratagem. You are now, in his opinion, persuaded that he is outside; you grant a truce, you keep guard carelessly; what is the result? he will try to slip through. Oh! I tell you he will try to slip through and escape; but we shall be there, I hope. The very thing that proves to you he is outside Montiel, proves to me that he is within."

Agénor passed from the tent of the king and the constable with an ardor that can be easily conceived.

"Musaron," said he, "seek the loftiest tent in the army, and fly my banner from it so that it can be easily seen from the castle. Aïssa knows it, she will see it, will be sure I am near, and will keep up all her courage.

"As for our enemies, when they see my banner on the intrenchment, they will believe me there and will not suspect we are about to slip again into the grotto of the spring. Courage, my brave Musaron, courage! one supreme effort and we arrive at our goal!"

Musaron obeyed, and the banner of Mauléon floated proudly above the others.

XLIV.

THE STRATAGEM OF THE VANQUISHED.

KING HENRY, with the constable and the army, left Montiel.

All who remained around the earthen rampart were Le Bègue de Vilaine and two thousand Bretons.

Love had inspired Mauléon, and each of his reflections was stamped with the impress of truth.

He spoke, in fact, as if he had heard everything that took place in the castle.

Hardly had Don Pedro arrived after the battle, — breathless, choking and foaming with rage, — when he threw himself upon a carpet in the chamber of Mothril, and remained dumb, motionless, unapproachable, making superhuman efforts to concentrate in the depths of his soul the fury and despair that were boiling within him.

All his friends dead! his fine army destroyed! so many hopes of vengeance and glory annihilated during what time the sun spends in making the tour of the horizon!

Henceforth nothing! Flight, exile, misery! Partisan skirmishes, shameful and fruitless! An inglorious death on some inglorious field of battle.

No more friends! This prince who had never loved any one experienced the utmost torture in having to doubt of the affection of others.

It was because kings, for the most part, confound the respect due them with the affection they ought to inspire.

THE STRATAGEM OF THE VANQUISHED. 355

Having the former, they think they can do without the latter.

Mothril, all bespattered with reddish spots, entered the chamber after him. His armor was riddled with holes through which blood flowed, and it was not the blood of his enemies.

The Moor was livid. A savage resolution gleamed in his eyes. He was no longer the abject, creeping Saracen; he was a haughty, stubborn man about to address his equal.

"King Don Pedro," said he, "so you are conquered?"

Don Pedro raised his head and read in the cold eyes of the Moor this change in his character.

"Yes," replied Don Pedro, "conquered beyond redemption."

"You despair," retorted Mothril; "then your God is not the equal of ours. I, too, am conquered, yet I do not despair; I have prayed, and I am strong."

Don Pedro bent his head, resignedly.

"'T is true," he said, "I had forgotten God."

"Unhappy king! and still you know not the greatest of your misfortunes. With your crown you are about to lose your life."

Don Pedro started, and shot a terrible look at Mothril.

"You would assassinate me?" said he.

"I! I, your friend! you are mad, Don Pedro. You have enemies enough without me, and I should not need to steep my hands in your blood, did I wish your death. Rise, come with me, and gaze on yonder plain."

And, in fact, the plain was covered with lances and coats of mail, which, touched with flame by the rays of the setting sun, were gradually forming an ever closer circle of fire around Montiel.

"Hemmed in! You see well we are lost, Don Pedro," continued Mothril. "For this castle, impregnable if we had provisions, cannot feed either the garrison or yourself; now, you are surrounded, they have seen you, — you are lost!"

Don Pedro did not answer at once.

"They have seen me! Who have seen me?"

"Do you believe it was to take Montiel, this useless eyry, that Le Bègue de Vilaine has planted his banner there? And, hold, see you yonder the pennons of the constable advancing? No, it is you they seek, you they would have."

"They shall not have me living," said Don Pedro.

Mothril, in turn, did not answer. Don Pedro resumed, with irony, —

"The faithful friend, the man full of hope! — and yet he is not hopeful enough to say to his king, 'Live and hope!'"

"I am considering how to get you out of here," said Mothril.

"You banish me?"

"I wish to save my life; I would not be forced to kill Aïssa to hinder her from falling into the hands of the Christians."

At the name of Aïssa, the brow of Don Pedro flushed.

"It is for her sake," he murmured, "that I have been caught in the snare. But for my desire to see her again, I should be now in Toledo; there, men do not die of hunger. The Toledans love me, are willing to die for me. Under Toledo, I could fight a last battle and find a glorious death, and — who knows? — not before that of Alfonso's bastard, Henry of Trastamare. A woman has led me to my ruin."

"I should have preferred you at Toledo," said the Moor, coldly, "for then I could have arranged my affairs better, — and yours."

"While here you will do nothing for me," cried Don Pedro, beginning to give free rein to his fury. "Well, then, wretch! I will end my days here, but not until I have punished you for your disloyalty and your crimes, not until I have tasted a last pleasure. Aïssa, whom you offered me as a decoy, shall belong to me this night even."

"You are mistaken," said the Moor, calmly; "Aïssa shall not belong to you."

"Do you forget that here I command three hundred warriors?"

"Do you forget that you cannot leave this room without my permission, that I shall stretch you dead at my feet, if you stir, and fling your body to the soldiers of the constable, who will receive my present with transports of joy?"

"A traitor!" murmured Don Pedro.

"Mad! blind! ungrateful!" cried Mothril, "say rather a saviour. You can fly; with liberty you can recover everything,—fortune, crown, and fame; fly, then, and lose no time. Do not anger God with your debaucheries and exactions, and do not insult the only friend you have."

"A friend! who speaks to me thus!"

"Would you prefer that he should flatter and betray you?"

"I am resigned. What would you do?"

"I am about to send a herald to the Bretons who are watching you. They believe you here; let us show them they are mistaken. If we see them losing the hope of so rich a prize, let us then turn the moments to account and provide for your escape on the first opportunity their negligence affords. Do you think you have a devoted, intelligent man you can send to them?"

"I have Rodrigo Sanatrias, a man who owes me everything."

"That is not a reason. Does he still hope something from you?"

Don Pedro smiled bitterly.

"'T is true," said he; "only those who hope are our friends. Well, I shall give him grounds for hope."

"That is right; let him come."

While the king was calling Sanatrias, Mothril summoned some Moors whom he ordered to stand guard over the chamber of Aïssa.

Don Pedro spent a part of the night in discussing the means of holding a parley with the enemy. Rodrigo was as ingenious as he was faithful; besides, he saw clearly that the safety of Don Pedro was the safety of all. To gain possession of the conquered king the conquerors would sacrifice ten thousand men, would demolish the rock, destroy every soul by sword and famine, but would attain their aim.

At daybreak Don Pedro saw with despair the banners of Don Henry of Trastamare.

It was certain, then, that a king would not turn from his route and a constable from his plans, except they expected to take something in Montiel beside a garrison.

Don Pedro at once despatched Rodrigo Sanatrias, who fulfilled his commission with the address and success we have seen.

The news he brought back to the castle filled all the prisoners with joy.

Don Pedro never wearied of asking details, and drew from each of them favorable deductions. The departure of the troops of the king and constable was a final proof of the wisdom and efficacy of the Moor's counsels.

"Now," said Mothril, "we have to fear only an ordinary enemy. Let a dark night come, and we are saved."

Don Pedro could not contain his delight; he became affectionate, confidential with Mothril.

"Listen," said he. "I see I have treated you badly; you deserve better than to be the minister of a dethroned king. I will marry Aïssa, and become united to you by the closest ties.

"God has abandoned me; I will abandon God. I will become a worshipper of Mahomet, since it is he who saves me by your voice. The Saracens have seen me at work; they know whether I am a good captain and valiant soldier. I will aid them in conquering Spain anew; and, if they deem me worthy to command them, I will place a Mahometan king on the throne of Castile, to shame Christendom, absorbed in intestine quarrels rather than seriously devoted to the interests of religion."

Mothril listened with gloomy distrust to promises dictated by fear or enthusiasm.

"Escape first," said he; "then we shall see."

"I wish you," answered Don Pedro, "to have a more assured pledge of my promises than mere words. Bring Aïssa hither; I will pledge her my faith. You will write down my promises, and I shall sign them; we shall make a mutual alliance instead of an agreement."

While entering upon this engagement, Don Pedro had recovered all his cunning and all his strength of other days. He knew well that, by restoring Mothril's hope in the future, he prevented him from entirely abandoning his cause; and that, without some such hope, Mothril was just the man to deliver him to his enemies.

On the other hand, Mothril had the same idea; but he saw a way to save Don Pedro, that is to say, to rekindle a war, all the gain from which would be for his cause;

while, if Don Pedro were taken or killed, the Saracens would no longer have any motive for keeping up a ruinous conflict with enemies henceforth invincible.

That Don Pedro was an able captain Mothril knew well. Don Pedro was acquainted with the resources of the Moors, and he could, by becoming reconciled with the Christians, do them incalculable harm.

Besides, Mothril was linked to him by crime and ambition, two mysterious and potent bonds whose extent and force cannot be measured.

He listened favorably then to Don Pedro, and said,—

"I accept your offers gratefully, my king, and intend to put you in the way of realizing them. You wish to see Aïssa. I shall show her to you; but do not alarm her modesty by too passionate discourses. Remember she is hardly yet recovered from her painful illness."

"I will remember everything," answered Don Pedro.

Mothril went for Aïssa, who was restless because she had no news of Mauléon. The noise of arms, the footsteps of servants and soldiers, proclaimed the imminence of peril, but what she most dreaded was the arrival of Don Pedro; and she was ignorant of his arrival.

Mothril, who had made so many promises, was again obliged to lie. He dreaded lest she might betray before the king the scene of Maria Padilla's death. This interview was fraught with danger, but he could not refuse it to the king.

He had avoided all explanation till now; this time Don Pedro would question, Aïssa would speak.

"Aïssa," said he to the young girl, "I come to announce to you that Don Pedro has been conquered, and is concealed in this castle."

Aïssa turned pale.

"He would see you, and speak with you. Do not

refuse him, for he commands here. Moreover, he leaves this evening; it would be well to keep on good terms with him for the time."

Aïssa apparently believed the words of the Moor. However, a painful agitation taught her that fresh misfortunes were in store for her.

"I do not want to see the king," said she, "nor to speak with him, until I have seen the Sire de Mauléon, whom you have promised to bring here, whether conqueror or conquered."

"But Don Pedro is waiting—"

"What is that to me?"

"He commands, I tell you."

"I have a means of escaping his authority; you know it well. What did you promise?"

"I will keep my promises, Aïssa, but aid me."

"I shall not aid any one in deceiving."

"'T is well; deliver up my head, then. I am ready for death."

This menace always had its effect on Aïssa. Accustomed to the speedy methods of Arab justice, she knew that at the gesture of the master a head falls. It was natural for her to believe that Mothril's was in danger.

"What will the king say to me," she asked, "and where will he speak to me?"

"In my presence."

"It is not enough. I wish others to be present at the conversation."

"I promise there shall."

"I must be sure of it."

"How?"

"This chamber overlooks the terrace of the castle. Station men on this terrace, and let my women attend me. When my litter is carried thither, I will listen to what the king has to say."

"What you desire shall be done, Aïssa."

"And now, what does Don Pedro want to say to me?"

"He will make you a proposal of marriage."

Aïssa made a violent gesture of refusal.

"I know it well," interrupted Mothril; "but let him speak. Remember he leaves to-night."

"However, I shall not answer."

"On the contrary, you will answer courteously, Aïssa. Look at all those men-at-arms, Spaniards and Bretons, around the castle. These people will take us by force and put us to death, if they find the king here. We must allow Don Pedro to leave for our own safety."

"But the Sire de Mauléon?"

"He could not save us, if Don Pedro was with us."

Aïssa interrupted Mothril.

"You lie," said she, "and you can no longer even expect me to believe you wish to unite us. Where is he? What is he doing? Does he live?"

At this moment Musaron, by order of his master, raised the banner so well known to Aïssa.

The young woman perceived the beloved signal. She joined her hands in ecstasy, and cried,—

"He sees me, he hears me! Forgive me, Mothril, I suspected you wrongly. Go, then, and tell the king I follow you."

Mothril turned his eyes on the plain, saw the standard, recognized it, turned pale, and stammered,—

"I am going."

Then with fury,—

"Accursed Christian!" cried he, as soon as Aïssa could not hear him, "wilt thou ever pursue me? Oh, I shall escape thee!"

XLV.

THE FLIGHT.

Don Pedro received Aïssa upon the terrace, in the midst of the witnesses she had desired.

His love was expressed without violence; his desires had been cooled considerably by his deep interest in the prospect of escaping soon.

Aïssa, therefore, had no occasion to find fault with Mothril in the present circumstance; and, moreover, during the entire conference, she never stopped gazing upon that blessed banner of Mauléon, which waved resplendent in the sun at the extremity of the intrenchments.

Aïssa saw a man-at-arms under this banner, whom, in the distance, she could take for Agénor, as our knight supposed she would.

Having thus found a means of reassuring Aïssa, while revealing his presence, and of banishing from the mind of Mothril the suspicion of any hidden enterprise, Don Pedro decided that three of his trustiest friends should hold themselves in readiness to reconnoitre the earthen ramparts at nightfall.

There was, certainly, one point of the ramparts more carelessly guarded than the others: it was the side of the rock which descended perpendicularly to a ravine.

Several considerations counselled the king to fly in that direction along a cable fastened to the window of Aïssa. But, once below, the king would have no horse to enable him to get away quickly.

It was resolved, then, to examine the ramparts, find the weakest point, and open a breach through which — the sentinels being somewhere else or poniarded — the king could fly, mounted on a good horse.

But the brilliancy of the sun gave promise of a clear night, and this would interfere with the success of the scheme.

Suddenly, as if fortune was resolved to favor every wish of Don Pedro, a breeze from the west raised burning whirlwinds of sand from the plain, and coppery clouds, spun out into long streamers, appeared at the back of the horizon, like the vanguard of a terrible army.

According as the sun died away behind the towers of Toledo, these ever thickening clouds grew blacker and blacker, covering the heavens as with a sombre mantle.

Copious showers fell, about nine in the evening.

Agénor and Musaron had come, after sunset, to their hiding-place near the spring, and buried themselves in its depths.

Men chosen by Le Bègue de Vilaine had dug under the outer side of the rampart a shelter, in soil dried up by the sun, so that there was around Montiel an interrupted cordon of these concealed men.

Apparently, and as Agénor, who took the initiative in everything since the departure of the constable, had directed, sentinels, stationed at intervals, watched or seemed to be watching the line of circumvallation.

The rain had forced the sentinels to muffle themselves up in mantles; some even lay down in these mantles.

At ten, Agénor and Musaron heard the rock quiver under the footsteps of men.

They listened more attentively, and finally saw three of Don Pedro's officers, who displayed the utmost caution, indeed, creeping rather than walking; they were examining the rampart at a place evidently decided upon beforehand.

The sentinel had been designedly removed from this spot; there was only an officer, who lay under the earthen casing on the outside.

The officers saw that this point was not guarded. They joyfully communicated this discovery to one another, and Agénor heard their mutual congratulations as they ascended the steep staircase.

One of them said, in an undertone,—

"It is slippery, and it will be some trouble for the horses to keep their footing coming down."

"Yes, but they will run the better in the plain," answered another.

These words filled the heart of Agénor with joy.

He sent Musaron to the intrenchments to announce to the nearest Breton officer that something new was about to occur.

The officer, who was lying down, communicated the tidings to his neighbor, who did the same in turn, and soon the information given by Agénor made its journey around Montiel.

Scarcely had a half hour slipped by, when Agénor heard on the summit of the terrace a horse's shoe striking the rock.

It seemed as if this sound was indenting his heart, so keen and painful was the impression.

The sound drew nearer; the steps of other horses were heard, but the noise they made was perceptible to Agénor and Musaron alone.

The king, in fact, had ordered the hoofs of the horses to be wrapped up in tow, in order that they might resound more softly.

The king was last; a little dry cough he could not restrain betrayed his presence.

He walked with difficulty, holding up his horse by the bridle, for its hind feet slipped during the rapid descent.

When the fugitives passed in front of the grotto, Agénor and Musaron recognized them. They had a perfect view of Don Pedro; his face was pale but confident.

As soon as the first two fugitives reached the intrenchment, they took horse and cleared the parapet. Scarcely did they advance ten paces, when they fell into a ditch prepared for them, and twenty men-at-arms gagged and bore them away without noise.

Don Pedro, who suspected nothing, leaped into the saddle in turn; suddenly, he was seized by Agénor, who clasped him in his sinewy arms, while Musaron closed his mouth with a girdle.

This done, Musaron pricked the steed with his dagger; it jumped over the intrenchment and fled, the sound of its rapid gallop echoing back from the stony soil.

Don Pedro struggled with the vigor of despair.

"Take care!" said Agénor in his ear. "I shall be forced to kill you if you make any noise."

Don Pedro succeeded in getting out these stifled words: —

"I am the king! treat me as a knight."

"I know well you are the king," said Agénor, "and I waited for you here. On my knightly faith, you shall not be ill-treated."

He took the king upon his robust shoulders, and, in this fashion, traversed the line of intrenchments in the midst of the officers, who leaped for joy.

"Silence! silence!" said Agénor, "no noise, gentlemen, no cries! I have done the work of the constable, do not make me fail in my own."

He carried the prisoner to the tent of Le Bègue de Vilaine, who jumped on his neck and embraced him tenderly.

"Quick! quick!" cried the captain, "couriers to the king, who is before Toledo; couriers to the constable, who is scouring the country, to inform him that the war is over."

XLVI.

A DIFFICULTY.

WHILE the entire camp of the Bretons was passing the night in the intoxication of triumph, and Don Pedro in the anguish of terror, cavaliers, mounted on the best horses in the army, were riding to notify Don Henry and the constable of what had occurred.

Agénor had spent the night with the prisoner, who, shutting himself up in a fierce silence, repelled all consolation and all assistance.

A king, a captain, could not be left bound; the prisoner, therefore, after giving his word of honor that he would not make any attempt to escape, was unbound.

"But," said Le Bègue de Vilaine, "we know what the word of Don Pedro is worth; double the post, and let the tent be so surrounded that he cannot even think of escaping."

The constable was found three leagues from Montiel, driving the remains of the conquered army before him like sheep, and crowning the fruitful returns of his important victory with a booty of prisoners rich enough to afford a generous ransom.

For the Toledans had refused to open their gates, even to their vanquished allies, so much did they dread one of those stratagems common in barbarous times, during which craft took as many strong places as force.

The constable had no sooner learned the news than he cried, —

"This Mauléon has more brains than we!"

And he pushed forward towards Montiel, with a joy hard to describe.

Scarcely had he arrived, — the new-born day was silvering the mountain crests, — when the constable took Mauléon, modest in his triumph, to his arms.

"Thanks, messire," said he, "for your courageous perseverance and for your sagacity. Where is the prisoner?" he added.

"In the tent of Le Bègue de Vilaine," answered Mauléon, "but he sleeps or feigns to sleep."

"I do not wish to see him," said Bertrand; "it is fitting that the first person to have an interview with Don Pedro be Henry, his conqueror and master. Is he well guarded? All that certain infernal spirits need to gain their freedom is a good prayer to the devil."

"There are thirty knights around his tent, messire," replied Agénor. "Don Pedro will not escape, unless an angel of Satan draw him away by the hair, as was formerly the case, with the prophet Habakkuk; even then, we shall see him coming forth."

"And I," said Musaron, "will send a shaft whizzing through the air that will bring him to hell before the angel of darkness."

"Let a camp bed be placed in front of the tent for me," ordered the constable. "I wish, like the others, to guard the prisoner and present him myself to Don Henry."

In compliance with this command, his bed, a bed of boards and heather, was erected at the very door of the tent.

"By the way," said Bertrand, "he is almost an unbeliever; he is capable of killing himself. Have his arms been taken from him?"

"We did not dare, seigneur; his is a sacred head. He has been proclaimed king before the altar of God."

"You are right. Besides, the orders of Don Henry are to give him all respect and assistance."

"You see, seigneur," said Agénor, "how deeply the Spaniard lied when he told you Don Pedro was not in Montiel."

"And, therefore, we shall have this Spaniard and the entire garrison hanged," said Le Bègue de Vilaine, composedly. "By lying, he has released our constable from his pledge."

"Monseigneur," replied Agénor, quickly, "these unfortunate soldiers are not culpable in doing what their leader orders them to do. Besides, if they surrender, you would commit an assassination, and, if they do not surrender, they will not be taken."

"They will be taken by famine," replied the constable.

The idea of seeing Aïssa dying of hunger carried Mauléon beyond the bounds of his natural discretion.

"Oh! messeigneurs," he said, "you will not be guilty of such cruelty!"

"We shall chastise falsehood and disloyalty," answered the constable. "Besides, ought we not all to rejoice that this falsehood gives us the opportunity of punishing the Saracen Mothril? I am going to send a flag of truce to this scoundrel, announcing that Don Pedro is taken; that his capture proves he was in Montiel; that consequently those in the castle lied, and that, to give an example to all felons, the garrison shall be decimated after its surrender, or condemned to perish of hunger if it does not surrender."

"And Doña Aïssa?" interrupted Mauléon, pale with anxiety and love.

"We shall spare the women, as a matter of course,"

replied Du Guesclin; "for cursed be the man of war who does not spare the old men, the little children, and the women!"

"But Mothril will not spare Aïssa, monseigneur; he knows she would belong to some one after him. You do not know him; he will kill her. Now, you promised, messire, to grant me whatever I should ask: I ask the life of Aïssa."

"And I grant it, my friend; but how do you expect to save her?"

"I must beg you, monseigneur, to send none but me as the bearer of a flag of truce to Mothril, and to leave me at liberty to speak what words I choose. If you do so, I answer for the prompt submission of the Moor and the garrison. But, for pity's sake, monseigneur, spare the unfortunate soldiers! They have done nothing."

"I see I must surrender. You have served me so well that I can refuse you nothing. The king also owes you as much as I do, since you have taken Don Pedro; and, but for that, our victory of yesterday was incomplete. I may then, in his name as well as in mine, grant your desire. Aïssa belongs to you; the soldiers, and even the officers of the garrison, are offered their lives, but Mothril must be hanged."

"Seigneur —"

"Oh, as far as that goes, you need not ask anything more; you will not obtain it. I should offend God if I spared that wretch."

"Monseigneur, the first thing he will ask me will be is his life safe; what shall I answer?"

"You will answer what you like, Messire de Mauléon."

"But you would have spared him, according to the conditions of the truce made with Rodrigo Sanatrias."

"Him? never! I said the garrison. Mothril is a

Saracen, and I do not reckon him among the defenders of the castle; moreover, this is a thing to be settled between me and God, I tell you. Once, my friend, you have Doña Aïssa, nothing further concerns you. Let me alone."

"Once more, monseigneur, allow me to entreat you. It is true that this Mothril is a wretch; it is true that God would be pleased with his chastisement; but he is disarmed, he can work no more harm —"

"It is as if you were speaking to a statue, Sire de Mauléon," answered the constable; "pray, let me rest. As to the words you will speak to the garrison, I leave you free. Go!"

There was nothing to answer. Agénor knew that Du Guesclin, once pledged to an undertaking, was inflexible, and never turned back.

He understood also that Mothril, when he learned that Don Pedro was in the power of the Bretons, would spare no one, because aware that no one would spare him.

Mothril, in fact, was one of those men who can bear the weight of the hatred they inspire and suffer its consequences. Implacable towards others, he renounced all mercy for himself stoically.

On the other hand, never would Mothril consent to surrender Aïssa. The position of Agénor was as difficult as can well be imagined.

"If I lie," said he, "I am dishonored; if I promise life to Mothril and do not keep my word, I become unworthy of woman's love and man's esteem."

He was plunged in these cruel perplexities, when the trumpets announced the arrival of King Henry before the tent.

The day was already advanced, and from the camp

could be seen the terrace upon which Mothril and Don Rodrigo were walking, all the while speaking earnestly.

"What the constable has not granted you," said Musaron, seeing that his master was crushed with sorrow, "Don Henry will grant; ask and you shall obtain. What matters the mouth that says yes, provided it says a *yes* you can without falsehood report to Mothril!"

"I shall try," said Agénor.

And he went and knelt by the stirrup of Don Henry, whom a squire was helping to alight.

"Good news, it seems!" said the king.

"Yes, sire."

"I wish to reward you, Mauléon; ask of me a county, if you wish."

"I ask of you the life of Mothril."

"It is more than a county," replied Henry, "but I grant it."

"Speak quick, monsieur," whispered Musaron; "the constable is coming, and it will be too late, if he hears."

Agénor kissed the hand of the king, who, after dismounting, cried, —

"Good-day, my dear constable; it appears the traitor is ours."

"Yes, monseigneur," answered Bertrand, who feigned not to have seen Agénor talking with Henry.

The young man began running as if he were carrying away a treasure. As the bearer of a flag of truce, he had the right to take with him two trumpeters; he chose them, and, with them before and the inseparable Musaron behind, he climbed the path leading to the first gate of the castle.

XLVII.

THE DIPLOMACY OF LOVE.

It was opened without delay, and he could, as he advanced, judge of the difficulties of the road he was ascending.

Sometimes the path was not more than a foot in width, and the rock on every side became more perpendicular according as the funnel widened; the Bretons, being little accustomed to mountains, were seized with dizziness.

"Love renders us very imprudent, messire," said Musaron to his master. "However, God is at the end of all!"

"Do you forget that our persons are inviolable?"

"Eh! monsieur, what does the accursed Moor care for that? Do you think anything on earth is inviolable, as far as he is concerned?"

Agénor imposed silence on his squire and went on climbing. At length he reached the terrace where Mothril was waiting for him, having recognized him while he was mounting.

"The Frenchman!" he murmured; "what means his presence in the castle?"

The trumpets sounded. Mothril made a sign that he was listening.

"I come, on the part of the constable," began Agénor, "to say this: 'I made a truce with my enemies, on condition that nobody left the castle. I granted life to every one on this condition; to-day, I must change my intention, since you have broken your word.' "

Mothril turned pale and answered, —

" In what ? "

" This night," continued Agénor, " three horsemen passed the intrenchments in spite of our sentinels."

" Well," said Mothril, making a mighty effort to recover his self-possession, " you ought to punish them with death, for they have perjured themselves."

" That would be easy," answered Agénor, " if we had them, but they escaped."

" Why did you not stop them ? " cried Mothril, unable to entirely moderate his joy, after having experienced such anxiety.

" Because our guards, trusting to your word, watched less carefully than usual, and because, according to the reasoning of Señor Rodrigo, who is here, none of you had an interest in escaping, as life was promised to all."

" And so you have decided ? " said the Moor.

" To change something in the conditions of the treaty."

" Ah ! I suspected as much," retorted Mothril, bitterly. " The clemency of Christians is as fragile as a glass; you must take care not to break it while drinking. You have come, then, to say, that several soldiers — were they soldiers ? — having escaped from Montiel, you will be forced to put us all to death."

" In the first place, Saracen," said Agénor, wounded by such a reproach and such a supposition, " in the first place, you must know who these fugitives are."

" Why should I know ? "

" Count your garrison."

" I am not their commander."

" Then, as you are not a part of the garrison," rejoined Agénor, quickly, "you are not comprehended in the truce."

"You are cunning for so young a man."

"I have become so through distrust, having seen so many Saracens; but answer."

"I am really their leader," said Mothril, who feared to lose the benefits of a capitulation, if capitulation there was.

"You see I was justified in being crafty, since you lied. But that is not the question. You confess you have violated the conditions."

"It is you who say so, Christian."

"And you should believe me," retorted Mauléon, haughtily. "This, then, is the order of the constable, our leader. The place must be surrendered on this very day, or a rigorous blockade will begin."

"Is that all?" said Mothril.

"That is all."

"You will starve us?"

"Yes."

"And if we wish to die?"

"You are free to do so."

Mothril regarded Agénor with a peculiar expression which the latter understood perfectly.

"All?" said he, emphasizing the word.

"All," replied Mauléon; "but, if you die, it is because you are anxious for death. Don Pedro will not succor you, believe me."

"You think so?"

"I am sure of it."

"Why?"

"Because we have an army to oppose him, and he has none, and because, long before he has one, you will all be dead of hunger."

"You reason closely, Christian."

"Save your life, then, since it is in your power to do so."

" Ah! you offer us life?"

"I offer you life."

" On the faith of whom? the constable?"

" On the faith of the king, who has just arrived."

"He has just arrived, you say?" asked Mothril, anxiously; "but I have not seen him."

"Look at his tent, or, rather, at that of Le Bègue de Vilaine."

"Yes — yes. You are sure our lives will be spared?"

"I guarantee it."

"And mine also?"

"For yours, Mothril, I have the word of the king."

"We can retire where we please?"

"Where you please."

"With our followers, baggage, and treasure?"

"Yes, Saracen."

"It is all very fine — "

"You do not believe it. You are mad. Why should we invite you to come to us to-day, when we are sure to have you, dead or alive, by staying here a month?"

"Ah! you are afraid of Don Pedro."

"I assure you we are not afraid of him."

"Christian, I will reflect."

"If, in two hours, you do not surrender," said the impatient young man, "consider yourself dead. The iron girdle will no longer be open."

"Well! Two hours! it is not a proof of great generosity," said Mothril, questioning the horizon anxiously, as if from beyond the plain some saviour was going to arise.

"Is that your full answer?" asked Agénor.

"In two hours," stammered Mothril, absently.

"Oh, monsieur! he will surrender, you have persuaded him," whispered Musaron, in the ear of his master.

Suddenly, Mothril gazed in the direction of the Breton camp with an earnestness he did not try to conceal.

"Oh, oh!" he murmured, pointing out the tent of Le Bègue de Vilaine to Rodrigo.

The Spaniard leaned over the parapet to see better.

"It would seem," said Mothril, "as if your Christians were fighting among themselves. Look, every one is running towards yon tent."

It was true. A crowd of soldiers and officers were running towards the tent and giving signs of the keenest anxiety.

The tent was rocking, as if it had been shaken from within by people wrestling.

Agénor saw the constable hurrying thither with angry gestures.

"Something strange and frightful is passing in the tent occupied by Don Pedro, Musaron," said he. "Let us return."

The attention of the Moor was distracted by this incomprehensible movement. That of Rodrigo was still more so. Agénor took advantage of their forgetfulness to descend the most difficult slope with his Bretons. In the middle of the way, he heard a horrible cry mounting to heaven from the plain.

It was fortunate for him that he reached the barriers; hardly was the last gate shut behind him, when the thunderous voice of Mothril shouted: —

"Allah! Allah! the traitor deceived me. The King Don Pedro has been taken. Allah! arrest the Frenchman as a hostage; to the gates! shut! shut!"

But Agénor had just cleared the intrenchment, he was in safety; he could even see in its entirety the terrible spectacle which the Moor had witnessed from the top of the terrace.

"God be praised!" said Agénor, trembling, and raising his arms to Heaven; "a minute more and we were taken and lost; what I see in yonder tent would excuse the bloodiest reprisals on the part of the Moor."

XLVIII.

WHAT WAS SEEN IN THE TENT OF LE BÈGUE DE VILAINE.

THE King Don Henry, after granting the pardon of Mothril to Agénor, and dismissing him, wiped his face, and said to the constable, —

"My friend, my heart is beating very fast. I am about to see in his humiliation one whom I hate mortally. My joy is mingled with bitterness, and I cannot, at the moment, explain this mixed feeling."

"That proves, sire," answered the constable, "that the heart of Your Majesty is noble and great; if such were not the case, the joy of triumph is all it could contain."

"It is odd," added the king, "that I enter this tent only with reluctance and, I repeat, a shrinking of the heart. How is he?"

"Sire, he is seated upon a stool; he is hiding his head with both his hands. He seems utterly prostrated."

Henry of Trastamare made a sign with his hand, and every one except the constable retired.

"Constable," said he, in an undertone, "a last counsel, if you please. I wish to spare his life; but whether ought I to exile him or shut him up in a fortress?"

"Ask no counsel of me, sire," replied the constable, "for I cannot give you one. You are wiser than I, and you have a brother before you. God will inspire you."

"Your words have made my decision irrevocable, constable; thanks."

The king raised a corner of the cloth that hung over the entrance, and went in.

Don Pedro had not abandoned the posture described to the king by Du Guesclin. His despair alone was no longer silent; it was revealed externally by cries, now hoarse, now clamorous. It looked like the beginning of madness.

At the sound of Henry's footsteps, Don Pedro raised his head.

As soon as he recognized his conqueror by his majestic demeanor and his crest, shaped like a golden lion, he was seized with a fit of fury.

"You come," said he, "you dare to come!"

Henry did not answer, and kept his reserved attitude and his silence.

"Vainly did I call to you during the onslaught," continued Don Pedro, growing more and more excited; "but you have only the courage to insult a vanquished enemy, and, even at this moment, you hide your face that I may not see its paleness."

Henry slowly unfastened the hasps of his helmet, and laid it on the table.

His face was indeed pale, but his eyes preserved their mild and humane serenity.

This calmness exasperated Don Pedro; he rose.

"Yes," said he, "I recognize my father's bastard,— him who called himself king of Castile, forgetting there can be no king in Castile as long as I live."

To the savage insults of his enemy, Henry tried to oppose patience, but anger gradually mounted in a flush to his forehead, and drops of cold sweat were beginning to run down his cheeks.

"Take care!" said he, in a trembling voice; "you are here, as it were, in my house; do not forget it. I do not insult you, and you dishonor your birth by words unworthy of us both."

"Bastard!" cried Don Pedro, "bastard! bastard!"

"Wretch! you wish, then, to unchain my wrath?"

"Oh! I am very tranquil on that score," said Don Pedro, approaching, with eyes aflame and livid lips; "your wrath will not lead you farther than the care of your safety demands. You are afraid—"

"You lie!" vociferated Don Henry, losing all self-control.

For answer, Don Pedro seized Henry by the throat, and Don Henry clasped Don Pedro in his arms.

"Ah!" said the vanquished monarch, "this is the battle we missed; you will find that it shall be decisive."

They struggled with so much fury that the tent was shaken; the canvas rocked to and fro, and the constable, Le Bègue, and several officers ran up at the noise.

In order to enter, they were obliged to cut asunder the canvas of the tent with their swords. The two enemies, locked together, entwined like two serpents, clung to the very curtains with their spur-armed feet.

Then were revealed the interior of this tent and the murderous struggle.

The constable lifted up his voice in a piercing cry.

A thousand soldiers ran at once in the direction of the tent.

This was what Mothril saw from the top of the terrace; this was what Mauléon began to see from the end of the intrenchment.

The two adversaries rolled and twisted, seeking, every time they had an arm free, to seize a weapon.

Don Pedro was the luckier of the two: he succeeded in getting Don Henry under, and, pinning him with his

IN THE TENT OF LE BÈGUE DE VILAINE. 383

knee, he drew from his belt a little dagger, and made ready to strike.

But the danger restored Henry's strength; he overturned his brother again, and held him on the side, and, side by side, they breathed in each other's faces the devouring fire of their impotent hate.

"This must have an end," cried Don Pedro, seeing none dare touch them, so much did the royal majesty and the horror of the situation restrain the by-standers. "To-day, neither king of Castile nor usurper. I cease to reign, but I am avenged. They will kill me, but I shall have drunk thy blood."

And, with unforeseen vigor, he rolled his brother, exhausted by the struggle, under him, seized him by the throat, and raised his hand to plunge the dagger in his enemy's body.

Then Du Guesclin, seeing him already thrusting at the coat of mail and cuirass in search of an opening, seized Don Pedro's foot in his sinewy grasp, and made him lose his balance. The wretch rolled, in turn, under Don Henry.

"I am neither making nor unmaking kings," said the constable in a hoarse, trembling voice, "I am aiding my lord."

Henry was now able to breathe; and, his strength renewed, he drew his cutlass.

With the quickness of a lightning flash, the steel was plunged through Don Pedro's throat. A stream of blood spurted out and smote the eyes of the conqueror, stifling the terrible cry that escaped Don Pedro's lips.

The hand of the wounded monarch relaxed, the light in his eyes was quenched, his brows, diabolically contracted, fell backwards, and the sound of his head, striking the ground heavily, was heard.

"Oh, what have you done!" said Agénor, who had rushed into the tent and was regarding, with hair on end, the dead body swimming in blood, and the conqueror on his knees, his weapon in his right hand, while with his left he tried to support himself.

An awful silence hovered over the assembly.

The royal homicide dropped his reddened poniard.

Next, a rivulet of blood was seen to stream from beneath the corpse and flow slowly down the slope of the rocky soil.

Each recoiled before this blood, still smoking, as if it still preserved the fire of hate and wrath.

Don Henry, when he was raised, sat down in a corner of the tent and hid his darkened face in both his hands. He could not endure the light of day and the looks of the by-standers.

The constable, as gloomy as he, but more energetic, gently lifted him up, and dismissed the spectators of this terrible scene.

"Certainly," said he, "'t would have been better had you shed this blood in the brunt of battle with your sword or battle-axe. But what God does he does well, and what he has done is accomplished. Come, sire, recover your courage."

"It was he who wished to die," murmured the king. "I would have pardoned him. See that his remains be not long exposed to the gaze of — Let an honorable burial —"

"Sire, think no more of all this, — forget; let us fulfil our task."

The king retired before a hedge of soldiers, who were in a state of silent consternation, and concealed himself in another tent.

Du Guesclin summoned the provost of the Bretons.

"You will cut off this head," said he, pointing to the body of Don Pedro, "and you, Bègue de Vilaine, will send it to Toledo. It is the custom of this country, where, at least, the usurpers of the name of the dead have no longer any right to trouble the reign and repose of the living."

He had scarcely finished, when a Spaniard came from the fortress, on the part of the governor, to say the garrison would lay down its arms at eight in the evening, according to the conditions offered by the constable's envoy.

XLIX.

THE MOOR'S RESOLUTION.

ALL this scene, so terrible and so swift, had been viewed from the castle of Montiel, thanks to the opening of the curtains in the tent and the agitation of the principal actors.

We have seen that, during the interview between Agénor and Mothril, the latter, while listening to the proposals of the bearer of the flag of truce, gazed frequently in the direction of the plain, where something seemed to attract his attention.

Agénor, in persuading him that the Bretons were ignorant of the names of the fugitives on the night before, also persuaded him that these fugitives could not have been taken.

This news reassured Mothril as to the fate of Don Pedro, for the darkness of the night had prevented the people in the castle from seeing the result of the escape, and the Bretons had kept the deepest silence while making the capture.

Mothril, then, had every reason to believe Don Pedro in safety.

This was why he began by treating the proposals of Mauléon with contempt. But, while looking over the plain, he saw three horses wandering on the heath, and recognized, beyond all possible doubt, — he whose glance was so unerring, — the horse of Don Pedro, all white except for its spots of fire, that noble animal that had borne its master back from the battlefield of Montiel, and which, it was thought, would carry him like a thunderbolt beyond reach of his enemies.

The Bretons in their excitement had seized the riders and forgotten the horses, which, seeing themselves free, and, moreover, frightened by the impetuosity of the aggressors, had fled beyond the intrenchments and gained the country.

During the rest of the night, they had wandered around, browsing and gambolling; but, at daylight, instinct, or, perhaps, fidelity, had brought them back to a spot near the castle, where Mothril perceived them.

They had not come to the circular path along which they had started, so that the ravine lay between them and the castle, and this deep, craggy ravine stopped them.

Hidden by the projections of the rocks, they gazed now and then at Montiel, then turned to graze, in the turnings and twistings of the rocks, upon the mosses and resinous madroños, whose berries resemble the strawberry in color and perfume.

When Mothril perceived these animals, he turned pale, and began to have doubts as to the veracity of Agénor. It was then he commenced to discuss the conditions and sought to have a promise that his own life would be spared.

But, suddenly, the scene in the tent appeared to him in all its horror. He recognized the golden lion of Henry of Trastamare, the reddish locks of Don Pedro, his energetic gestures and his vigor; he recognized his voice when the last cry, the cry of death, escaped, strident and despairing, from his gaping throat.

At one time, the Moor was determined to hold Agénor in order to keep him as a hostage or else tear him limb from limb; at another, he lost all hope; then, again, seeing the massacre of Don Pedro, and seeing neither the cause nor meaning of the struggle, he told himself that he was indeed lost, — he, the tempter of the assassinated king.

From that moment he understood all the tactics of Agénor.

The latter promised him life, but would allow him to be massacred on leaving Montiel, so that he himself might have Aïssa freely and forever.

"I may die," said the Moor to himself; "still, I shall try to live; but, as for the young girl, Christian, thou shalt not have her, — rather shalt thou die along with me."

He arranged with Rodrigo that they should be silent about Don Pedro's death, and he had the officers of Montiel assembled.

All agreed that it was necessary to surrender.

Mothril vainly tried to persuade these men that death was better than submission to the discretion of the conquerors.

Rodrigo himself combated his proposal.

"They hate Don Pedro, and, perhaps, some other grandees," said he; "but we, whom they have spared in battle, we who are Spaniards like Don Henry, why should we be massacred, when the promise of the constable guarantees us from harm? We are neither Saracens nor Moors, and we invoke the same God as our conquerors."

Mothril saw well that all was over, when his officers were thus resigned. He bent his head, and shut himself up alone in the circle of an immutable and terrible resolution.

Rodrigo announced to him that the garrison would surrender immediately. Mothril requested that the capitulation should not take place till evening.

His wish was obeyed for the last time.

It was then the bearer of the flag of truce came to propose eight o'clock in the evening as the hour for the surrender of the fortress.

Mothril shut himself up in the governor's apartments, "to pray," he told Rodrigo.

"You will," said he to him, "march out the garrison at the appointed hour, that is to say, at nightfall, the soldiers first, the lower officers next, then the officers and yourself; I shall be the last to leave, with Doña Aïssa."

As soon as Mothril was alone, he went and opened the door of Aïssa's chamber.

"You see, my child," said he, "that everything turns out as you wish. Not only is Don Pedro gone, but he is dead."

"Dead!" cried the young girl, with an expression of horror in which there was, however, a slight trace of doubt.

"Come," said Mothril, calmly, "come and see."

"Oh!" murmured Aïssa, divided between her terror and her desire to know the truth.

"Do not hesitate, do not force me to drag you; I want you to see how Christians treat their vanquished enemies, once they have made them prisoners, those Christians you love so much!"

He drew the young girl outside the room and to the terrace, and showed her the tent of Le Bègue de Vilaine, with the dead body of Don Pedro still lying stretched within it.

At the moment Aïssa, dumb and pale, was gazing upon this frightful spectacle, a man knelt beside the body, and, with a Breton cleaver, separated the head from it.

Aïssa uttered a piercing cry and fell almost fainting into the arms of Mothril.

The Moor carried her to her chamber, and, kneeling at the foot of the bed upon which Aïssa was reposing, —

"Child," said he, "you have seen; you know! The fate which has stricken Don Pedro awaits me. The Christians have offered me life if I surrender; but they also had promised life to Don Pedro. You see how they keep their word. You are young and inexperienced, but your heart is pure, your judgment is upright; advise me, I entreat you."

"I! advise you!"

"You are acquainted with a Christian—"

"And a Christian," cried Aïssa, "who will not break his word, and who will save you, because he loves me."

"You think so?" said Mothril, shaking his head, dubiously.

"I am sure of it," added the young girl, with all the enthusiasm of love.

"Child!" said he, "what authority has he among his people? He is a simple knight, and has above him captains, generals, a constable, a king! That he might pardon me I grant you; the others are implacable, they will kill us!"

"Kill me!" cried the young girl, showing something of a selfish emotion she could not repress, and baring to the Moor the depths of her soul, that is to say, the depths of his peril and the need of a prompt resolution.

"No," said he, "not you; you are a young girl, beautiful and desirable. All these captains and generals, this constable and this king, will pardon you in the hope of being rewarded by a smile, or a guerdon more flattering still. Oh, Frenchmen and Spaniards are gallant!" he added, with a baleful smile. But I am simply a dangerous man in their eyes; they will sacrifice me—"

"I tell you Agénor is there, and will defend my honor at the expense of his life."

"And, if he died, what would become of you?"

"I, too, can find a refuge in death."

"Oh! I see death with less resignation than you, Aïssa, because I am nearer it."

"I swear I shall save you."

"Upon what will you swear?"

"Upon my life. Besides, you are altogether mistaken as to the influence Agénor exercises. The king loves him; he is a good servant of the constable; they confided an important mission to him, you know, — at Soria."

"Yes, and you know, too, Aïssa, as it seems," said the Moor, his eyes laden with a gloomy jealousy.

Aïssa blushed with shame and fear, recalling that, for her, Soria was a name of love and of ineffable delights.

Then she resumed, —

"My knight will save us both. If necessary, I will make this condition — "

"Listen, then, my child," cried the Moor, losing patience, when he saw every step of the road along which he would hurry impeded by this amorous obstinacy; "Agénor has so little power to save us, that he came here a while ago — "

"He here," said Aïssa, " and you did not warn me?"

"So that every eye might be watchful of your love? You forget your dignity, young girl! He came, I say, to beg me to find some way of delivering you from the outrages of the Christians. If I did so, he promised to defend me."

"Outrage to me! to me, who will become a Christian!"

Mothril uttered a cry of rage, which imperious necessity forced him to repress immediately.

"What shall I do?" continued Mothril; "time

presses; advise me. This evening the castle will be delivered to the Christians; this evening, I shall be dead, and you will belong to the chiefs of the Christians as a part of the spoil."

" What did Agénor say? tell me."

" He proposed a terrible means, a means that will prove to you how great the danger is."

" A means of safety?"

" A means of escape."

" What was it?"

" Look through this window. You see that, on this side, the rock of Montiel is perpendicular, impracticable, and runs down to the bottom of the ravine in such fashion that guards at this point would be superfluous, for only flying birds and crawling snakes can rise or descend along this rock. Moreover, since they no longer watch Don Pedro, the French have totally abandoned this point."

Aïssa looked with dismay down into the gulf, already tinged with black by the approach of night.

" Well! " said she.

" Well! the Frank has advised me to tie a rope to the bars of this grating and to have this rope reach down to the ravine, as we would have done for the king, and as he would have done, were it not that he could not find a horse at the bottom.

" The Sire de Mauléon advised me to knot this cord around me, and, with you in my arms, to glide down to the bottom, while the Christian army was engaged at the gates in relieving the garrison, which will file out unarmed at about eight in the evening."

Aïssa, with eyes on fire and quivering lips, listened to the Moor, and went a second time to look down into the yawning abyss.

"He gave you that advice?" said she.

"'When you have descended,' he added," continued Mothril, "'you will find me waiting for you; I will help you to escape.'"

"What! he will abandon us? he will leave me alone with you?"

Mothril turned pale.

"No," he said. "You see the three horses browsing yonder on the jaras and madroños along the other slope of the ravine?"

"Yes, yes, I see them."

"The Frank has already kept half his promise. He has sent his horses for us. Count them, Aïssa."

"There are three."

"And how many are needed for our escape?"

"Oh, yes, yes!" she cried, "three for you, me, and him! Oh, Mothril! oh, to fly with him I would be willing to plunge into a gulf of fire! Let us start."

"You will not be frightened?"

"And he waiting for me?"

"Be ready, then, as soon as the drums and trumpets announce that the garrison is in motion."

"The rope —"

"Here it is. It would support a weight three times greater than ours; and as to its length, I have measured it by letting a leaden ball attached to a string drop to the bottom of the ravine. You will be courageous and strong, Aïssa?"

"Strong as if I were going to my wedding feast with my knight," answered the young girl, intoxicated with joy.

L.

SWORD AND SHAFT.

Night fell on Montiel; a night dark and cold, which enveloped in a damp winding-sheet forms and colors.

At half-past eight the trumpets gave the signal, and a long line of torches was seen descending the steep, rocky road which ended at the principal gate.

Officers and soldiers appeared one by one, each making submission, and each kindly received by the constable, who, standing near the intrenchment, watched the departure of the men and of the baggage.

Suddenly, an idea came to Musaron; he approached his master and said in his ear, —

"That infernal Moor has treasures; he is capable of throwing them down some precipice, so that we may not profit by them. I think I'll take a turn round the fortress, for, like a cat, I can see clear by night, and, certainly, I don't find much pleasure in looking at these scurvy Spanish prisoners filing out."

"Go," said Agénor; "there is a treasure Mothril will not throw down any precipice, the most precious of all treasures to me! That treasure I am watching for at this gate, and I am going to seize it as soon as it comes in sight!"

"Oh, you are, are you?" returned Musaron, with an air of sinister doubt; then he slipped down among the brushwood in the ditch, and vanished.

The soldiers were still filing out; next came the cavalry. Two hundred horses take a long time to descend, one by one, such roads as that of Montiel.

The heart of Mauléon was eaten up with impatience. A fatal presentiment was piercing his head like a keen-edged sword.

"Fool that I am!" he said to himself. "Mothril has my word; he knows that his life is safe; he knows that the least misfortune happening to this young girl would expose him to the most horrible tortures. Then Aïssa, who has seen my banner, must have taken her precautions. She will appear; I am about to see her; I was mad."

Suddenly, the hand of Musaron rested on Agénor's shoulder.

"Monsieur," said he, in a whisper, "come quick."

"What is the matter? how excited you are!"

"Monsieur, come, in the name of Heaven! What I have foreseen is happening. The Moor is moving off through a window."

"Well! what does that matter to me?"

"I am afraid it matters much to you. The objects being let down from the window looked to me like living objects."

"We must give the alarm."

"Let us do nothing of the sort. The Moor, if it is he, will defend himself; he will kill some one. The soldiers are brutal and are not in love; they will spare nothing. Let us manage our own affairs ourselves."

"You are mad, Musaron; you would, for some wretched coffers, expose me to the risk of losing the first look of Aïssa."

"Then I am going alone," said Musaron, impatiently; "if I am killed, it will be your fault."

Agénor made no reply. He quietly separated

from the group of captains and took his way to the intrenchment.

"Quick, quick!" cried the squire; "let us try to arrive in time —"

Agénor doubled his pace. But nothing could be more difficult than this race through creepers, brambles, and brushwood.

"Do you see?" said Musaron, showing a white form to his master that was gliding along the black wall down to the bottom of the ravine.

Agénor uttered a cry.

"Is that you, Agénor?" asked a sweet voice.

"Well, monsieur! what do you say now?" queried Musaron.

"Oh!" cried Agénor, "let us run quick to the edge of the ravine and surprise them."

"Agénor!" repeated the voice of Aïssa, which Mothril tried to silence by energetic appeals in a low voice.

"Let us lie down on the coping, monsieur, and neither speak nor show ourselves."

"But yonder is the way they are flying!"

"Oh! it will always be easy to catch a young girl, especially when that young girl asks nothing better than to be caught. Lie down, my dear master, I tell you!"

But Mothril had heard, as the tiger hears, when he enters his lair, bearing a great prey between his teeth.

Hearing nothing further, he again took courage and climbed with agile step the slope of the trench.

With one hand he held Aïssa; with the other he seized the branches and roots.

He reached the crest and recovered breath.

Then Agénor rose up and cried, —

"Aïssa! Aïssa!"

"I was sure it was he," answered the young girl.

"The Christian!" howled Mothril, furiously.

"But Agénor is yonder, yonder; let us go yonder," said Aïssa, trying to free herself from the arms of Mothril and run to her lover.

The only reply of the Moor was to clasp her tighter and drag her towards the spot where he had seen the horse of Don Pedro.

Agénor ran, but stumbled at every step, and Mothril was gaining ground and drawing nearer to one of the horses.

"This way! this way!" cried Aïssa; "come, Mauléon, come!"

"If you say a word, you are dead!" articulated Mothril in her ear; "do you wish to bring every one here with your stupid cries? do you wish to prevent your lover from being able to come to find us?"

Aïssa was silent. Mothril found a horse, laid hold of the mane, jumped into the saddle, and flung the young girl before him; then he started at a gallop. The horse had belonged to one of the officers taken with Don Pedro.

Mauléon heard the horse's gallop, and uttered a roar of anger.

"He flies! he flies! Aïssa, answer!"

"I am here! here!" said the young girl, and her voice was lost in the thick veil which Mothril pressed against her lips, at the risk of stifling her.

Agénor ran like a madman; he fell on his knees, exhausted, breathless.

"Oh, God is not just!" he murmured.

"Monsieur, monsieur, here is a horse!" cried Musaron; "courage! come, I have him."

Agénor leaped with joy; he recovered his strength, and placed his foot in the stirrup Musaron held for him.

He galloped like lightning in the track of Mothril. His steed was that marvellous courser, with the spots of fire, which had not its equal in Andalusia, so that Agénor flew over the ground and was soon close to Mothril. He cried to Aïssa, —

"Courage! I am near you!"

Mothril plunged his poniard into the side of his horse, which neighed with pain.

"Give her back to me! I will do you no harm," cried Agénor to the Moor. "By the living God! I will let you escape."

A disdainful laugh was the Moor's answer.

"Aïssa! Aïssa! Slip down from his arms, Aïssa!"

The young girl was choking, and uttered groans of despair under the strong hand that was stifling her.

At length, Mothril felt on his back the burning breath of Don Pedro's horse. Agénor was able to seize the robe of his mistress and pull it violently towards him.

"Give her up," said he to the Saracen, "or I shall kill you!"

"Let her go, Christian, or you are dead!"

Agénor twisted the skirt of the white woollen robe around his wrist, and raised his sword over Mothril; the Moor, with a stroke of his poniard launched sidewise, beat down Agénor's right hand.

The hand was pinned to the stuff, and Agénor uttered a cry so heart-rending that Musaron howled with rage.

Mothril thought he could escape now; but it was no longer Agénor who pursued; it was the courser, put on its mettle by the race.

Moreover, rage had doubled the strength of the young man; his sword rose a second time, and, if Mothril had not made his horse swerve, it was over with him.

"Give her up to me, Saracen," said Agénor, in a voice that was growing weaker; "you see well I will kill you; give her up to me, I love her!"

"And I, too, love her!" answered Mothril, spurring his horse.

A voice, that of Musaron, pierced the darkness. The honest squire had found the third horse, he had cut his way through briars and stones, and was coming to the aid of his master.

"Here I am; courage, monsieur!" he cried.

Mothril turned round and felt he was lost.

"You want this young girl?" said he.

"Yes, I want her and I shall have her!"

"Well, then, take her!"

The name of Agénor, followed by a stifled rattle, issued forth from behind the veil, and something heavy rolled under the feet of Agénor's horse, and, with it, the long, undulating folds of the white scarf.

Mauléon leaped down to seize what Mothril was abandoning to him. He knelt down to kiss the veil that covered his mistress.

But, as soon as he looked, he lay upon the ground fainting, lifeless.

When the dawn shed its pallid light upon this horrible scene, the knight, wan as a spectre, might have been perceived gluing his lips to the cold and violet lips of the severed head which the Moor had flung to him.

Three paces away, Musaron was weeping. The faithful servitor had found means to dress the wound of his master during his long swoon; he had saved him in spite of himself.

At a distance of thirty yards lay Mothril, his temples pierced by the sure and deadly shaft of the worthy squire, still holding under his arm the mutilated corpse of Aissa.

In death he smiled triumphant.

Two horses wandered here and there among the herbage.

EPILOGUE.

THE good knight of the iron hand was mistaken in assigning a week's duration for the narrative of his exploits and misfortunes. In fact, he was one of those who tell a story quickly, because their words are pointed and picturesque, and, as for his audience, never did impassioned narrator meet with one more intelligent and responsive.

It was well worth seeing the ardor wherewith each of his auditors followed, with equivalent pantomime, every emotion which the knight was interpreting in language at once vigorous and artless.

Jehan Froissard, with eyes, now sparkling, now moist, devoured every word; he looked as if he were forming in his own mind an image of the places, the skies, the acts, and everything he grasped was reflected in his quick-sighted eyes.

And as for Messire Espaing, he was all on fire, as if he had heard the clarions of Spain or the horns of the Moors.

The squire alone, in the darkest corner of the chamber, remained silent and unmoved.

While so many glowing memories were being unravelled by the brilliant words of his master, his head was sunk on his breast; but he raised it for a moment, if one of his own deeds of prowess was rehearsed, or if the knight grew so excited as to make him fear a revival of his sorrow.

Eleven, twelve long hours of the night passed thus, or rather flew away like the sparks of the vine-branch fire which warmed the chamber, like the smoke of the lamps and tapers that whirled above the heads of the audience.

When the narrative was near its close, their hearts were despondent, their eyes filled with tears.

The voice of the Sire de Mauléon became visibly troubled, jerked out each phrase, tore asunder each emotion, as does the pencil stroke of inspired artist.

Musaron riveted on him a soft and melancholy look, and, with that familiarity that recalled the friend rather than the servant, placed a hand on his shoulder.

"There, there, seigneur!" said he, "enough, enough, for the time."

"Ah!" murmured the knight, "these ashes are not yet cold. They still burn if you stir them."

Two big tears rolled down the cheeks of the chronicler, tears of compassion and interest, no doubt, but which a bad mind, that always tries to belittle the best intentions of chroniclers and romancers, has since attributed to the joy of hearing so fine a tale from the very lips of the hero of the adventure.

When the history was finished, the sun was already glinting on the roof of the hostel and the greenery of the forest.

Jehan Froissard could then see the face of the knight, and that face deserved the attention of a man who studies men.

Upon that intelligent and noble brow, thought, or rather sorrow, had furrowed a deep wrinkle. Already at the corners of the eyes were spreading those diverging networks, which seem like threads destined to draw back the eyelids and then shut them violently before death comes and closes them forever.

The bastard's look asked not for either applause or consolation from his audience.

"Oh, what a touching history," said Froissard, "what a fine picture! and what delicacy in the portrayal!"

"In the tomb lies all this, master," answered the knight, "in the tomb; all this is dead indeed. Doña Aïssa, that beloved being, is not the only one I have to weep for: all my loves, all my friendships, have not chosen the same field for their sepulture. When he," said the knight, pointing with tender eyes to his squire who was leaning over the back of his chair, "when he, who, alas! is older than I, has closed his eyes, I shall no longer have any one on earth, and, *vrai Dieu!* I will never love any one again. My heart has died, Sire Jehan Froissard, because it has too much lived in too little time."

"But, *Dieu merci!*" exclaimed Musaron, with an effort to give a free and joyous tone to his voice, which was choked with emotion, "*Dieu merci!* I am as fresh as a rose, my arm is good, my eye steady: I send an arrow as far as ever I did, and riding tires me very little."

"Sir knight," interrupted Froissard, "you will, then, allow my unworthy pen to retrace the glorious deeds and tender misfortunes I have just heard from your lips? It is a great honor you do me, and a pleasure at once sweet and bitter."

Mauléon inclined.

"But for the love of Jesus! good knight," continued Froissard, "do not despair. You are still young; you are handsome. You ought to have everything in this world a noble man and a noble heart require; the brave never lack friends."

The knight sadly shook his head. Musaron gave a shrug, which the stoic Epictetus or the sceptic Pyrrho might have envied.

"The man who has been noted in the army for his valor," continued Froissard, "and in the councils of princes for his wisdom,— the man who has an arm that executes vigorously and a head that plans surely, is always a man sought after. He does not approach the court without receiving its favors; and you, Sire de Mauléon, you have two courts that protect you, and dispute for the prize of making you rich and powerful. Has Spain a better claim to it than France? Do you prefer a countship in the one to a barony in the other?"

"Sire Froissard," resumed Mauléon, with extreme calmness and with a profound sigh, "that was a great sorrow that spread over France on the thirteenth day of July, thirteen hundred and eighty! On that day a soul breathed its last sigh to the Lord; and that soul was by far the most noble and generous that has ever appeared in the world. Alas! Sire Jehan Froissard, it touched my breast while passing; for I held in my arms, I on my knees, the head of the valiant constable, and that head grew rigid on my bosom."

"Alas!" said Froissard.

"Alas!" repeated Espaing, crossing himself piously, while Musaron frowned, in order that the emotion the recollection called forth might not overpower him.

"Yes; messire, once the constable, Bertrand Du Guesclin, lay dead at Castelneuf de Randon, — he who seemed the god of battles! — I felt that all my strength had left me. I had centred much of my life in his life, messire, and every fibre in my heart was connected with his."

"But you had still the good king, Charles the Wise, sir knight."

"I had to weep for his death at the very moment I was weeping for that of the constable; from these two blows I have never recovered.

"I suspended my sword and shield from the joists of the little house which my uncle had left me, and there buried four years of sorrows and memories.

"However, a new reign was rejuvenating France; I saw sometimes joyous knights riding by, and heard the minstrels singing their fresh songs. Oh, messire! what blows did not these trouvères strike at my heart as they passed on their way to the Pyrenees, singing to the sad air of the romance the Spanish verses made on Blanche of Bourbon, and Don Frederic the Grand Master: —

> "'El rey no me ha conocido
> Con las virgies me voy
> Castilla, di que te hize!'"

"What, seigneur! all this did not draw you to the court of Spain, to King Henry, who reigned so gloriously and loved you so much?"

"Sir chronicler, the moment came when I dreamt of nothing but Spain. The memory I retained of all my past exploits was so sad and so blurred that it really did seem to me to be the result of a dream. My life, in fact, appeared to be divided by a long sleep, and, but that Musaron sometimes said to me, —

"'Yes, seigneur, we have seen all that these people sing,'—but for Musaron I should have believed in sorcery.

"Every night I dreamt of Spain. I saw again Toledo and Montiel, the grotto where we witnessed the death of Hafiz, and where Caverley came and sat. I saw Burgos and the splendors of its court, — Soria! Soria! seigneur, and the ecstasies of love. My life was consumed in desires, in disgusts. It was torpor; it was fever.

"One day trumpets passed, sounding in the country. It was the soldiers of Monseigneur Louis de Bourbon, who was on his way to Spain to the court of King Henry. The latter, fearing to be beaten in a war with Portugal, had asked France for assistance.

"The Duc de Bourbon heard of a knight who had fought in Spain, and who knew many secrets connected with the expeditions of the Companies. I saw pages and knights filling my little court, and astonishing my servants very much.

"I was at a window, and had just time to descend and hold the prince's stirrup. Then the latter, with much courtesy, questioned me on my wound and my adventures; he wished to hear me relate the death of Don Pedro and my combat with the Moor. However, I concealed from him all that concerned Doña Aïssa.

"Carried away by enthusiasm, the duke begged, implored me even, to accompany him. It was during one of these moments of hallucination, when my life appeared to me as a dream; and, during these periods, I wished to know again, I burned to see again. Moreover, the trumpets intoxicated me, and Musaron, who is here present, looked at me with greedy eyes; he had his arbalist already in his hand.

" 'Well, Mauléon,' said the prince, 'what do you say to it?'

" 'Be it as you wish, monseigneur,' I answered. 'To tell the truth, the King of Spain will be glad to see me.'

"We started; and I will admit I almost felt joyous. I would bow my head, then, over that land which had drunk my own blood and that of my beloved. Oh! messeigneurs, memory is a beautiful thing: many know how to live but once; others live over and over again the days they have already lost.

"A fortnight after our departure we were in Burgos, and in another fortnight at Segovia with the court.

"I saw King Henry again, older indeed, but still upright and majestic. I cannot explain the secret repugnance that kept me apart from him, — from him I had loved so well when youth, with its golden trust, showed him to me noble and unfortunate, that is to say, perfect. When I beheld him now, I read cruelty and dissimulation on his face.

"'Alas!' I said to myself, 'a crown changes face and soul.'

"It was not the crown had changed Henry, it was looking on me who could read what lay beneath the darkness of that crown.

"The first thing the king showed the duke in the tower at Segovia was the cage in which were imprisoned the sons of Don Pedro and Maria Padilla. Unfortunates, growing up wan and famished within the narrow enclosure of these bars, ever menaced by the lance of a sentinel, ever insulted by the ferocious smile of a warder or a visitor!

"One of those children, messeigneurs, was the faithful portrait of his unhappy father. He fastened on me looks that pierced my heart, as if the soul of Don Pedro had taken refuge in that body, and, knowing all, was silently reproaching me for his death and the woes of his race.

"This child, or rather this young man, knew nothing, however, and had never seen me before. He regarded me aimlessly and heedlessly, but my conscience spoke, although that of King Henry said little.

"In fact this prince, holding the Duc de Bourbon by the hand, led him to the cage, remarking, —

"'These are the children of your sister's murderer. If you wish to have them put to death, I will deliver them up to you.'

"To which the duke replied, —

" 'Sire, the children are not guilty of the crimes of their father.'

" I saw the king frown and order the cage to be closed.

" I would gladly have embraced the brave prince. So when, after the inspection was over, monseigneur wished to present me to the king, who had regarded me attentively,—

" 'No, no!' I answered, 'I could not speak to him.'

" But the king had recognized me. He came to me, in presence of his whole court, and hailed me by my name, a thing that, in any other circumstance, would have made me weep for joy and pride.

" 'Sir knight,' said he, 'I have a promise to fulfil towards you. You remember?'

" 'No, sire,' I stammered, 'I do not.'

" 'Well, to-morrow I'll remember it for you!' answered the king, with a gracious smile that did not make me forget his cruel look at the two prisoners.

" 'Do it at once, then, if you please, sire,' said I. 'Your Highness once promised to grant me a favor.'

" 'And I will keep my promise, sir knight.'

" 'Do me the favor, sire, to grant me the liberty of these two poor children.'

" King Henry darted at me a glance sparkling with anger, and replied,—

" 'Not that, sir knight; ask something else.'

" 'I have nothing else to ask, seigneur.'

" 'But that cannot be realized, Sire de Mauléon. I promised to grant you a favor that would enrich you, not one that would destroy me.'

" 'Enough, seigneur,' I answered.

" 'Still, I would see you to-morrow,' said the king, trying to retain me.

" But I did not wait for that to-morrow. With the

duke's permission, I started at once for France, and sojourned in Spain but a quarter of an hour to say my prayers at Aïssa's tomb near the castle of Montiel.

"Poor we set out, my brave Musaron and I, and poor we returned, when others returned very rich.

"And now you have the end of my story, sir chronicler. You may add to it that I await death impatiently; it will, surely, unite me with my friends. I have just made my annual pilgrimage to the tomb of my uncle, and am returning to my house. If you pass by it, messires, you will be well received, and you will do me honor. It is a little castle built of bricks and quartz; it has two towers, and a wood rises above it. Any one in the country will point it out to you."

Then Agénor de Mauléon courteously saluted Jehan Froissard and Espaing, called for his horse, and slowly and tranquilly took the road to his house, followed by Musaron, who had paid the charges.

"Ah!" said Espaing, as he gazed after them riding away, "what fine opportunities the men of other days have had! what glorious times, and what noble hearts!"

"It will take me a week to write down all this," said Froissard to himself; "the good knight was correct. And then, shall I write it as well as he has told it?"

Some time after, the two children of Don Pedro and Maria Padilla, beautiful as their mother, proud as their father, died in the cage at Segovia. However, Henry of Trastamare reigned happily and founded a dynasty.

THE END.

CPSIA information can be obtained
at www.ICGtesting.com
Printed in the USA
BVHW041303200819
556326BV00015B/107/P

9 781167 671500